JOURNEY TO JAVA

D1378065

ALSO BY HAROLD NICOLSON

Sainte-Beuve
Good Behaviour: Being a Study of Certain Types of
    Civility
King George V: His Life and Reign
The Evolution of Diplomatic Method
The English Sense of Humour
The Congress of Vienna 1812–1822
Lord Carnock
Peacemaking 1919
Curzon: The Last Phase 1919–1925
Benjamin Constant
Byron: The Last Journey
Tennyson: Aspects of His Life, Character and Poetry
Helen's Tower
The Desire to Please

JOURNEY

Harold George Nicolson

TO JAVA

Doubleday & Company, Inc.

Garden City, New York, 1958

G
550
.N5
1958

G 550
.N5
Copy 1

Library of Congress Catalog Card Number 58–8106
Copyright 1957 by Harold Nicolson
All Rights Reserved
Printed in the United States of America
Designed by Alma Reese Cardi
First Edition

DEDICATION

On the approach of my seventieth birthday, which fell on November 21, 1956, two hundred and fifty-five of my friends conspired to give me an enormous cheque. I decided to spend this present on a visit to the Far East, which I had not seen before. V. and I sailed from England in the liner Willem Ruys *of the Rotterdam Lloyd on January 15, 1957, and returned on March 17. It is to the generosity of my friends that I owe two of the happiest months which, in a life of wholly unmerited felicity, I have ever enjoyed. It is to them therefore that my travel diary is dedicated.*

H.N.

Sissinghurst

AUTHOR'S NOTE

With one obvious exception, all the people mentioned in this book are real people and have been given their real names.

Only those who have enjoyed their life have the right to say that they are not made wretched by the thought of death. It needs a certain amount of management to enjoy life properly. I enjoy it twice as much as most people, since the degree of pleasure it affords is related to the amount of attention that we give it. Above all, now that I feel my life to be brief in time, do I seek to extend it in weight. I try to delay the velocity of its flight by the velocity with which I grasp it; and to compensate for the speed of its collapse by the zest which I throw into it. The shorter my hold on life, the greater the sweetness of contentment and well-being; I feel it just as much as they do, but not by letting it just slip away. Rather I seek to study it, reflect on it, and savour it, in order to be able to render just thanks to him by whom it has been accorded.

Montaigne
III CH. XIII

CONTENTS

officer— The Americanisation of Europe— Pillow fight at the swimming pool – Jupiter's moons – Meganyctiphanes – The Indonesian trades unions – Passengers are not give sufficient information – Leonard Forman and his herbal – Test Matches – I feel an outsider.

It would have been good for me to have studied Kierkegaard when young – I might have been alienated by his egoism and hallucinations – But I might have been fortified by his sense of sin, despair, and dread – I might have learnt that not to agree with his views was a sign of ethical stupidity – Heidegger regards dread as an inevitable component of human personality – I read William James to cheer me up – The electric storm – Ronald Firbank's cousin – We reach Cape Town on our return visit – We go with Peter Lycett Green to Kirstenbosch, Groot Constantia, and Morgenster – Passage in praise of Captain Thibault and Groot Constantia – The curiosity shop – *The Unquiet Grave* – Colin Wilson's *Outsider* – The ship's entertainment after dinner makes me feel an Outsider myself.

Conversation with Culpeper on the subject of dread and despair – He tells me that he has served a prison sentence and is terrified always of this episode being either

I. NORTH ATLANTIC

1

Tuesday, January 15. The Albany, Piccadilly

We are called at 7.15. I turn on the wireless and hear the 7.55 weather report and the news. There has been a gale in the Channel and the Ostend boat has been obliged to return to Dover. I keep this disturbing information to myself.

We have some coffee. The Albany porter comes to fetch our luggage and wheels it along the Rope Walk in his little truck. He then packs it into the large Daimler hire car which is waiting in the courtyard. Considering that we shall be away for two months in the tropics, our luggage is not too numerous or bulky. As always, I seem to need more luggage than V. does, having six pieces to her four. I have a revelation suitcase, an ordinary suitcase, a dressing case, a case for books and papers, and an attaché case—all in rawhide with a large red label "DJAKARTA," which is what people now call the capital of Java. In my young days it was called "Batavia" and one knew where one was. Then I also have my typewriter in a black box. It is not the Remington Portable that I acquired more than thirty years ago in Berlin and on which I have typed more than a million words. That machine is old and frail, slips frequently, and is unsuited for nautical expeditions. In its place I have brought the typewriter that I got when working on the archives in the Round Tower at Windsor. I dislike it since it has a red gadget marked "self-starter" which, when pressed inadvertently, induces it to pounce and whirr.

We leave Albany at 8.27. Colin, looking young and gay, stands on the steps of the front door waving us farewell. We reach Waterloo Station at 8.45.

The platform from which the boat train is to leave for Southampton docks bears a red board inscribed "Rotterdam Lloyd Special." Having disposed our luggage in the rack, tipped the porter, and thrown newspapers on our seats, we return to the platform and watch our fellow passengers arrive. It is curious to reflect that these flustered men and women have reached this platform with identical intentions but from all manner of different homes and places and in all manner of different circumstances. For the present they are as impersonal and indistinguishable as those whom I have so often watched flocking on or off the boat at Folkestone or Dover; but in a few days they will have acquired separate identities, have become static, lying stretched on deck chairs in quite different clothes, laughing distinct laughs. Their luggage is labelled "Baggage Room," or "Not wanted on voyage," or "Colombo," or "Singapore." They seem to consist mainly of dominating women, with bold Teutonic busts, dressed in tight astrakhan jackets, with *articles de Paris* on their lapels and brass bracelets jangling round their wrists. They have tight golden ringlets, carefully compressed like those of Tissaphernes. They are fussed and cross.

The whistles shrill; the doors slam; green flags wave; the train slides out of the station at 9.15; we have left London.

We have an excellent breakfast in our compartment, brought us by an engaging steward. We read the newspapers and learn therefrom that Dr. Adams of Eastbourne has been committed for trial; we regret that we shall miss what promises to be a most interesting case. We reach Southampton docks at 10.25 or 10.28. Our luggage is placed upon a truck and disappears into a lift. We ascend the stairs and enter the vast waiting room of the Ocean Terminal, which is assuredly an improvement on the cold damp sheds I remember when leaving for America between the wars.

As we enter the room we are greeted by Nigel and Philippa who have, in spite of petrol rationing, motored over to see us off. Nigel lends me his movie camera to take with me and tells me of the latest developments in his battle with the Bournemouth East and Christchurch Conservative Association. They have "repudiated" him for having dared to warn his constituents that the invasion of Egypt was a violation of existing treaties and was unlikely to attain its objectives. He had annoyed them still further by abstaining from voting in favour of the government in the crucial debate.

As always, my younger son is objective, good-humoured, and tolerant: his fault as a politician is that he has an irresistible tendency to see the other person's point of view. He explains that the members of his Executive feel just as deeply and sincerely about the whole business as he does himself. To him the government have behaved dishonourably in breaking the spirit and even the letter of the United Nations Charter, the North Atlantic Alliance, the Tripartite Declaration, and their own election pledges; they have been shifty and even tricky in explaining the real purpose of the operation and in not stating how far they were aware of collusion between France and Israel; and they have been foolish in undertaking this action at the moment of the presidential election in the United States and in not foreseeing that they would have against them, not merely the Labour and Liberal parties, but the mass of American opinion and the majority of United Nations. The constituency committee, on the other hand, take the "my party right or wrong" point of view and regard Nigel as unpatriotic and even treacherous in voicing opinions which may be correct but which they deeply dislike. I can see that he is distressed by the situation, and his predicament casts a shadow on our embarkation.

We are then summoned by loud-speaker into the enormous customs hall, find our luggage piled under the initial "N," are passed through with a quick scribble of violet chalk, and accompany the porter through a covered gangway into the bowels of the *Willem Ruys*. The gangway is so neatly covered and so neatly illumined that it is not clear at what moment we actually leave our native shore and step into the boat. Anyhow, we find our cabins, which are on different decks. Nigel and Philippa accompany us on a visit to the saloons and the observation gallery and then say good-bye, since they are lunching in Bournemouth. "You see," says Nigel gallantly, "there are at least some of my constituents who still have the courage to ask us to luncheon." But it was kind of them to come, and the gratification they gave us was worth at least a month's petrol in human values.

2

We much dislike having cabins on separate decks and V. takes me to the purser's office to try to have them changed. Women are so much better at that sort of business than men are; they do not accept inconvenience so supinely and have none of the male aversion from being a nuisance. The purser is most obliging. A passenger from Rotterdam had cancelled his booking at the last moment and there is now a cabin for me available on the same deck as V. and bang opposite her cabin, across a little landing. Thus I move into No. 123 on the port side of A deck, whereas she is installed in No. 122 on the starboard side. We are entranced by this arrangement. The cabin stewards who do the housemaid work are Indonesians. V.'s is called "Tiwar" and mine "Matt." They are supervised on each deck by a Dutch steward. Ours is called "Van Ruy," is tall and handsome, and speaks the most perfect English. Our luggage arrives and we unpack. We then have luncheon in the saloon. The final tables have not been yet allotted and we just sit down at the first table we find. The food is rich and good.

We cast off at 2.30 and slow tugs nose and prod us round. By 3.20 we are out of the Solent and passing the Needles. It is a grey and wintry afternoon but there is a shaft of watery sunlight out at sea. The houses of Bournemouth and Christchurch can be observed in the dim distance, but I notice that they are unvisited by any shaft of sunlight. Then out we throb into the open sea; it is rough and cold with a fierce following gale. We have boat drill for the passengers. Each of them has taken down from the ledge above his hanging cupboard a puffy orange life jacket which he or she ties rightly around the neck, giving to the body the appearance of those little *poussahs* which as a child I use to buy in the toyshop of the rue de Rivoli. I discover that V., being starboard, is allotted to lifeboat No. 3, whereas, I, being port, am destined for No. 4. If we really had to take to the boats I am quite sure that we should refuse, whatever discipline were enforced, to be separated. But fortunately V. regards boat drill as a ridiculous formula, and as she dislikes all formulas it does not dawn upon her that we shall either have to mutiny if a crisis occurs or be separated from each other on the angry waves.

Before we left Sissinghurst, V. and I discussed what work and what books we should bring with us on our holiday. Our cabins are large and well heated, and we were delighted to find that under the lid of the dressing tables there slides out a shelf or flap which serves as an excellent writing table and on which my typewriter and V.'s papers can rest with ease and comfort. The table and chair are situated near the bunk, and upon the bed-spread thereof we can set out our documents and our books of reference. We foresee therefore that, unless it becomes too rough, we shall be able in tranquility to get through a great amount of work.

V. has with her typescript copies of the letters which Virginia Woolf wrote to her over several years. She proposes to go through these carefully and, since many of them are undated, to arrange them in their approximate sequence. The copyright of these letters rests, not with her, but with Leonard Woolf, who is considering some form of publication. Like all good letter writers, Virginia adapted her mood, and therefore her style, to the person whom she was addressing. Her letters to V.

are written in a uniform key of affectionate derision and pleasure. She had complete confidence in V.'s devotion and understanding, and there is no note in these letters of that rather acrid self-distrust which, to my mind, marred her correspondence with Lytton Strachey, of whom she was afraid. She was fond of V. and admired her serene integrity, but she was not in the least afraid of her; these letters display therefore the gay and sunlit aspects of Virginia, which were clouded in her correspondence with Lytton and in the published sections of her diary. I hope therefore that Leonard will agree that her letters to V. should be published uniformly and not confused with other letters written to other people in different moods. But it is for Leonard to decide.

V. has also got with her the notes, and some of the essential books of reference, for the biography of *La Grande Mademoiselle,* on which she has been engaged for several years. At home she is distracted by so many interruptions, or by the prospect of so many interruptions, that she finds it difficult to concentrate. She will settle down to *Mademoiselle* and then someone will come to tell her that a cow has strayed into the rose garden, or that the roof of the oasthouse needs repairing, or that a coachload of American tourists has turned up, and *Mademoiselle* is lost to her for the whole day. It may well be that in the blessed void repose of this journey she will find that she and *Mademoiselle* can resume their private colloquy.

I myself have got one or two articles of polish off—a long article on the design for living for a symposium that Lord Inman is editing, and an article for America upon the relation between government offices and their sources of information. The Americans, it seems, are under the impression that our embassies at Washington and elsewhere were gravely at fault in that they failed to warn our government of the probable reaction of the Suez adventure upon public opinion abroad. The Americans can scarcely believe, (and I do not blame them for their incredulity), that in fact most of our representatives in the countries affected were kept totally uninformed of what was intended. I shall seek to explain that, in diplomacy at least, the part played by Intelligence, by which is often meant the Secret Service, is very small indeed.

Apart from these immediate tasks, we have been considering our general reading. We have agreed to divide the books which we take with us into three categories, namely serious study, instructive reading, and bunkside books. I seldom read modern novels and it is high time that I started to do so. I have therefore acquired a number of slim volumes in the Penguin fiction series which I shall read when I retire to rest. They include H. E. Bates, William Faulkner, James Cain, C. P. Snow, Nancy Mitford, and Joyce Cary. Under the heading of "instructive reading" I have included a few biographies and some books of travel, whereas V. has got some horticultural dictionaries and monographs.

For more serious stuff, I propose to examine a problem that has for long interested me, namely the problem of contentment. I always have the feeling that, considering that we live in a world of chaos and transition, I ought to be more unhappy than I am. I have protected myself from this form of self-reproach by the reflection that the average human being is capable of absorbing only an average amount of worry; he is a vessel of a certain capacity and if more is poured into the vessel than it is designed to contain then the liquid overflows. Moreover apathy and anxiety—acceptance and denial—would seem to be distributed in fairly stable proportions, generation by generation. Thus, while it is true that my grandfather and his friends took for granted the stability of the existing order, our island security, and our status as a Great Power, they lay awake at night tortured by such problems as that of the Holy Trinity or the Thirty-nine Articles, problems which leave me unmoved. In my lifetime I have witnessed disasters and triumphs, wickedness and virtue, on a scale infinitely greater than any that my grandfather (who was a selfish man in any case) could possibly have conceived. Yet, being an average insider, *un homme moyen sensuel,* I cannot sincerely affirm that I have been more distraught by these manifestations than he was by Dr. Pusey. In emotional reactions also there is such a thing as the law of diminishing returns.

Incidentally I want to examine whether the disillusion bequeathed by the French Revolution to the nineteenth century is in any way different from that which has been left us by our own social revolution and by two horrible wars. Is it a fact that the *maladie du siècle* of the nineteenth century produced languorous melancholy, whereas that of the twentieth century is distinguished by fear and anger? How far are the feelings of guilt and apprehension from which the young intellectual of today suffers, or pretends to suffer, different from the *"immortel ennui"* of the romantics? Is it commendable or the reverse to escape from self-concern, and is contentment to be purchased only by the banishment of desire? Are energy and apathy, courage and anxiety no more than personal accidents or are they symptomatic of an age? By reading the works of representative malcontents and escapists I hope to find some sort of answer to these questions. It will at least prove an interesting, selective, and perhaps profitable, enquiry.

I shall begin with health, since I am convinced that contentment or dissatisfaction is closely associated with the bodily humours. I shall go back to the fountain of medical science. I shall begin with Galen.

3

Dusk and darkness descend and I go up to the smoking room, which is warm and bright. I am reading my Galen when I am accosted by a Dutchman of distinguished aspect, who holds a passenger list in his hand. He has evidently identified me from my appearance. Inwardly I am feeling vivacious, inquisitive, and young; delighted to find myself alone with V. on this, a second honeymoon, fascinated by the problem of my own contentment, and anxious to get down to Galen in order to discover whether a melancholy disposition is in fact due to defective secretion on the part of the ductless glands. My interlocutor can have noticed none of these things. To him I must have seemed a typical Englishman of the upper-income group; well advanced in age; rubicund and stout; slightly ruffled about the hair and collar and therefore probably an intellectual; and certainly reading a small green book. So he asks me whether I am in fact the person whose name he indicates on the passenger list. I say that I am indeed. He then says that he has been Dutch minister in Bucharest, Madrid, and Rio, where he knew several people with whom I also must have been acquainted. He mentions particularly Elizabeth Bibesco and Horace Rumbold. He then introduces me to his wife, and I sit at their table for a bit and have a martini. Then V. joins me and also has a martini. He tells us that he has retired from the diplomatic service and is now on his way to Java to see about his estates at Surabaya and to join his son. He had been there at the time of the Japanese invasion and had been shut up in a concentration camp for three years. He shows no sign of this ordeal, being a hale old man, spruce and courteous. His wife is a woman of culture with a gentle rather shy face. I take to them immediately. His name is Jan Hubrecht and she is Leonora Hubrecht. They will provide agreeable and congenial company on board.

Before dinner I return to my Galen. The bore about this Pergamene is that he is so anxious to contradict and expose his opponents that he can find little time to expound his own ideas on medicine. When he does get down to his own theories he is as lucid and concise as Euclid, but then off he goes again gabbling sneers at Erasistratus and the Asclepiadeans. It may be, as Dr. Arthur Brock suggests in his excellent introduction to the Loeb edition, that Galen inherited his disputatious manner from his mother, who must have been an intolerable woman, bullying her acquiescent husband and screaming invectives at her neighbours across the flat rooftops of Pergamum.

The importance of Galen to medicine was that he insisted that the physician should take account, not of the actual symptoms only of his patient, but also of his general constitution. Only thus, he contends, as Hippocrates also contended, can "nature" be allowed to practise her consummate curative arts.

What is more to my purpose is his insistence that the psychological condition of an individual is determined by the proportions in which the humours are present in his body. He defines the four humours as blood, phlegm, black bile, and yellow bile. These four condiments, when present in excess or deficient in quantity, are the cause of all the ills that flesh and bone are heir to. Primary diseases, moreover, can be classified into hot, cold, moist, and dry, and should be treated by their opposites. He also believed in what he called "the life spirit," or the *élan vital,* which was an essence of energy independent of the four humours. And he contended, and rightly, that what rendered a man contented or discontented was the state of his liver and the quality of his bile.

I find Galen an enjoyable authority. He remarks incidentally that honey is excellent for a young man but that an old man should avoid it like poison. I must ask John Hunt when I get back to London to confirm this fascinating fact.

We dine; we go to bed early; as a bunk book I read *The Diary of a Nobody,* which was composed in the house in Canonbury where Raymond Mortimer and Paul Hyslop now reside. In the middle of the night I get up to see whether the light of Ushant is blinking at us across the waves. In order to lower the shutter of my window I kneel on my bed and also on my hot-water bottle. The latter explodes. I have known many hot-water bottles to leak secretly, but this one broke right across the neck and deluged my bunk with water. With immense effort I turned my mattress upside down and put on my dressing gown and raincoat. I sleep a dreamless sleep.

4

Wednesday, January 16. M.S. "Willem Ruys" at sea

We wake up in the Bay of Biscay. It is very cold, very rough, and very stormy. I go on deck after breakfast and take photographs of the great waves roaring beside and behind us. My Indonesian steward, Matt, is overjoyed by the spectacle of my hot-water bottle with a jagged neck and its head toppling; to him it must convey a Dyak effect. He holds it up and giggles like a child.

I enjoy *The Diary of a Nobody,* which I have wanted to read ever since I found Mr. Pooter figuring so frequently in Rupert Hart-Davis' biography of Hugh Walpole. It gives a vivid picture of the period and social status against which H. G. Wells reacted so truculently, and it thus throws light upon his strange spasms of peevishness. Charles Pooter is both an example and a victim of the respectability of the lower middle class at the end of the nineteenth century. He stands in awe of his boss, Mr. Perkupp; he is much flattered by an invitation to a reception at the mansion house; he is pleased when the curate asks him to hand round the plate in church. His taste is not good. He buys two stag heads in plaster painted chocolate colour and puts them up in his hall; he is delighted by his wife's decoration of the looking glass above the chimney piece, which she has hung with flags, ribbons, and "Liberty silk bows." He calls evening tails "swallowtails," disapproves of driving on Sundays, and is shocked by his son playing billiards. His wife is even more respectable. She regards it as ungentlemanlike of him to use the expression "good old Broadstairs." I am not surprised that Wells, with his contradictory temperament, his arrant egoism, his petulant self-assertion, should have been enraged by such conventions. Yet, until saddened by diabetes and insulin, Wells was not a melancholy man or one who suffered from ennui or the denial of self-fulfilment: he was irritable and combative rather than angry. It was only in the last years of his life, when he had ceased to be a gay critic of contemporary conventions and imagined himself to be a disregarded prophet, that he became embittered and ceased to be either agreeable or amusing. Mr. Pooter makes me realise that Wells was a man of great talents who reacted violently against his early environment and yet was never able to fit easily into any other. The impress of Victorian class consciousness went deeper than that of today.

It is rough all day but the *Willem Ruys* is an excellent sea boat when the gale is behind her, and although the things in our cabins slide about a bit we are not really inconvenienced. There seems to be some theory that the ship has not finally settled down to her voyage until we are out of the bay. It is not, for instance, until we are past Finisterre that V. and I are allotted permanent places in the dining saloon. We are given a table to ourselves, which is a great relief. We go to bed at 10.00. and I read Nancy Mitford—very chatty and gay. I am wakened by the howling of a child. The acoustics of this ship are excellent, and I imagine that there is some sound-absorbing material encased in the partitions between the cabins. But this child yells loud enough to penetrate into Broadcasting House itself; it is not a cry of pain or fear; it is a cry of sustained rage, of *saeva indignatio*. I suppose the child had been put in the same bunk as her brother and wished to be with the grown-ups. With my left ear I hear the Atlantic thudding and hissing against the ship; with my right ear I listen to this child howling. Then I go to sleep again, lulled by the ocean and the pursuit of love.

Thursday, January 17. At sea

There is a heavy swell during the night, due to the northeast gale we had all yesterday. I pull down the shutter and gaze out of my porthole at the dawn. Great downs of black water are sweeping beside us. I use the term "porthole," since that is the expression usually applied to windows on boats. Yet in fact the windows in the *Willem Ruys* bear no relation at all to the portholes which, in former days, used to admit a quivering light into the emplacements which were then called cabins. These apertures were circular and opaque and were tightly closed by a large nut revolving on a really enormous screw, the grooves of which were smeared with grease. The windows in the *Willem Ruys* are in comparison magic casements opening on the foam. As I look out on the swelling, sweeping Atlantic, I observe upon the horizon a sharp coruscation which I first take to be a rick on fire; but there can be no ricks in mid-ocean and I conclude that it must be a three-masted schooner ablaze from prow to stern, from topmast to water level. I then realise that it is neither of these things but just the sun rising in a cold sky over Portugal. I sleep again.

While shaving, I reflect whether yesterday's reading of Galen has left me with any useful information as to the nature of discontent. He has certainly convinced me that it is caused mainly by some defect in the ductless glands, leading to an unbalanced distribution of the four humours. It is their recognition of this fact that has induced the French to associate discontent with such words as "spleen" and "phlegm." How right they are. I realise also that Robert Burton, whose *Anatomy of Melancholy* was composed some fourteen hundred years later than Galen's lectures, was also of this opinion. I share with Dr. Johnson, Tristram Shandy, and Charles Lamb a warm affection for Robert Burton. When, after pouring for hours over manuscripts in the Bodleian or over his own books in his room at Christ Church, he would feel the shadow of discontent beginning to chill his heart, he would walk down to Folly Bridge and listen to the bargees hurling insults at each other as they punted past. He would roar with laughter at their sallies and invectives, bending double in his exhilaration and slapping his thighs hard. This process would set the bile moving and mixing: he would return to his study radiant with recovered zest. Not that I can read the *Anatomy of Melancholy* without skipping, although to his contemporaries it must have represented a rich anthology of all the many books which they were unable to obtain. It is provided with such excellent chapter headings and summaries that one can easily find one's way and can extract from these cluttered anecdotes and quotations what it was that Burton really wanted to convey.

To him discontent was "a kind of dotage without a fever, having for his ordinary companions fear and sadness, without any apparent occasion." Burton used the word "dotage" in the same sense as we should use the word "obsession," not implying any association with senility; in fact he clearly recognised that the malady was more likely to affect adolescents than men of mature age. The causes of melancholy, in his judgement, were both supernatural and natural. In the category of supernatural causes he included God, "and the Devil with God's permission," witches, sorcerers, magicians, and astronomical conditions at the hour of birth. The very worst thing that could happen to a baby was to be born at a moment when Saturn and the moon met in Scorpio. Such a child was predestined for a life of gloom.

Among the natural causes he included such misfortunes as heredity, poverty, imprisonment, religious mania, hypochondria, loneliness, a too vivid imagination ("which invites the Devil to come to us"), shame, disgrace, envy, malice, ambition, greed, gambling, overwork, self-centredness, which is "a slie insensible enemy," and "the frightful malady of love." Yet, like Galen before him, he attributes immense importance to health. No man can avoid discontent if he be permanently constipated, if he denies himself the pleasures of the flesh (what Burton charmingly calls "Venus omitted"), or if, conversely, he indulges in sexual excess. A man should be careful about diet. Such foods or liquids as beef, pork, venison, hare, milk, butter, cheese, peacocks, waterfowl, melons, cabbage, onions, garlic, peas, beans, red wine, cider, beer, and all varieties of fruit, cake, and biscuits are certain to engender melancholy. Burton admits that his list of substances liable to create discontent in human beings is perhaps too comprehensive. "It were a meer tyrannie," he writes, "to live after these strict rules of Physick." Yet he who wishes to avoid the black choler should in all matters of diet practise strict moderation.

Burton is excellent upon the theme of fresh air and exercise. He contends that those who fuss about taking exercise become in middle age terribly addicted to melancholia. "School boys in

Germany," he writes, "are so often scabed because they use exercize presently after meals." And this leads him to one of those purple passages which combine acuteness of observation with sensible advice:

Opposite to Exercize is Idlenesse, (the badg of gentry) or want of Exercize, the bane of body and minde, the nurse of naughtinesse, step-mother of discipline, the chief author of all mischief, one of the seven deadly sins, the sole cause of this and many other maladies, the Devil's cushion, his pillow and chief reposal. . . . This body of ours, when it is idle, and knows not how to bestow itself, macerates and vexeth itself with cares, griefs, false fears, discontents and suspicions; it tortures and preys upon its own bowels and is never at rest.

From personal experience Robert Burton had acquired the conviction that those unfortunate people who were subject to discontent were generally lean, sallow, hirsute, and of a dark complexion. Men who had thick eyebrows, stammered slightly, became prematurely bald, had black spots in their nails, perspired immoderately, laughed to themselves, or made "mimicall gestures" were specially liable to melancholy. Those who were subject to this dotage should first pray to God, and if that failed they should consult a doctor, adopt a moderate diet, and enjoy good company, music, and philosophy. He is not very positive on the subject of medicines, pointing out that the inhabitants of the Shetland Islands, who know no medicine, generally live for one hundred and twenty years. Yet there is no doubt that the following herbs are excellent in relieving the black choler: borage, hellebore, bugloss, betony, wormwood, marigold, rosemary, maidenhair, endive, and tobacco. There are some minerals also which can prove of great assistance. There is the granatus, a kind of ruby imported from Calicut, which "if hung about the neck or taken in drink much resisteth sorrow and recreates the heart." A topaz is also useful in allaying fear or anger. Whereas the onyx helps "against the phantastic illusions which proceed from melancholy" and the sapphire "is the great enemy of black choler."

It is not recorded whether Burton himself followed his own prescriptions. But he certainly walked down to Folly Bridge, listened to the bargees shouting at each other, and enjoyed his laugh.

At noon I go up on deck. We have covered 521 miles since midday yesterday and are now parallel with the Strait of Gibraltar, but well out to the west of it. It is still wet and cloudy: the wood of the taffrail is still cold to the touch and there are but faint skids of sunshine that shine over the distant sea and then skim quickly across our boat. No land is to be seen—just the soup-plate edge of the horizon. Thinking of Robert Burton's instructions, I begin to pace up and round the deck. V. comes up and tells me to desist from so absurd an exercise, since with the ship pitching as it is I shall be bound sooner or later to fall down a gangway or into the hold. We cling to the taffrail and look out upon the furious sea. "If it were calm," says V., "we should be seeing porpoises in these latitudes," and as she says the words a young porpoise springs and flops a few yards only from the ship, being a truant from its school.

V. works all day putting Virginia's letters in order; I get on with my two articles and then read hard. But it is still January all around us.

Friday, January 18

The sun comes out of the surrounding sea punctually at 8.00. It is difficult in my cabin to estimate the outside temperature, since it is air-conditioned. In the corner, close to the ceiling, an apparatus is affixed which is larger and more effective than the neat little nozzles one finds in the sleeping cars of the Scottish night express. It contains two large globes the size almost of a diver's helmet, which rotate or oscillate in their sockets like the eyes of some gigantic sea monster. One can turn the machine off or on and direct it upon one's body or away from it so that it puffs only at the cabin door. It spurts into the cabin and keeps the temperature at between 65 and 75 degrees. I expect I shall be glad of it when we reach the tropics, but at present it makes me feel northerly. I open my casement and the roar and swish of the sea fills the cabin. It is still rough with the wind blowing from the north as it has done ever since we left Calshot and watched "the sun's feet stride across the sea," carefully omitting in its passage to throw a single ray upon the bunched houses of Bournemouth East and Christchurch. So far, I have not cast a clout.

I find it unexpectedly refreshing to be released from the sense of time. The little red engagement book which Bruce Lockhart gave me for Christmas lies listless and unrequired in a drawer. For the first time in my life since I was eight years of age I appreciate timelessness, and rejoice to feel that it is of no importance whatsoever whether today be yesterday or tomorrow. This is in truth a physical and intellectual luxury.

The log at noon shows that we have been 522 miles in the last twenty-four hours and are are now approaching the Canaries. V. is convinced that we ought to be further advanced, that the captain must have made some error in calculation, and that, if he only knew it, we have already passed the Canaries and are on a level with Dakar. She even suspects that he has turned north during the night and that we must now be heading back to Southampton instead of towards Table Bay. It is curious that a person who has so good a bump of locality should become so confused by the points of the compass. To her the words "east" or "west" have no instinctive significance and she has to work out in her mind on which side, port or starboard, America lies and on which Asia. While working this problem out, she makes sign-post gestures in the air.

It is warm but not hot. We lean over the taffrail, if that be the correct nautical expression, and discuss the mistakes in navigation which the captain has committed. We are thus engaged when suddenly bang in front of us, there looms the island of Teneriffe. We have a quick luncheon and then, by invitation, go up onto the bridge.

Teneriffe by then is close to us and dark. The peak is unfortunately hidden in clouds, but the captain shows us where it lies. As we sweep past the island its eastern flank comes into view and we see a small town with churches and oil tanks flashing in the afternoon sun. V. is delighted at being able to identify through the telescope a white farmhouse which is so isolated that it must be almost inaccessible. This stimulates the hermit side of her character. She would, if she were free from all responsibilities, like to live on a desert island which no boats ever visit, at which no postman ever knocks, and on which there is no Bench, which, as a J. P., she is summoned to attend. As the *Willem Ruys* to the throb of its mighty engines swings past the island she remains fascinated by the loneliness of that small white farm. I assure her that it is not a farm but one of Franco's police stations. She says that she can identify vineyards through the telescope and that no police station was ever sited in a vineyard. We swing to the southeast again and the outline of the Grand Canary appears on our left. As the sun sets it throws a pink light upon the bare mountain sides of the Grand Canary, crinkling in the crevices and gorges like tissue paper as in the Aegean Islands. But the peak of Teneriffe remains hidden from us under its dome of cloud.

They have set out the deck chairs in a thin tight row along the taffrail. They are made of wood and have a little footrest which can be adjusted. V. thinks them uncomfortable and prefers the smaller dryad chairs in which she can sit upright. But I like my own chair and sit in it for a while reading Diogenes Laërtius. But it is cold and the Canaries have faded behind us in the mist of dusk.

At 6:45 the captain throws a cocktail party in the saloon. We sit at a table where there is a senior colonial civil servant, aged about thirty-seven, with his wife, who has sprained her ankle. His name is Boumphrey and he is in the audit department at Singapore. He is dressed in a sports coat and grey flannel trousers and is intelligent and earnest. He has been stationed in the Falkland Islands, in Nigeria, and in Malaya. He seems the sort of sensible person who will not mind talking shop and from whom I shall derive much reasonable information.

Dinner this evening is what in liners subject to American influence is called "a get-together party," but what the Rotterdam Lloyd prefer to call a "Welkomstmaal." We are offered wine and liqueurs at the expense of the company, which strikes me as hospitable and even lavish. The stewards have exchanged their blue suits for white duck. It makes the Dutch stewards, who are chosen largely for their looks, seem like Olympians ministering to our needs; even the Indonesian stewards look clean and neat. Some of the male passengers have also donned white dinner jackets, which seems premature. The women are arrayed in sumptuous evening frocks. V. and I feel very dowdy in comparison.

There is a dance in the saloon afterwards. We watch it for a while and then go down to our cabins and to bed. But the sound of revelry continues to reach us as the great ship plunges onwards in the African night.

II. EQUATOR

1

Saturday, January 19

It is cold and grey with a northeast wind driving long waves beside us. At noon I go on deck and find it deserted except for two young Englishmen who are pacing round and round rapidly in football sweaters and scarves. The clouds, which are the colour of army blankets, drift above us the whole day. I and my fellow passengers are still wearing our winter clothes. Yet the log tells us we have been 526 miles since yesterday and are now parallel with the Río de Oro and in the same latitude as Miami, where American men and women are at this moment basking in bikinis.

At 12.30 the captain gives a cocktail party in the smoking room in honour of the birthday of Princess Margriet, who was born in Canada and is now the godmother of the Netherlands Merchant Marine. We are given pink drinks at the expense of the Rotterdam Lloyd; the orchestra play the Dutch national anthem, the passengers stand up and raise their glasses, and the captain shouts "Hoch! Hoch! Hoch!" The Hubrechts have orange bows pinned to the lapels of their coats. Jan Hubrecht, who is a fervent royalist, is moved by the occasion; there are tears in his loyal eyes. And at luncheon we are given *Gateau Margriet*, which is a spongecake decorated with oranges and daisies in marzipan.

The *Oceaanpost*—which is a radioed newssheet written in Dutch and English and containing the main items of the wireless bulletins—informs us that Edward Boyle has been appointed Parliamentary Secretary at the Ministry of Education and that Julian Amery obtains a similar post at the War Office. This means that Harold Macmillan wishes to repair the split caused by the Suez adventure by including in his government two prominent rebels. But if Edward Boyle can be forgiven and rewarded, why should Nigel, whose protest against Suez was no more resounding than his, be boycotted as a traitor? I hope the significance of these two appointments will be appreciated by the Conservative Association of Bournemouth East and that Nigel will now be forgiven for having stuck to his election pledges. They cannot be as unfair as all that.

V. and I find this boat one of the best designed that we have ever seen. The cabins are wonderfully comfortable, the bunks resilient, the water hot, the lighting and ventilation perfectly arranged. The public rooms—the saloon, the smoking room and bar, the library, and the gallery that connects them—all open into each other and should serve as a model of design for an embassy or government house. The furniture is soft and unobtrusive, the carpets of thick grey pile, and the decoration restful. The rooms are so skilfully lit that one can read even small print and yet there is no glare at all.

The menus in the dining saloon are printed in Dutch and English. The Indonesian waiters can speak no known language and are unable to read. Thus each item on the menu bears a number and all one does is to write down the number one needs and hand it to the steward. Writing pads and little stubby pencils are provided beside each plate for this purpose. Passengers are warned only to write down one number at a time, since if they hand the waiters two numbers, confusion is apt to result. Either the passenger is provided with tapioca and prunes, to be shortly followed by beefsteak, or else the waiter will drop his tin tray in panic upon the linoleum floor, producing a splashing noise so powerful that it must reverberate throughout French Equatorial Africa and beyond.

I am fascinated by these Indonesian stewards and watch them with attention. Hubrecht tells me that they are not for the most part natives of Java or Sumatra but that they come from the adjoining island of Madura, which possesses a long nautical tradition. When dressed in their white duck suits and wearing their sandals or black shoes they look delightfully cool and span. But in the early mornings, when they are employed on housemaid work in the cabins, they wear pyjama suits of cotton waste and their feet are bare. While waiting for the passengers to leave their cabins, they squat on the floor of the passage, playing with their toes and from time to time flicking jokes at each other in their native tongue. I am unable to catch the drift of their remarks. When one of them will suddenly say to the other *"tulangbelakangsujaadashute,"* I am unaware whether he is saying "I have a slight touch of lumbago this morning" or "I see the South Africans are all out for 254." It may be sex only which they discuss with each other, relating how, when on leave in Madura during the last voyage, they climbed up a palm tree at full moon and watched the village girls bathing naked and ritually at Pamekasan. Their legs appear to me to be double-jointed and to fold neatly, each below or into the other, like the wings of little bats, or like those spectacle frames which are designed to collapse upon themselves and thus to fit into cases no larger than a dollar piece. When seated at ease (and they are frequently at ease) they seem not so much to be seated upon as spilled over, and adhering to, the linoleum of the floor, as if wet dishcloths flung down there by some hurried charwoman.

Ageless these anthropoids seem to us, their hair remaining thick and black, their faces unwrinkled until, at the age of seventy or eighty, time leaps like a jaguar upon them, leaving them suddenly haggard, with scrannel necks and with but three or four gold-capped teeth stuck here and there. It does not strike me that their intellectual development has been rapid or prolonged. I have heard their voices giggling in the pantries and have come across them ogling and pinching each other, not as becomes the grandfathers that they probably are, but in the manner of little boys of seven. Among them the Dutch stewards pass and repass, aloof and majestic, like Apollo or Ares, or Dionysus, or Hermes visiting the Pygmies.

They seem to be an amiable race, in whom the young wine of self-determination has created uncertainty of status. When in the smoking room I wish to summon one of them in order to sign a chit for a glass of beer or a martini, I find it difficult to attract their attention. They lean against the wall in abstraction, reflecting doubtless on the purpose of life or the nature of the beautiful and the good. I am averse from shouting "Boy!"

at them, since this seems to me a degrading appellation. So I asked Hubrecht, who has lived long in Indonesia, what I should say. He told me that "Boy!" was permissible, since it was English and customary in the Far East. If they refused to respond to that call, I might experiment with *"Bung!"* which means "Comrade" or "Brother." Two things I must never do, either to shout *"Jongens!"* which is a Dutch word and as such obnoxious to the liberated, or to snap my fingers, which in the Far East is a gesture reserved for summoning dogs or other domestic animals. But when I do call *"Bung!"* their abstraction becomes even more impenetrable.

I go to the library in the hope of finding a copy of *Die Leiden des jungen Werthers* but the books provided for passengers are either in the Dutch language, which I can only read with difficulty, or they are the novels of the more popular British and American authors.

In the evening after dinner there is a round game called "Bingo" played in the saloon. One purchases a card or piece of paper on which numbers are printed and, as the games instructor calls out the numbers he draws from a bag, one strikes out the corresponding number on one's card. When all the numbers on one's own particular card have thus been called and cancelled, one exclaims "Bingo" in a loud voice. The other passengers applaud sympathetically; and one walks up to the table to receive a prize. Now that I have realised that the game is not one of skill but solely one of chance I shall take part in it when played in future. For the moment V. and I just master the rules and then retire below decks to bunk.

2

Sunday, January 20

I wake up at 4.30 A.M. and look out of my casement. I see a lighthouse winking patiently and below and around it a tiny coruscation of lights quivering. It is Dakar. I get up, put on a dressing gown, cross the passage, and rouse V. It is not, I know, really worth it, but I hate seeing anything of the slightest interest without sharing it with her. She will be interested to observe that the African continent, which until now has kept away from us, could swing or bulge so suddenly and so close that we can see lights at four in the morning twinkling beside a tower. To me those lights recall de Gaulle and the agony of his failure to capture Dakar and French Africa. We were told at the time that some of his staff had spoken indiscreetly of the coming venture and that the Vichy Government had thus been warned in advance and had been given time to prepare their resistance. Only a man of de Gaulle's superhuman faith, resolution, and self-confidence could have survived such a fiasco. As it was, the utter failure of his expedition embittered the already taut personal relationship between him and Churchill and confirmed our General Staff in their suspicion that the Free French represented a security risk. Thus in the future our plans were concealed from them and de Gaulle was deeply hurt by our unwillingness to keep him fully informed in advance of such operations as the North African and Normandy landings, with which he claimed with some justice that he was intimately concerned. Curious that a little nest of lights sparkling across dark waters should recall to me so vividly the picture of this tall man actually trembling with suppressed rage in his study at Carlton Gardens. I sympathised with his mortification, I profoundly admired his courage, and kneeling there on my bunk watching the lights of Dakar swing past us, I exclaim *"Vive de Gaulle. Vive de Gaulle!"* Then I pull up my little shutter again and go to sleep.

All morning after breakfast I work at my article for Lord Inman's anthology on the design for living or the pursuit of happiness. I have promised to send it him by air from Cape Town, and although I regard eight thousand words as far too long for any such contribution, I am not sorry to do it since, it helps me to clear my mind for my present theme, for my examination of the nature of discontent and of the remedies which wise men throughout the ages have suggested against melancholia.

At 12.45 we come up on deck. It has suddenly become hot. They are filling the oval swimming pool, pumping in the waters of the Atlantic through a large orifice in the floor of the bath. The salt sea water when it first enters gurgles and seethes ferociously and is then hushed into a steady bubbling which in its turn subsides as the bath fills. This process, they assure me, will take place every morning at 7.00, so that if I bathe before breakfast I shall have water fresh and clean from the Atlantic. I am encouraged and a trifle intimidated by this prospect. Dr. Parish has forbidden me to bathe, but he did not forsee that I should cross the Equator backwards and forwards six times in the course of this journey, or that the temperature of the water would rise to 85 degrees.

When after luncheon I go up on deck for my daily round of

exercise I find that the bath is already peopled with swains and nymphs splashing in the sunshine. I go up to the sports deck and look down upon them. There are two notices suspended on the side of the bath; the one in English reads "Diving forbidden"; the one in the Dutch language reads *"Verboden te duiken."* But the young rubber planters, tea planters, civil servants, and employees of the Burmah and other oil corporations pay no attention, I am glad to say, to this prohibition. In they jump with arms stretched forward, and one can see as they propel themselves like frogs in the clear water that their hair is parted by the pressure into curious seaweed fronds.

How correct was Kenneth Clark in making so sharp a distinction between "the naked" and "the nude." The bodies of Western whites do not gain by being unveiled. I had admired the elegance of these young men, now puffing naked in the pool, when I had watched them playing deck quoits on the sports deck arrayed in flannels, or dancing in the saloon after dinner in their neat white tuxedos. Lissom they had seemed to me and limber, whether their arms were taut or pendulous, whether their legs were moving to the music or relaxed. I had envied their muscular shoulders, their straight limbs, the way in which their waistcoats were concave and not convex, the neat manner in which their torsos fitted above the pelvis, their tidy little necks, *teretesque suras*. But when I saw them in the swimming pool this illusion was dispelled. Here was one whose right shoulder was demonstrably higher than his left; here another round whose knees puffy pouches had already formed; and there a third—a mere lad with the milk of Uppingham still wet upon his lips—whose forearm remained permanently

flexed, as if he were prancing outside a football scrum waiting for the ball to dribble out.

Moreover, I reflected, whereas the skin of the coloured races appears smooth, immaculate, and glistening, that of the white races is patined with bright spots. Across the shoulders, the backs, and even the fronts of these youths varied blemishes were spread like constellations. Here was the Great Bear, there Cassiopeia, here an angry little rash of Hyads and Pleiads, and there, striding boldly, the belt of Orion. Moreover, as they laughed and splashed they snorted wetly, and from time to time indulged in that displeasing gesture whereby bathers, having no handkerchief upon their persons, pass or smear the thumb and finger down the nose, expelling moisture.

I was saddened by this spectacle, recalling how, in the vicinity of Rouen on one occasion I had spent the afternoon with a distinguished but inarticulate professor of mathematics, watching some village sports or festival upon the heights of Bois-Guillaume above the Seine. He had remained silent all the afternoon and it was not until we returned to the city and were drinking beer at a café on the quay that he opened his lips. *"Dieu,"* he exclaimed with a profound sigh, *"que l'humanité est laide!"* He would have agreed with Kenneth Clark that a marked difference can be observed between the naked and the nude.

Later in the afternoon we pass a fellow Dutch liner, the *Barnevald,* of the Nederland line. We greet each other in passing and the children in our ship scream shrilly and wave their bathing towels. Dusk descends and the lights go up on the promenade deck and in the saloons. An Indonesian steward comes out from the smoking room and flings into the darkening waves a cluster of forsythia which has accompanied us all the way from Rotterdam. There is a feeble sunset which disappoints me. I move into the saloon and continue reading.

After dinner we sit and talk to the Hubrechts and they give us much interesting information about Java, the Indonesian Republic, and the shabby way in which, after the Japanese surrender, the British political and military authorities in the Far East behaved to the poor Dutch.

I go to bed and read Bates's "Colonel Julian." He is an admirable writer and his style is more muscular than that of Somerset Maugham; but there is a sense in the background of the loud lustfulness of a sergeant's mess, which I find unattractive. It is strange that I, who am so tolerant of sex behaviour in practice, should be so readily shocked when it is described in print. It was not for nothing that I was born in the reign of Queen Victoria.

3

Monday, January 21

I get up at 7.25 and put on my dressing gown and the *zapatos* I bought at Cadaqués. I had felt it preferable that this elder at least should reach the swimming pool before any Susannahs were about. I had endeavoured, before leaving London, to acquire a bathing suit which comprised both top and bottom, a pair of pants below, and above it a sort of vest or singlet by which the upper part of the body should also be concealed. But the man at Simpson's, with a smile in which contempt was not unmixed with compassion, informed me that this form of bathing wear was no longer worn or sold. It was quite the thing today even for elderly gentlemen to wear bumbags and nothing else. Hoping that he was correct in this assumption, I came up on deck in the warm fresh morning, swinging my little pants audaciously to show that I was not really ashamed.

The bathing pool in the *Willem Ruys* is, as I have said, of oval construction and two decks deep. When it is filled, the water sways with the movement of the ship, taking leave of one end of the blue tiles with a long succulent kiss, and smacking the opposite end with a brisk wet splash; it reminds me of the Wellenbad in Berlin. To my relief there are no other bathers at this early hour, with the exception of a sad Dutch engineer of middle age, who, before he enters the water, places his pince-nez neatly on a bench. Obedient to the instruction that I am not to dive, I descend the steep steps into the water and then fling myself upon my back. The water is warm, the sky is blue, the accompanying sea gulls are white: I feel forty years younger. There is a notice beside the door of the men's dressing room informing one of the daily water temperature; today it is 74. There is also a weighing machine which I glance at with some distaste. But, in that I am feeling adventurous this morning, I step upon the little contraption and am delighted to observe that I weigh only eight stone; yet as I continue to gaze in some surprise at the needle it quickly mounts to fourteen, and I then realise that as the ship rolls and pitches my displacement upon the step of the machine is displaced. I strike a comforting average of twelve, which John Hunt tells me is "more or less what you ought to be." I have a shower of sweet fresh water in the dressing room and then return exuberant to my cabin.

Richard Rumbold has often told me that the reason why I am impatient with melancholy people is because I have never either experienced or witnessed acute suffering. Had I served in the trenches in Flanders during the winter of 1916, or had I spent years in a Nazi or a Japanese concentration camp, I should have learnt that, whereas squalor can be endured, fear mastered, and the nerves conditioned to the spectacle of horror, no man can see hatred triumphant and love banished without his character being deepened and changed. I have been mortified by this criticism and for a while I believed it to be profoundly true. But I am not so sure.

In the first place, as a little boy at my private school, with my parents living abroad and my schoolmaster a sadistic bully, I was certainly, between the ages of eight and thirteen, atrociously and continuously unhappy. Yet it has left no scar upon my soul. The abominable shyness which has been a curse to me throughout my life is, I am sure, not due to this experience, but to natural timidity. All that remains to me from those wretched years is a deep pity for the little boys whom I see at Charing Cross Station in September on their way back from their summer holidays; and a "sudden glory" when the Golden Arrow on its way to Dover slides past the playing fields of The Grange, Folkestone. On the other hand many of my closest relations and most intimate friends were in the trenches in 1916 or spent years as prisoners of war and even in the hands of the Japanese. It may be that, when suffering from indigestion, they recall these months or years of misery in nightmare dreams; but I am positive that this memory does not warp their waking minds or souls. In this very boat is Jan Hubrecht, who was interned by the Japanese in circumstances of fear and degradation, who is today as eupeptic as any of us and who, although even an older man than I am, dances lustily in the saloon after dinner, beaming with the *douceur de vivre*. Conversely, many of the most melancholy men whom I know have been spared these frightful experiences and have, to all seeming, spent their lives in unruffled tranquility. Thus, although wounded by Richard Rumbold's criticisms, I am not convinced of their relevance.

The melancholy disposition is, I am sure, occasioned in the first place by what both Galen and Burton called "black bile" and what today I suppose, we should describe as a functional defect in the ductless glands. In the second place it is caused by what Burton called "sloth" and what the ecclesiastics refer to as "acedia," or "accidie." This odd word derives from the Greek "*akedia*," meaning quite literally "the state of not caring." In the Middle Ages the term was applied to the condition of torpor or moral prostration into which nuns, anchorites, monks, and solitaries were inclined to relapse, owing to low diet, lack of exercise, and denial of practical occupation. It was denounced by the Church as one of the main sources of restlessness and rightly included in their list of the seven cardinal sins.

Dr. Josef Pieper, in his excellent book *Leisure, the Basis of Culture*, recognises acedia as Kierkegaard's "despairing refusal of oneself." When a man is unable to acquiesce in his own existence, when he begins to have doubts (as all melancholics have doubts) regarding his own identity, when he feels himself unable to be at one, either with the external world or with his own temperament, then he is surrendering to the capital sin of acedia. In contemporary life, when I hear a man or woman use the odious words "I couldn't care less," I know that I do not wish to see or hear that person again.

Before I left England I had been reading Georg Brochmann's book *Humanity and Happiness*. He had served in the Norwegian resistance movement, had been arrested by the Gestapo, had been interrogated and interned. During the months he spent in a concentration camp he reflected on the problem why, when faced with suffering, danger, and the deprivation of all that had formerly been regarded as important, he had experienced greater "happiness" than at any previous period in his comfortable bourgeois life.

He makes an interesting comparison between Hjalmar Ekdal in Ibsen's *The Wild Duck* and Dr. Stockmann in *The Enemy of the People*. The latter was a happy man, in that he was able to express his tremendous vitality in an ideal attuned to his own personality: the former was miserable since he was a weak man, who indulged in "life-lies" or daydreams, and was shattered when the falsity of his position was made plain to him by Gregers Werle. In the same way Dr. Brochmann contends that many Norwegians of the resistance movement were rendered "happy" because they found that they could express in action their ideals of faith, freedom, and decency. Under the German occupation such concepts as honour, humanity, and dignity acquired overwhelming practical significance and rendered men "happy" by providing them with a dominant ideal, which they had lacked during the years of security. He is convinced that this is a fundamental fact which no casuistry can explain away.

He learnt from this experience that the happiness which the young intellectuals despised as a bourgeois opiate to deaden desirable pain was in essence "a harmonious development of our instinctual energies in the direction of an ideal." He makes some interesting suggestions. He suggests that in young people idealism is often but a superficial emotion and that cynicism might prove a better path towards the attainment of authentic idealism. He suggests again that the aim of culture is to render civilisation human and to preserve the capacity for happiness. Thus every technical invention is worthless that does not provide us with opportunities to develop our natural instincts: he compares the delight afforded to Robinson Crusoe by his own inventive adaptability with the torpor engendered by a modernized flat, in which there is nothing left to discover, to adapt, or to do. He contends also that a major cause of unhappiness is the failure of an individual to integrate, not his character merely, but the objectives of his energy. "Without concentration on the object," he writes, "no experience will give a satisfactory release of happiness-potential." These are interesting comments and injunctions.

There is another point which Brochmann makes which seems useful. He contends that between the ages of thirty-eight and forty-two most individuals pass through a climacteric as important and disturbing as that of puberty. Instinctual energy, at that period of life, diminishes or changes, and if new energy be unavailable or be misdirected, then acute unhappiness will result. A man, when he reaches this period, must realise that material success has nothing to do with happiness and must develop a stronger sense of responsibility for others. If he manages to do this he may experience a form of regeneration, and acquire a living happiness such as he never knew before. "Every age of life," he writes, "creates in its own way a high point of happiness for those who have recognised its potentialities." There is truth in this. But one is not obliged to join a resistance movement or be imprisoned by the Gestapo in order to discover it. It has been thought of before.

Thus to the two main sources of causeless melancholy, ill-health and acedia, I add a third, the absence of any realisable ideal.

4

The Indonesian steward who summons us to meals possesses a musical gong. In Victorian days, in the great country houses of England—at Chatsworth, at Hatfield, and at Knole—there was a large circular gong in the lower regions which the butler would strike with a powerful drumstick, spreading the monotonous reverberation of a single deep note throughout the rooms. In the evening there would first come the "dressing gong," warning people that the moment had arrived when they should go upstairs and dress. This was followed half an hour later by the "dinner gong" itself, announcing that they must now come downstairs and be ready to be taken in to dine. Only in very few, very old-fashionable country houses does this gong now boom. Its place was taken, about the time when King Edward VII ascended the throne, by a musical gong which played scales, or even, in extreme circumstances, little tunes, such as "Home, Sweet Home" or "The Eton Boating Song." This musical accompaniment was, for some reason, regarded by the aristocracy as middle class and the practice has now been dropped. Yet I suppose that in the boarding-houses of Bayswater it still survives, and I have certainly seen these gongs for sale in the ironmongery department of Harrod's or the Army and Navy Stores. What is so charming about the

Indonesian steward is that he manages to extract from his little gong an oriental tune. Instead of scales or "Home, Sweet Home," there is a sound, as he hurries along the decks and up into the observation saloon, of temple bells ringing from pagodas among palms rustling in the morning or the evening breeze. As he rings his bells his face assumes the rapt expression of a hierophant or acolyte and we become aware that he is the product of a civilisation distinct from that of Bayswater or the Army and Navy Stores. We are reminded that we are travelling to the Far East.

In the afternoon, as I read on deck, the children of the passengers play around me. One of the most admirable features of Rotterdam Lloyd efficiency is that they have realised that children upon board ship can prove a constant anxiety and nuisance. Thus they are not allowed to enter the main saloons or to have their meals with the adults. They have an early breakfast somewhere, and during the morning they are placed in a concentration camp or cage and supervised by competent Dutch nurses. The prison in which they are confined is a delightful prison, containing swings, shoots, seesaws, rocking horses, and even a little shop where they can play at shoplifting and a small cottage or house to scale with doors that they can enter, and a thatched roof. Then in the afternoon, between the hours of two and five, they are allowed to play on the promenade deck under the eyes of their parents. Out come their private teddy bears, their trains, and their small tin motor cars. Although, when I am going on my constitutional walk around the deck from 3.30 to 3.55, my passage is obstructed by these infants and their possessions, I find that with a little skill I can pick my way among them, and I enjoy their *gentil babil* and their stout tottering gait.

They are a cosmopolitan bunch of children, of different colour and origin, being English or Dutch or Indonesian or Chinese. "Singho!" they shout to each other, or "Jackie!" or "Dieck!" Coming down the staircase this morning, V. stopped to listen to two little girls who were exchanging confidences cheek by jowl. "What was your first foreign language?" one said to the other. "Italian," her friend replied. "Liar," exclaimed the other, "why should it be Italian?" "But it was," protested the second. *"Uno, due, tre*—so there!" "Mine was Dutch," the first one answered. *"Ja! Ja! Ney! Ney!"* mocked her companion. And most of them speak Malay and chatter gaily with the Indonesian stewards.

I sit in my deck chair reading the admirable Amiel. For some reason V. does not care much for the deck anyway, and when she consents to leave *La Grande Mademoiselle* and her cabin, she prefers to sit bolt upright on a hard teak bench in the sun. I join her for a moment, and while we are gazing at the turbulent blue water we suddenly see a shoal of flying fish dart out of the sea and then fall again into the next wave. "The flying fish," wrote Alun Lewis:

> *The flying fish like kingfishers*
> *Skim the sea's bewildered crests . . .*

This is poetic licence. They are not in the least like kingfishers, they are like small tin model aeroplanes bought at Woolworth's; and their motion is not correctly described as "skimming"; it is far more curious and complicated than that. We gaze at them entranced and I go downstairs to fetch my binoculars and to have a closer view. It is clear that they have been ill-equipped by nature either with the apparatus which enables an animal to leave the water for the air, or with the apparatus which thereafter enables it to return to the waves without pain or disturbance. It takes them some time, and many quick beatings of their fins, to leave the water, and even when they do so they are not immediately air-borne but continue to imprint a scratch or wake upon the water with their keel. Then they do not seem to dive back into the waves with any surety or elegance but just to fall or flop with a splash. They are delightful animals and the sight of them enlivens V.'s dear romantic soul. To her they are flashing liberated spirits, lovelier even than Shelley's larks or Swinburne's gulls; she is quite cross when I remark that they are metallic objects. But we sit there in the sunshine gazing at them with deep pleasure and hoping that a large school of porpoises will come tumbling in their wake. How memorable are such occasions!

For dinner this evening I put on the neat white dinner jacket which I bought at Moss Bros. and which fits me, as V. remarks, "like a glove." After dinner we sit in the warm air on the deck and talk to the Hubrechts and the Stedalls. Mr. Stedall is something of an ornithologist and has his binoculars permanently swung round his neck for purposes of bird watching. Mrs. Stedall, whom I had met before, lunching with the Houses at Wellington College, is a charming woman who is busy sewing little quadrilaterals or pentagons of chintz on to some other material in order to make a quilt. We are joined by Mrs. Ault who is taking her two children to Kuala Lumpur where her husband is waiting for them. He is an Englishman with some official job; she is either French or Belgian. She is so graceful and gay that, without being exactly a beautiful woman, she makes everybody else look drab. She is the most popular of all the passengers and when she comes and sits at our table Jan Hubrecht actually purrs with pleasure.

The sky is veiled in a heat mist, and we are still unable to see the southern stars.

5

Tuesday, January 22

The sun rises earlier, about 7.20. I go up on deck and have my bathe. I am joined by Hubrecht, who splashes about furiously, wreathed in smiles. V. wrote a poem once which contained the line "this blessed void repose," but never until we embarked upon this journey did we savour the full sense of those words. I change into white trousers, and the sight of the flannel shirt in which, only a week ago, I embarked at Southampton, makes me feel hot all over. I have closed my casement, and the air-conditioning apparatus hums sturdily in my cabin roof, reducing the temperature to 75. We had looked forward to an empty morning but are interrupted by the ceremony of crossing the Equator.

I agree with V. that it would be nice if they could designate the Equator by a row of red and green buoys encircling the globe, so that one knew exactly at what moment one had passed from the Northern into the Southern Hemisphere. Strange as it may seem I actually had this experience when visiting Uganda with the De La Warr mission in 1936. Across the dining-room floor at Government House, Entebbe, was drawn a broad green line, similar to those with which one marks out a hard tennis court. I was assured by the A.D.C. that this line marked the exact line of the Equator. Although to this day I am uncertain whether the A.D.C. was not making a mock of me, I accepted his statement with my wonted gullibility. I stepped with a great stride and without ceremony across the Equator, and then I stepped back again into the Northern Hemisphere. I then straddled the line, which gave me the impression of being titanic, bestriding the globe with all the majesty of Atlas, King of Mauretania and brother of Prometheus. It was a pleasurable experience. So when Hubrecht asked me whether this was the first occasion that I had crossed the line, I could reply with sincerity that I had already crossed it in Lady Mitchell's dining room. He imagined that I had not heard his question and assumed the expression of bored pity that one adopts towards the deaf.

In the *Willem Ruys* the ceremony of crossing the line is celebrated with customary cordiality. There was a notice in Dutch and English affixed to the board outside the dining room informing us that His Majesty King Neptune would come on board at 9.30 that morning. I was displeased by this, partly because I dislike my timetable being interrupted, and partly because I have a profound reverence for the more elderly Olympians and shall not enjoy seeing Poseidon (who after all was the son of Saturn and own brother to Zeus himself) being treated as a comic character. When at breakfast I explained to V. my apprehensions regarding the impending ceremony she reproved me for being snooty and for having no sense of fun. I replied that for a man of my age, who from a safe distance had witnessed two world wars, I had an excellent sense of fun: what I did lack—and I was proud of it—was a taste for

farce. She said that she rather liked farce sometimes. I said that
this must be due to her Spanish blood. So we went up somewhat silently together to the sports deck, looking down on the
bathing pool, prepared to watch the event.

It began with a long loud hoot on the ship's foghorn, indicating that Neptune and his court had come on board. My
heart sank. The first-class passengers were grouped around us
so tightly that I saw that I should be unable to use my bioscope
to film the event. The second-class passengers were jammed in
a wedge opposite to us, on the other side of the empty pool,
filling what is called "the Lido," in honour of that long wide
beach near Venice, where Byron used to go for his afternoon
rides and where today the gay young people recline amid the
orange peel and the banana skins. At the forward end of the
pool were three thrones or chairs prepared for Neptune and his
consort and facing them, on the very lip of the swimming bath,
the chair which was to serve as a ducking stool. Many of the
Indonesian stewards were grouped behind us, already grinning
in anticipation but being unable, owing to their small stature,
to see through the phalanx of whites who barred their view.
Even some of the engineers had come out of the bowels of the
ship and were clinging to the derricks and the rigging with
bare black forearms. Then, amid much clapping, Neptune and
his household arrived.

I reflected that of all the older gods, Poseidon had been the
most amorous and inventive. He had obtained the favours of
Amphitrite with the assistance of a porpoise; he had seduced
Ceres in the disguise of a horse, Theophane in the semblance
of a ram, and Tyro by pretending to be the river Enipeus; he
had possessed several other women and produced several bas-

tards, most of whom reached positions of high distinction in the hierarchy of Olympus. And here he was, under his later title of Neptune, striding up to the forward end of the bathing pool, wearing a long flaxen wig and a long flaxen beard, under which I detected the fine feathers of the games instructor. The part of Amphitrite, who until the porpoise episode had been condemned, like Tennyson's sister, to "perpetual maidenhood," was taken by the assistant games instructor, who wore an even more flaxen wig, adopted postures of giggling coyness, and wore a green linen tea gown. Their chief attendant carried a large pantomime trident; the secondary attendants were stripped to the waist and wore heavy necklaces formed of cockleshells. The ceremony began by Neptune reading aloud a long address in Dutch. The victims filed up. To my dismay I observed that the lovely, the elegant, Mrs. Ault had, like Iphigenia, offered herself to the sacrifice. One by one the victims were placed on the ducking stool, lathered with semolina coloured green, shaved with a large wooden razor, and then pitched backwards into the pool. Mrs. Ault was loudly applauded, and indeed it was sporting of her to submit to the indignity; she managed somehow to carry through the performance with consummate grace and with an air of gentle detachment which would have done credit to the Lorelei. The passengers guffawed as one by one the victims splashed into the pool; it was a delight to see the children twisting themselves into knots in an ecstasy of enjoyment; V., owing to her Spanish blood, was much amused. And I, not wishing to be an outsider, smiled with the utmost benevolence. Then we returned to our cabins and worked and read all day.

In the evening there was a film in the second-class dining

room. It was preceded by a newsreel and views of the canals at Amsterdam, which I always enjoy. The main film was a Hollywood discard depicting the adventures of a tough American p.t. instructor in a mixed school kept by nuns. We crept away in the middle and once again vainly sought to catch a glimpse of the southern stars. To our regret there was no sign of phosphorus in the foam made by the great ship as she ploughed through the southern Atlantic.

III. SOUTH ATLANTIC

1

Wednesday, January 23

The sun rises at 6.40. I have my bathe. It is less hot than yesterday although the water temperature is 79. When I have finished splashing in the pool I have a shower of sweet water in the dressing room. I then sit on deck basking in the sun. I realise that today is Wednesday and not Thursday as I had supposed. I am pleased by this error, partly because it proves that I really have lost count of time, and partly because I feel that I have eluded the winged chariot and filched a whole twenty-four hours from death. Who, sitting on such a morning in the southern sun, could fail to be contented?

I am aware that many of my younger friends, such as Hugh Thomas or Philip Toynbee, regard contentment as bourgeois or even vulgar. To them it suggests a trivial view on life and even a lack of sympathy for the afflicted. What right have I, they would snort, to feel happy at a moment when many far more worthy men and women in Budapest are suffering atrociously for their faith in the eternal verities? What right have I to experience any form of satisfaction at a time when Abdul Nasser, with all his arrogance and untruthfulness, has openly humiliated the governments of Great Britain and France? "And what about inflation?" Philip Toynbee would snarl, mocking my complacency. When confronted by these deep indignant minds I feel as shallow as a puddle in the pavement.

Yet I also have my moments of melancholy, when I retire to the uncouth cell:

> *Where brooding darkness spreads his jealous wings*
> *And the night-raven sings.*

I also find it difficult at times to contemplate my body or my soul without disgust. Yet I hope that my resilience is due to satisfaction in general and not at all to self-satisfaction. I really do regard self-satisfaction as a stupid and hampering defect. As I sit there, a line of T. S. Eliot's swoops down like a black crow upon me: "Those who sit in the sty of contentment." I rise quickly and walk back along the promenade deck, flapping my damp bathing pants against my dressing gown, flagellating myself in self-contempt. *"Epicuri,"* I murmur, *"de grege porcus! Porcus! Porcus! Porcus!"* I repeat, giving myself a whack as I say the word. For what am I but an old man driven by the trade winds?

a pig of the herd Epicu

Then, as I descend the staircase, a further picture, another and a more solemn voice comes to solace me. I am there in the Fifth Circle of the Inferno where those who in their lives have given way to accidie or anger wallow in a bog, bubbling slime at each other. Encased in mud, they cry: "We were those who were sad in the sweet air which the sun enlivens":

> *Fitti nel limo dicon: 'Tristi fummo*
> *nell' aer dolce che dal sol s'allegra.*

I feel better after that. I shave and anoint my hair with bay rum. I go down to breakfast.

The menus in the *Willem Ruys* are, as I have said, beautifully printed in the Dutch and English languages. They have on their outside successive reproductions of some of the lesser known pictures from the Boymans museum at Rotterdam or the Ryks museum. There is a charming one today of a young woman with her back to the painter, wearing a red velvet jacket trimmed with fur and receiving a plate of oysters from a stout young man dressed in blue and silver. It is by Jacob Ochtervelt. There is another one that we had yesterday of an old woman cooking pancakes by the fire. It is called *De Pannekoekenbakster* and is by Adrian de Lelie. At breakfast these reproductions are varied by water-colour sketches of monuments at Haarlem, Delft, or Sneek. I have porridge for breakfast which they call *havermout;* the coffee is first class. Then we return to our cabins, looking forward to a long uninterrupted morning.

It is interesting to observe how insistent, even when one has transformed the external circumstances of life, is the force of habit. I have already noted in this diary how often I have been startled by the realisation that, when both time and space are regulated by forces utterly beyond one's own control, it ceases to concern one whether one is in Latitude 38° or Latitude N. 04°, whether today is tomorrow, or whether it be 11.55 in the morning or 3.24 in the afternoon. This liberation from engagements and appointments has shown me how, in my English routine, I am at the mercy of a timetable. I had hitherto assumed that my days were more or less my own and unregulated by anything but my own whims or volition. I was called at 8.00, had my breakfast at 8.30, read the newspapers, dictated my letters, wrote a review or an article during the morning, went out to luncheon, attended some committee or visited some gallery or flower show in the afternoon, read a book during the evening, had some friends to visit me, had my bath and changed, dined somewhere, and eventually retired to bed, wholly unaware that throughout the day I had been disciplined and harassed. On Fridays, by the 3.15 from Charing Cross, I would go down to Sissinghurst, work during the mornings, do some light gardening in the afternoon, read books all evening, and perhaps look at television for half an hour or so after dinner.

I now realise that always I was being bullied by the clock on the mantelpiece (I am not among those who say 'chimney piece' when they mean mantelpiece) and that my engagement book had become a despot ordering me to do this or to do that and to be up and about. My engagement book, as I have said, now lies idly in a drawer of the dressing table, and no telephone can shrill. There is no reason at all why I should not allow the hours to drift by me, sitting in the sunshine looking for flying fish or discussing with my fellow passengers whether it is profitable or the reverse to nip off the minor shoots of the delphinium in the month of May.

Yet such is the force of habit that I have evolved for myself a marine timetable for the purpose of this voyage. Being a romantic, V. regards this reversion to the automatic with contempt. I explain to her that if one is by nature orderly one cannot slough off this disposition merely because one has crossed the Equator. Moreover I believe that the human brain is largely mechanical in its functioning, that it requires a certain regular rhythm, and that a timetable is a flywheel which sets the whole apparatus on the swing. "Nonsense!" she answers, "you are sacrificing the whole benefit of the journey owing to an illusion which you acquired when you were a civil servant. You are incapable of leisure." I have noticed, however, that she also spends the whole morning and the whole afternoon working in her cabin at *La Grande Mademoiselle:* but I do not say so. I merely elaborate my own timetable with greater detail and in greater precision. Obstinacy is among the more unexpected components of the bourgeois mind.

I wake at 6.30; I pull down my shutter and gaze at the sea outside; I read or think till 7.25; then I bathe in the pool and get back to my cabin about 7.55. We then breakfast and return to our cabins where we work till 12.50. We then go on deck, check our position and the twenty-four hours' run on the log and map, and have a cocktail in the smoking room. We then have luncheon, and after luncheon I read or sleep in my bunk until 3.15. Then up I go on deck and walk round and round it until 3.55, when I have a cup of tea. Thereafter I sit on my deck chair reading until 7.15, when V. joins me and we have another cocktail. Then I have a bath and dress for dinner, and after dinner we sit in the saloon, watching some show or indulging in conversation. At 9.45 punctually we go back to our cabins and by 10.45, having read a little, I am fast asleep. I call this a sensible régime. V. thinks that, did I possess greater will power, I should take this opportunity to waste my time.

2

Before leaving England I had decided that, if I am to examine the nature of causeless melancholy, I must study with attention the lives and characters of those malcontents who have exercised the greatest influence upon their contemporaries and successors. I must begin with Jean Jacques Rousseau. I have therefore brought with me the Pléiade edition of the *Confessions* and of the *Rêveries d'un promeneur solitaire*. I have hitherto merely read a few salient passages from these books: I must now read them carefully from page to page.

Ever since reading *Emile* and the *Contrat social*, (the latter of which struck me as being based on false logic and the former as a long exhalation of sloppiness), I have viewed Rousseau with suspicion. It seemed to me a misfortune that a man of his warped character and chaotic emotions should have been able to erode, and eventually to destroy, the mighty bastions of eighteenth-century taste and reason. I quite see that the romantic is an inevitable reaction from the classic mood; that when people have become bored with the rectilinear they come to enjoy the serpentine; and that when for two generations men have been taught to repress their individuality and to follow a prescribed formula they tend to rejoice in exposing the pageant of their bleeding hearts. I fully sympathise, moreover, with those men and women who, being wearied by the conventions of a rigid society, being exhausted by the discipline and fatuity of Versailles or Marly, sought to discover in nature a less trammelled scope for self-expression, and to exchange the artificiality of a too polite world for the apparent simplicity and directness of rural solitude and unsophisticated minds. What I fail to appreciate or applaud is that the intellectuals of the second half of the eighteenth century should, owing to the infection of a blubbering Rousseau, have become so sentimental about it all; or that, in rebelling against the tyranny of reason, they should also, and to their lasting disadvantage, have rejected its guidance.

Rousseau begins his *Confessions* by assuring us that his aim is to depict "a human being as Nature really made him." He seeks from the outset to filch our confidence by confessing some of his schoolboy misdemeanours, hoping thereby to convince us that he is being refreshingly outspoken and frank. Yet these admissions do not create in me any impression of veracity: they create the impression of indecent exposure. So far from convincing us that he is presenting the portrait of "the natural man," he convinces us that, as a man, he was physically, mentally, and morally abnormal. And when, halfway through the book, persecution mania leads him to take leave of his senses, we reach the wearied conclusion that his autobiography is a tissue of hallucinations. The result is not pity, but disgust.

He could, had he been less of an ape, have drawn a true but still idyllic picture of Les Charmettes. One summer, when on the way to Italy, V. and I spent a night at Chambéry. We visited the garden at Les Charmettes and walked through the rooms of the house. There were attractive dry-walled terraces, gay with petunias, geraniums, morning-glories, and plumbagos. The bees, as in Rousseau's day, were busy around the hives. There were bright wooden shutters to the windows, which Madame de Warens, on rising from her bed, would throw wide open to the morning sun. The rooms inside were cool, and dark, and rich with the simplicity of rustic panelling. Yet the account of *Les Charmettes,* as given in the *Confessions,* is an inaccurate account. It was not there that Rousseau and Madame de Warens spent a protracted honeymoon. By the time that amorous lady acquired Les Charmettes, she was already living with Monsieur Vintzenried in her house in Chambéry, and Rousseau was sent away to the suburbs, since his protectress feared that she might cause grave scandal and thereby lose the pension, which she had been drawing from King Victor Amadeus II of Sardinia, if she lived overtly with two lovers at the same time.

Nor, even at the best, was the relationship between Rousseau and Madame de Warens an agreeable relationship; it was perverse and false. She was twenty-eight years old when he entered her service and he was only sixteen. At first her attitude towards him was strictly maternal: she would address him as *"Mon petit"* and he would always refer to her as *"Maman."* She emerges from the pages of the *Confessions* as a most equivocal person—living precariously on her pension as a Sardinian secret agent; sleeping with her butler, Claude Anet; the victim of every passing charlatan and soothsayer; small, extravagant, feckless, and very fat. On his return from a visit to Switzerland, she informed him that he "was now a man" and insisted that he also should become her lover. He was horrified by these instructions but would creep obediently to her bedroom at nighttime, well aware that the sexual disability with which nature and his own habits had afflicted him would only be increased by the inhibitions of emotional incest. In the end, she became dissatisfied with his lack of ardour, and on his return from a second journey he found that his place had been finally taken by Monsieur Vintzenried, a hairdresser's assistant whose father was the concierge of the Château de Chillon. So Rousseau was sent to live at Les Charmettes and eventually took a post at Lyons as tutor to the abominable children of Monsieur de Mably.

In his *Confessions* he represents Madame de Warens as a woman of great vivacity, sensibility, and charm, and one whose life, apart from her addiction to soothsayers and her unfortunate investment in a soap factory, was regulated by the deepest religious convictions. She was, he asserts, in no sense a voluptuary; it was merely that, having fallen under the influence of the encyclopaedists, she had acquired the idea that it would be "philosophic" on her part to go to bed with anyone who might ask her to do so. In the end she was reduced to abject penury, a misfortune which Rousseau much regretted but did little to assuage. Yet in the tenth of his "Promenades," which was composed but a few weeks before his death, he indulges in much retrospective sentiment in regard to Madame de Warens, repeating that his five years at Les Charmettes and Chambéry were the only truly happy years of his life. The whole story, we now know, is defaced by wilful distortion of truth. The fact that, as he would say, it is also *"inondé de larmes"* increases my repulsion.

3

In the late afternoon, after I have finished my walk, I am joined by V., who consents for once to be released for half an hour from the tyranny of *La Grande Mademoiselle*. She has found a place in the front of the promenade deck which is enclosed by windows and where she can sit on a hard dryad chair undisturbed by wind and spray. There she finds a Major and Mrs. Green who will also be doing the return journey. He has been suffering from bronchitis and asthma ever since we left Southampton and has been given M & B by the doctor. This has relieved him of his bronchial trouble but left him dispirited and indeed depressed. Moreover he is afflicted by arthritis and can no longer indulge in the violent sports to which he has all his life been accustomed. In spite of these misfortunes, he is a most courteous old gentleman and I admire his endurance. She is younger than her husband, over whom she watches with tender solicitude. I am glad that this agreeable couple will be with us during the return journey.

There are plenty of flying fish and then suddenly a large school of porpoises starts leaping and splashing in the evening sun. I have a talk with Boumphrey, the colonial civil servant who is in charge of the audit department at Singapore. He is an interesting man who has seen service in remote places and does not mind talking about them. For three years he had been posted in the Falkland Islands and had made several expeditions into the Antarctic. He tells me that the silence of the polar regions is far more impressive than that of the desert and that the effects of light are indescribably beautiful. I suggest to him that the extreme silence may be due to the total absence of all colour. He disagrees with this suggestion, since he says that the light itself, apart from the green caverns in the ice cliffs, throbs with a colour all its own. He has camped in deserts at nighttime when one can almost hear the stars singing, but he says that the hush of the Antarctic is even more exhilarating than that. I like people who notice and recount such things.

I ask him about porpoises and what it is that distinguishes them from the dolphins which played so dramatic a part in Greek mythology. He says that whereas dolphins have long hard beaks, porpoises merely have soft noses and teeth. I ask him whether the porpoises leap and splash in the waves because they are trying to catch flying fish or merely from pleasure in the sparkle of the sun. He says that he believes it to be due to constant cuticular irritation, in that the porpoise is worried by lice and hopes by jumping to shake them off. I say that I do not believe this and he then tells me that a few years ago he was travelling on a small cargo steamer which, unlike the *Willem Ruys,* drove slowly and quietly through the waves: the porpoises would play for hours around the ship, and if one watched them carefully one would see that they would often actually jump onto the prow and scrape themselves along the sides. The captain had assured him that this was in order to scrape off the parasites. I suggested that a porpoise who wished very much to scrape or scratch himself could surely find some remote Calabrian cove in which at night, and without hurry or bumps, he could scrape himself against the rocks. Boumphrey insisted that this was not so; that they liked scraping themselves on the bows of small, slowly moving steamers; and that in any case the captain of his cargo ship, who knew far more about porpoises than he or I did, had assured him that this was an acknowledged fact. I was sorry to hear this, since I have always regarded porpoises as symbols of the *joie de vivre,* and it is disappointing that their antics should be ascribed to the wish to rid themselves of vermin.

V. has been reading a book on marine zoology and raises

a question which interests us much. According to this book, and according to all reasonable supposition, the deep-sea fish, being deprived of light, are not only blind but colourless. How is it therefore, that the film we saw in London called *The Silent World*, which we took to be a portrayal, not of rock-pool fish, but of those inhabiting the lower strata of the sea, depicted animals of the most glowing colours—pink, coral, green, and sapphire blue? V. contended that it was quite true that the fish, living in submarine darkness, were generally both blind and grey; but that when the frogmen descended into the depths with their arc lights the fish suddenly acquired both sight and the most flamboyant colouring. Warming to her theme, she allowed her poet's imagination to illumine such conditions. For years, she said, a blind black fish had been living under some submarine rock with his blind black wife in terms of mutual esteem and habit, but deprived of passion. Suddenly the frogmen with their arc lights would descend and the dull rock would become a Pavillon d'Armide and the blind black wife would twist and turn, displaying her naked azure body and waving veils of emerald and gold. "Cymothoe," her husband would exclaim in ecstasy, "how beautiful you are!" "Then the frogmen," I said, "would return to the upper air and the rock would become a shadow again and Cymothoe no more than the scraping of a sightless fin." Boumphrey, I could see, preferred V.'s version to my own.

After dinner there is a horse race in the saloon. A long green strip, representing a race course, is rolled out upon the centre of the room and six wooden horses on little stands are aligned. Each horse, according to the number it bears, is then auctioned by the games instructor, and some passengers, fevered by the incertitudes of chance, stake high sums. This is a long process and we become rather bored. But when the dice begin to be thrown and the horses are advanced to the numbered section marked on the racecourse, excitement is aroused. From time to time a horse which is in advance of its companion is accorded by the dice a number which is inauspicious and which obliges it to retreat five or six stages further back. These inauspicious numbers occur more frequently as the horses approach the winning post, with the result that anticipation is seasoned by misfortune. Hubrecht, who is radiant with the zest of life, bets recklessly and wins about £7.7.0. I do not bet, not because I do not enjoy games of chance, but because I should hate being stared at by the other passengers if I happened to win.

4

I continue to read the *Confessions* of Jean Jacques Rousseau, striving to master the repugnance which the sentimentalist inspires. It is evident that when serving on the staff of the French ambassador in Venice, the Comte de Montaigu, he committed some act of folly or dishonesty that led to his being expelled in disgrace. "I drove him out," the ambassador reported to the foreign office in Paris, "like a dismissed footman for the insolence he showed me." Rousseau himself seeks to explain away the episode on the ground that he was denounced by personal enemies and informers and that the ambassador "took a dislike to me merely because I strove to serve him faithfully." The story is unconvincing, but it was as a result of his experience in Venice that he developed the conviction that he was

the victim of universal animosity and injustice, a feeling that
later developed into persecution mania. He persuaded himself
that he was being pursued by spies; that when he entered a
room there occurred a sudden hush, since all those present had
before his appearance been indulging in slander against himself; that the members of the orchestra of the Paris Opera had
formed a plot to assassinate him in the streets; and that his
intimate friends, Diderot, Grimm, and Marmontel, were resolved on his destruction, not only because they were jealous
of his genius, but because they envied his superior virtue. His
self-pity is to me unbearable. He is forever lamenting "the
long chain of my misfortunes" and the horrible injustice to
which he had been exposed. It is true that *Emile* was condemned and burnt by the Parlement of Paris and that he
considered it wiser to leave France. Yet his influential patrons,
such as the Maréchal de Luxembourg, Lord Keith, and the
Prince de Conti, never failed to protect him, and his self-imposed exile was profitable and most enjoyable.

The sufferings of Rousseau can thus be attributed less to
external causes, scarcely at all to the quirks of ill fortune or the
malignity of his fellow men, but almost entirely to the flaws in
his own temperament. I could commiserate with his unhappiness, even as I could condone his self-absorption, were it not
for the strain of hypocrisy which defaces his life and memoirs.
One can scarcely forgive this professional sentimentalist for his
atrocious treatment of his mistress Thérèse Le Vasseur, and of
the five babies that she bore.

As with so many malcontents, one can, if one so desires,
attribute his melancholia to masochism, induced probably by
an embarrassing physical defect. As a little boy, he had been

spanked by a Mademoiselle Lemercier and he records the lasting effect of this experience. "Who would have imagined," he writes, "that this punishment, inflicted on a boy of eight by a woman of thirty, should have had so decisive an effect upon my tastes, my desires, and my passions for the remainder of my life?" In addition he suffered since childhood from an enlarged prostate which rendered his bladder incontinent and for many years afflicted him with a dread that he might prove incapable of sexual intercourse. For a man of his animality this was in truth a distorting apprehension. It rendered him hypochondriac, shy, awkward in the presence of women, tortured by the fear of incurring ridicule, and convinced that he would for ever remain an outsider. *"J'étais désolé,"* he wrote in his *Confessions, "de ma lourdise."* "I was overwhelmed by my social incompetence." And in the sixth of the *Rêveries* we come upon the following admission: "The more I look back upon my life, the more convinced do I become that I was never properly adapted to the society of my fellow men".

Being thus hampered and afflicted, it is not surprising that he should have developed the familiar symptoms of a frustrated man. He was haunted by a sense of guilt, not so much for the many dastardly actions that he had committed as for the indolence that had prevented him from doing justice to his gifts. He excused his sloth on the ground that "to write for my living might have stifled my genius and destroyed my talent." We have heard that excuse before and since. He persuaded himself that his superficiality, of which he was sometimes conscious, was not due to any laxity of mind, but to his own wonderful sensibility. "I always feel," he wrote, "before I think." "In my constant dreams of ecstasy," he wrote, "I intoxicate myself with torrents of the most delicious sentiments such as have never hitherto been conceived in the heart of man." He therefore "abandoned the world and its pomps" and decided that, dressed in the garb of an Armenian, he would become an eccentric solitary, rejoicing in "rocks, torrents, conifers, dark woods, rough paths that ascend and descend, mountains, and precipices which fill me with terror." He therefore retired to his hermitage in search, not of happiness, since that was no more than a "rare instant of elation," but of contentment.

Although Rousseau was not as visionary as Shelley, or so deeply afflicted with melancholia as Cowper, or assailed, as was Dr. Johnson, by a panic fear of death, it is evident that he suffered from hallucinations. He describes how he was often distracted by "dark presentiments," how he felt that he was encased "by a whole structure of shadows built around me," and how there came moments of "indescribable disturbance, when I ceased to be myself." Yet in all this prevarication and self-display there do occur some authentic notes. Like so many disintegrated people he was conscious of arrested adolescence. "Although," he writes, "I was in some respects born an adult, I remained a child for many years, and even today I strike many of my friends as having retained several childish attributes." The malcontent, like the homosexual, has often been denied a normal passage from adolescence to manhood: he becomes obstructed somewhere about nineteen.

Although all malcontents are not as warped as was Jean Jacques Rousseau, his inability to distinguish between adult concepts and childish emotions, his pathetic endeavours to "talk grown-up," are illuminating symptoms of the scattered self.

People who are cursed with this peculiar form of disintegration inevitably attribute their misfortunes to the structure of society, to lack of understanding on the part of their parents or school-teachers, to the envy or hostility of the world at large. I agree of course that Rousseau had some slight grounds for feeling that he was persecuted. In 1761 he had published *Emile* in which he had written that "a man who cannot fulfil the duties of a father has no right to beome one." In 1764 Voltaire published his pamphlet entitled "Sentiment des Citoyens" in which he revealed the fact that Rousseau had abandoned his five bastard children in a foundling hospital. The scandal was great, and in January 1766, accompanied by David Hume, he left France to seek asylum in England. Just before his departure a lampoon had been circulated in Paris, purporting to be a letter to Rousseau from Frederick the Great in which the latter offered to provide him with as much persecution as his self-pity required. This lampoon was mainly the work of Horace Walpole, but Rousseau was convinced that Hume had also contributed. Hence arose the quarrel between them which, on the part of Rousseau, was carried to insane excess. His sojourn in England was a failure. After a few weeks at Chiswick he retired to a house owned by Mr. Richard Davenport in the Peak district. Thérèse quarrelled with the English servants and encouraged Rousseau to believe that there was a plot against him, financed and organised by Hume, and operated through the Derbyshire gentry and the household staff at Wootton. One night he and Thérèse disappeared and were missing for several days. Eventually, under the name of Monsieur Renou and in elaborate disguise, he managed to reach Dover and returned to France. The last years of his life were poisoned by the belief that, in spite of the protection of the Prince de Conti, he was being persecuted by the Duc de Choiseul. He died almost demented.

Although I consider it unfair of Voltaire to have denounced him as "a bastard Diogenes," and although I do not agree with Henry James that he was a "pitiable weakling" and a "nerveless sentimentalist and dreamer," I cannot regard Rousseau as a typical malcontent. He was physically afflicted and ended by becoming almost certifiably insane. But I am glad to have read through the *Confessions* and the *Rêveries* undisturbed by any interruptions other than the sighs of the surrounding sea.

5

Thursday, January 24

It is cool and the sky is grey. None the less I bathe under a slight drizzle. I spend the morning writing letters to be posted in Cape Town on Sunday. My article for Inman costs me ten shillings and more in stamps. What happens is that we buy Dutch stamps and post our letters on board. They are then put in a mailbag by the purser and the bag is handed to KLM, which flies them to Rotterdam. The bag is then opened, the letters for England being posted in the ordinary way with their Dutch stamps and flown on by KLM. Thus the letters we post on Sunday should reach London by Friday at latest. Having written my letters, having had them weighed and stamped by the amiable and efficient deck steward, I post them in the letter box on the promenade deck. V. says that this is a wistful thing to do, since what I imagine to be a letter box is in fact a fire alarm. She takes her letters to the purser's office and explains to the clerk there that the mail which she expects to receive at Cape Town will be addressed to her, partly under my name and partly under her own name. The clerk, who is young and not such a master of the English language as are his older colleagues, is bewildered by this information. "Certainly, Lady West," he answers, blinking long sandy eyelashes. "No, not Lady West," V. expostulates. "They will be addressed V. Sackville-West." "I quite understand, Lady Sackville," the poor man replies. "You see," V. explains patiently but with mounting indignation, "I always write under my own name and people generally correspond with me under that name, so there will be many letters in the Cape Town mail thus addressed." "I understand," he answers, flushing slightly. "You need not worry, Miss Nicolson." The conversation becomes so intricate and embarrassing that I leave them to their controversy and return to my cabin.

Every day has its particular tone of character and today has been a series of cross-purposes and misunderstandings. When studying the log and chart before luncheon I tried to measure our distance from St. Helena, which is now alongside us but far to the west. I was interrupted by a brisk, stout little man of military appearance. I had not spoken to him before but had observed him in the smoking room and had realised that he was the type of person who enjoys imparting information. "I see," he began, "that you are trying to work out how far we have come since Teneriffe." "No," I answered, "I am trying to estimate how far we are from St. Helena." "Interesting thing about Teneriffe," he persisted. "Do you know why we call them the Canary Islands?" "No," I answered. "You probably imagine that it has something to do with the birds called canaries?" "No," I repeated. "Well," he went on exultantly, "it hasn't. When the Spaniards got there the island was full of wild dogs so they called them the 'Caninas Islands,' '*canina*' being the Spanish for dog. This was corrupted by our sailors into 'Canaries' and the name stuck." "But," I protested, "the Spanish for dog isn't '*canina*,' it is '*perro*.'" "Not a bit of it," he concluded. "It is *canina*, straight from the Latin, you remember, *cave canem*, what?" At this he laughed horribly and I moved away.

Then at 4.15 V. and I had an assignation with the games instructor, who operates the small wireless machine from which, when the band is not playing, tunes are relayed for our pleasure, either on gramaphone disks, or, I suppose, on short wave from Hilversum. Before I left England I had recorded a talk for the Overseas Service on the B.B.C. which was timed to go out at 1.15 today from London. I asked the games instructor whether he could on his machine manage to capture this wave length and enable V. and me to hear my talk on headphones. He said that it was all very difficult. The ship's own wireless, which was immensely powerful, interfered with all lesser receptions, and in addition the Atlantic caused atmospherics. In any case he would do his best; 1.15 in London, he explained, would be 4.15 at St. Helena, so if we came at that time to the cabin where he installed his machines he would see what could be done.

Never in my life have I been able to establish with games instructors relations of confidence or amity. This Dutchman, although as always perfectly polite, did not enter into my proposal with any zest. He fiddled with the screws of the several boxes which were set out on shelves in his cabin and suddenly, with the utmost distinctness, came the accents of the B.B.C., swaying slightly in the long wash of North and South Atlantic seas. They were giving an intolerably long report on football results. We listened patiently and then came the pips. It was two in the afternoon in London and we had missed my talk by three quarters of an hour. We thanked the games instructor for his co-operation and returned, in a mood of what younger people all too frequently call "frustration," to the saloon. Being bad at mathematics I did not try to calculate how and where he had got the time wrong. V. was disappointed and blamed both the Rotterdam Lloyd and the B.B.C. for this discomfiture. I was privately much relieved.

We talk to the Hubrechts after dinner and I introduce myself to Dr. Neumayer, who was recently a member of Adenauer's cabinet and who looks a most distinguished man. His wife is younger than he is and has a gentle face.

Friday, January 25

There is a southwest gale, hurtling at us straight from the Antarctic. We are in the latitude of Walvis Bay. V. and I spend most of the day working in our cabins. It is so cold that I slip on a jersey. We play Bingo after dinner in the saloon.

Saturday, January 26

It is still very rough and the swimming bath is closed since, when gales blow, the movement inside the pool is so violent that even powerful swimmers are hurled against the hard blue tiles. We go up to the bridge and the captain invites us into his cabin where we are given coffee and cake. V. dislikes the bridge in bad weather, not that she suffers from seasickness, but that up there the violence of the elements seems concentrated and ferocious and everything seems to bang and swing. It is only a little quieter in the captain's cabin, which is next the adjoining chart room and is comfortable and furnished with care.

Captain de Jonge is a mighty mariner and a courteous and amusing gentleman. For three hundred years his family have served in the Netherlands marine or navy, and one of his ancestors was with Admiral de Ruyter when, in June 1667, he broke the boom across the Medway and burnt three British battleships at Chatham. He is the last of his line and it is sad to feel that this long nautical tradition will die with him.

He tells us that the *Willem Ruys* was named after the nephew of the present chairman of the Rotterdam Lloyd, a man of exceptional character and courage. When, after their outrageous bombing of Rotterdam, the German army occupied the port, the officers established themselves in the local yacht club. Willem Ruys the younger, who was president of the club, appeared in their mess and addressed them with cold politeness.

"Gentlemen," he said, "I am unaware that the committee of this club have invited you to be honorary members." The German officers withdrew from the club and established their casino elsewhere. But they did not forgive or forget. Willem Ruys was arrested as a hostage and shot.

The captain tells us that the Greek shipowners, Onassis and Niarchos, had the foresight to construct enormous tankers which could ship such vast quantities of oil that it would become cheaper for them to use the Cape route than to pay dues by going through the Suez Canal. Other countries will now follow their example and in a few years Abdul Nasser may find that the canal is too expensive to maintain. The sands of the desert will resume possession. He asks me how it came that our government failed to foresee the effect which our violation of the charter and the Tripartite Declaration would produce upon world opinion and especially upon UNO and the American public. I could find no answer to this question.

After dinner Hubrecht, who is something of an astronomer, took us to the sports deck to see the southern stars. I had always told V. how, at Kigoma once, Rob Bernays and I had seen the Southern Cross blazing like a crucifix above Lake Tanganyika. And how, on the next morning, we had gone on to Ujiji with the governor, Sir Harold MacMichael, and watched him present an ebony and silver walking stick to an aged cripple who, as a young man, had been one of Dr. Livingstone's servants. The ceremony took place under the very tree which had echoed Stanley's famous remark. That night, that day, remained vivid in my memory. But tonight the Southern Cross was in no sense like a crucifix; it was faint, supine, and as shapeless as a cat's cradle. In fact the stars of the Southern

Hemisphere are a sad disappointment. V., who has been reading *The Lusiads* on this voyage, remarked that Camoens had got it absolutely right:

And here at length [he wrote in Canto V] we crossed the Equator and said goodbye to the familiar constellations of the northern world. In this new southern hemisphere we had already discovered one constellation, the Southern Cross, that before us had never been seen by any. The heavens here sparkle less brilliantly and, having fewer stars, impress less with their beauty. And still we could not tell whether the ocean stretched on for ever, or would give way eventually to some other continent.

IV. CAPE OF GOOD HOPE

1

Sunday, January 27

There is a heavy swell and the swimming pool is closed.
There are fiddles on the tables at breakfast, which is a
rare precaution and ominous. After breakfast we go on
deck. Passengers are gazing expectantly towards the south.
Through the morning mist can be seen a faint line of what
might be hills or might be mountains—in any case indubitably
land. As I watch, a strange bird, which I take to be a cormorant, sails close to the side. It is a glorious, sun-flooded, morning. I return to my cabin and write my diary for yesterday.

At 10.00 we come up on deck again. There straight in front
of us, but still some miles away, lies a jumble of peaks and
sugar loafs and in the centre a long blue precipice with its
summit drawing a sharp straight line against the sky. "That,"
I remark to V., "is Table Mountain."

Each of us was taken by surprise. We had seen many
photographs, films, and paintings of this natural phenomenon,

but had never yet realised how vast, how proud, how dramatic it really was. This confirms me in my belief that no pictorial representation of the works of nature can communicate the actual impression, owing to the fact that no photograph or painting conveys the proportions of scenery or the true relation between masses. One must always see places for oneself.

We go up to the observation saloon, where we find Mrs. Ault with her two children, Michael and Patricia. As we approach nearer, the lesser hills subside and the great mountain stands up behind them. Solitary, dominant, and superb. It is coloured indigo and there is not a cloud upon its straight dark upper rim. "But this," I exclaim excitedly, "is better far than Rio or the Bay of Naples. Why is it that nobody had ever told me about Table Bay before?" V. smiles silently at this remark, since she contends it is one I always make in moments of enthusiasm.

As we get closer we can make out the signal station on the Lion's Rump and the road that climbs beside the Lion's Head. Through my glasses I see the cable that runs straight up to the top of Table Mountain with a small white gondola creeping slowly up it across the cliffs and gorges. "Look! Look!" I exclaim. "One can see the *nacelle* going up." "What," asks Mrs. Ault, "is the English for *nacelle?*" "Gondola," I answer. "But why gondola?" she says. "It isn't in the very least like a gondola." And why indeed?

We nose our way in through the narrow opening of the Duncan dock and edge up to the side of the quay. I had expected to see rows of rickshaws lined up with Kaffirs lolling between the shafts dressed in ostrich feathers and cockleshell necklaces. But not at all. There were several neat taxicabs, painted light green or blue, some engines shunting and puffing along the quays, and a group of dock hands dressed in cloth caps and white shirts, already beginning to handle the sections of the heavy black oil pipes through which our motive power would be pumped into our tanks. The sun blazed. It was as hot as Rome in August.

Before I left England I had written to my old friend Peter Lycett Green saying that we should be reaching Cape Town today and suggesting tactfully that he should give us luncheon and take us to the botanical gardens at Kirstenbosch. I had received no reply and V. said that she thought someone had told her that Peter had got rid of his house and garden at Constantia and had decided to return to England, bringing with him his collection of pictures which, it seems, the National Gallery of South Africa had refused to accept. I therefore scrutinised the motor cars lined up along the dock side in the hope of spotting Peter's great Rolls-Royce. But there was no sign of anything at all like Peter or his motor car, and I therefore concluded that V.'s informant must have told the truth. We decided therefore to have an early luncheon on board and thereafter to take a taxi to Kirstenbosch by ourselves.

We are still gazing at the scene on the dock side and watching passengers descending and visitors coming on board when the steward comes to say that a lady and gentleman are enquiring for us. We turn to see a man and his wife who introduce themselves as Mr. and Mrs. Kramer and who tell us that Alvilde Lees-Milne has sent them a cable announcing our arrival and asking them to show us round. They carry with them a large bouquet of August flowers (plumbago, tiger lilies, and gladioli) which Alvilde has ordered. We go down to our cabins with them in order to put these flowers in water. They say that they propose to drive us to Kirstenbosch, to give us luncheon, and then to see that we are back on board in time. We accept all these offers gratefully, but scarcely have we done so before a Mr. Burnham appears with a note from Peter, saying he is not well enough to come himself to the dock but that he has sent his car and expects us to lunch with him. Having a moment before agreed to lunch and spend the afternoon with the Kramers, we are embarrassed by this double entry and I scribble a note to Peter saying that we are already engaged for luncheon but hope to see him when we return to Cape Town in March. I am worried by this confusion, since I do not like more or less chucking an old friend in favour of two people whom neither of us had ever seen before. But there it was. Mr. Burnham goes back on shore discomfited and we descend with the Kramers and drive away.

We cross the large *terrain vague* extending between the frontage of the town and the harbour. These ugly acres were some years ago thrown out into Table Bay by a firm of Dutch engineers, and the citizens of Cape Town call them "The Reclaimed Foreshore." One day a civic centre and a new railway station will rise upon the site, but for the moment it is a treeless plain, traversed by forlorn railway tracks, and recalling in its arid desolation the earlier landscapes of T. S. Eliot.

We drive past the Van Riebeck statue, past the war memorial, and down Adderley Street and Parliament Street. We see Government House, a nice low white building, where my dear Aunt Lizzie ruled in the eighties and where Lady Anne Barnard, that inquisitive and courageous woman, must also I suppose have resided.

I am appalled by the brainless way in which the town planners of Cape Town have used their unique natural opportunities. One would have supposed that with such splendid examples before them as Groote-Schuur and Groot-Constantia they would have evolved a national tradition of architecture; but not at all. Dull grey office buildings alternate with reproductions of the Grand Hotel at Leicester, interspersed with apartment blocks having balconies with wrought iron railings in imitation of those of New Orleans and Sydney. We drive west, past the Rhodes Memorial and past the zoo park, in which I can see wildebestes and hartebestes and I think gnu grazing peacefully among stone pines. We drive through the suburbs of Mowbray, Rosebank, Pinelands, and Claremont with their neat little villas set among shrubs and creepers. From these there is a fine view over the Cape flats with their factories and corrugated iron roofs glittering in the blazing sun. We stop at Kirstenbosch and enter the botanical gardens.

It is the wrong time of year to visit these famous gardens, since the collection of Cape wild flowers which blaze in January are now just beds of dried grass. There are some magnificent trees, skilfully planted, a few streams which ooze rather than babble down from the mountain, and a pool or two in which blue lilies raise their heads. For the rest there are wide beds of plumbago, agapanthus, and many varieties of hibiscus. Huge cactuses raise their spikes against the blue gorges behind them, and there is a tumble everywhere of bignonia and morning-glory. What impressed us most was the African silver tree, which we had not seen before and the leaves of which are a striking alternation of blue and silver. I gaze up the rock gorges and precipice paths which back the gardens and recall how

Smuts used to tell me how in the mornings he would walk up these gorges clambering, as in his malachite statue in Parliament Square in London, up into the heights.

We then drive on to the Kramers' house, which is called Oakridge and is situated in the suburb of Kenilworth. It is a pleasant house and we are glad to have a rest and a drink under a huge oak tree in which two doves are exchanging love songs in Afrikaans. Mr. Kramer is a wine merchant and she was once a concert singer who was taught by Olga Lynn. They are most hospitable and give us an excellent luncheon with a superb Cape Colony white wine. I try to telephone to Peter to make my apologies, but his servant says that he is resting and must not be disturbed.

The Kramers then drive us back to the dock and we return on board. The mail has been distributed and we sit in the saloon reading our letters. There are two letters from Nigel giving us the latest news of developments in Bournemouth East. He is hoping that the tide of opinion may change now that it is obvious that the Suez adventure was in fact the fiasco that he had foretold. Some of the more experienced of his local constituents, including Sir Horace Wilson and Brigadier Windsor, who was his first chairman, are indignant at the way that the Association have treated him. The Prime Minister has sent him a message of encouragement, the Whips have been very kind, and Central Office, although it is their policy not to interfere in the affairs of local associations, have begged him not to resign his seat.

We weigh anchor at 5.00, and V. and I lean over the side looking at the *adieu suprême des mouchoirs*. I am still feeling worried and unhappy about Peter and write him a detailed and submissive letter of apology. We stay on deck watching the evening mist pouring like Niagara down the rim of Table Mountain. Thereafter we gaze in amazement at the succession of precipices that fringe the coast, standing up violet and purple in the setting sun. We round the Cape of Good Hope and when we come up after dinner there is a single light pulsating across the still swelling waves, repeating interminably the same single word. It is the light of Cape Agulhas, the southernmost point, I imagine, of the African continent.

2

Monday, January 28

When we come up on deck before luncheon we find that we are still running along the blunt southern fringe of Africa and are opposite Port Elizabeth. It is now quite grey and cool again, and I tell V. that it is because we are so close to the Antarctic. She for her part is convinced that the captain has again committed an error, that the southern coast of Africa is not as prolonged as all that, and that in fact we are going due north in the direction of Walvis Bay.

What one notices after a fortnight on board is that those of our fellow passengers whose personality is pronounced or whose behaviour is unreserved have become detached from the rest, whereas there are still many modest people whom we have not yet identified. I am sure they all recognise V. and me, since we look so odd.

Now that we are entering the Indian Ocean and have eight clear days ahead, I shall resume my examination of causeless melancholy. My difficulty is to find a satisfactory specimen or exhibit. So many of the eminent exponents of, and sufferers from, the *maladie du siècle* either espoused melancholy as a temporary attitude which they subsequently discarded, or else were afflicted by pessimism owing to adventitious circumstances, such as ill-health, a disagreeable childhood, the denial of opportunity, an unhappy love affair, or prolonged and grinding poverty. What I want to discover is somebody who was sad and frightened without any real reason and who remained sad and frightened for the whole of his life. The stock examples of this illness do not provide the material that I need.

Jean Jacques Rousseau is not a good specimen, since he was born with a humiliating physical defect, was abnormally sensitive, was tortured and warped by feelings of inferiority, and was so obsessed by his inability to give full expression to his own talents that in the end he became demonstrably mad. He may well have been the pioneer and analyst of sensibility: but he does not provide a pure example of the causeless melancholy that I wish to consider.

Werther again, although generally acclaimed as the type of youthful unhappiness, as the progenitor of *Sehnsucht,* as the supreme exponent of *Weltschmertz,* was rendered miserable owing to the chance circumstance that the girl he loved was engaged to, and eventually married, another man. *Die Leiden des jungen Werthers* is a study in sensibility rather than a description of causeless melancholy. I do not agree with Philip Toynbee that this novel is "ludicrous, vulgar and trivial," and indeed I wonder how a man of his intelligence should use such inappropriate terms. But I agree that the book is artificial and was motivated by Goethe's practice of "writing off a passion."

By this he meant that one could chill and calm an emotional disturbance by describing it on paper. It may well have been that, when practising law as a young man of twenty-two at Wetzlar, he fell much in love with Charlotte Buff and that when she married a worthy but dull young man he thought for a night or two of committing suicide. But the very next year he was in love with Maximiliane von Laroche and the year after that with Lili Schönemann: his Lotte was soon forgotten. Thus the passion described in *Werther* was no very authentic or durable passion. As Benedetto Croce remarks, "it is less a malady than the recovery from a malady: a vaccination fever, rather than a fever after infection." And in any case the melancholy it engendered, which is analysed in such detail and rendered in such beautiful prose, was not a causeless melancholy. It began and ended as an episode and, even as a young man, Goethe did not care for episodes which ruffled his calm.

In other ways, however, *Werther* does illustrate some of the components of a melancholy disposition. It reflects the sensibility which Rousseau had rendered fashionable, the love of solitude, of rustic life, of simple virtues. Charlotte shares with her admirer a passion for *The Vicar of Wakefield*, a tendency to cry readily, and an awed veneration for the works of Ossian. *Werther* is certainly an example of a man who fears that he may not be able to give expression to the gifts with which he has been endowed. He reproaches God for not having accorded him greater self-confidence, even as he reproaches himself for his own "restless lassitude." Much as he enjoys the beauties of Nature, it frightens him that she should be eternally either "*mangeant ou mangée*" and that she should seem at times to be a monster constantly swallowing and then regurgitating her own children: *"ein ewig verschlingendes, ewig wiederka-uendes Ungeheuer."* In such passages one can recognise the components of guilt and fear. I agree with Croce that Werther is essentially a spineless creature who tries to escape from "the command to accomplish some effort." Strange it seems to me that this incidental work should have exercised so lasting an influence and that Bonaparte, who was not given either to pessimism or sensibility, should have tucked the novel under the pillow of his camp bed during his early campaigns.

It might seem that in Chateaubriand's *René* I should find a perfect exhibit of the type that I am seeking to discover. The early part of the story certainly describes a typical mal-content with all the symptoms and components. But the climax of the story is so unusual and indeed eccentric that our dis-belief is aroused.

Among what were then the wild forests and swamps of Louisiana, a young French aristocrat recounts to the Indian chief, Chactas, and to an aged Christian missionary, Father Souel, the reasons why he had been driven into self-imposed exile. His mother had died when he was born; his father treated him with indifference; he was brought up by strangers. His only friend and confidante was his sister Amélie. His father dies; his brother inherits the family property; he goes off with Amélie to live with relations. His sister is deeply religious and for a while he himself contemplates entering the Church. He decides to travel; he visits Greece and Italy and we find him reciting Ossian in the Scottish Highlands. He discovers that the past is a heap of ashes and that the present is no more than emptiness and vanity. Chactas intervenes at this stage of the story to assure him that great souls always suffer more than small souls. René explains that nothing could assuage the "anxieties and the passionate aspirations by which he had been continually haunted." He was at first totally unable to account for his depression. He felt himself to be "crushed under the weight of his own corruption"; he felt "that there must exist something which could fill the void of his existence." But although he left the world and lived alone in a hut in the forest he could not rid himself of his disgust with life. He decides to commit suicide and his sister, divining his intention, comes to pay him a surprise visit in his hermitage. She entreats him to become "more like ordinary people," to marry, to adopt a political career. She then suddenly abandons him, leaving a note on the dressing table to say that she has decided to enter a convent. He pursues her and arrives at the very moment when she is about to take the veil. In that instant he realises that her odd manner was due to the fact that she was deeply in love with him. Horrified by this incestuous passion, he falls in a faint upon the floor. Amélie takes the veil and after many years of exemplary piety dies when nursing the victims of an epidemic. René crosses the ocean and seeks to hide his shame and misery among the noble savages. A few weeks after making his confession to Chactas and Father Souel, he is tomahawked by unfriendly Indians.

Chactas, the old Indian chief, was deeply moved by the story and cried for long. Father Souel was less impressed. "One is not," he said, "a superior being merely because one sees this world in an odious light." "Presumptuous young man," he says, "he imagines that any individual can suffice unto himself! Solitude is an evil thing for any creature who does not live in God. Whoever has been accorded talents must devote them to the service of his fellow men: if he leave them unused he will be devoured by private unhappiness and sooner or later heaven will send him some atrocious punishment."

What is interesting about René is that, so long as he was assailed by causeless melancholy, his very soul was devoured by ennui. His sudden realisation of Amélie's guilty secret rendered his distress less meaningless. "I had," he confessed, "no longer any desire to commit suicide. My sorrow had become an occupation to me; it filled my every moment." According to this theory, a man who suffers from causeless melancholy can be cured if he be provided with even the most horrible cause. Chateaubriand himself quickly recovered from his adolescent lassitude and thereafter became active, ambitious, amorous, and almost inconceivably self-satisfied.

3

To many of his contemporaries and successors—to Goethe, Lamartine, Musset, Pushkin and Amiel—it was Byron who furnished the supreme example of the discontented young man. It was he who, although well born, beautiful, and rich, became obsessed by the vanity of human desires, by the utter falsity of the life around him, and decided to seek in more primitive civilisations, and in converse with less sophisticated minds, that authenticity for which his nature yearned. "A character of such eminence," remarked Goethe to Eckermann, "has never existed before and probably will never occur again." *"La maladie du siècle,"* wrote Taine, *"n'a pas eu de plus illustre proie."* Lamartine and Musset could each celebrate the "*immortel ennui*" with which Childe Harold was afflicted, and even Stendhal, who was not given to facile enthusiasms, could write of his amazing "Apollonian" quality. He became the symbol of an age.

There is no positive evidence, in so far as I am aware, that Byron was influenced directly by *René*, or even that he had ever read the story. It may be that as a young man he was affected merely by the climate of the time. It is significant however that, whereas in his poems, journals, and letters there are copious references to others among his literary predecessors and contemporaries, the name of Chateaubriand is only mentioned once in all those volumes, and then as a purely incidental allusion in *The Age of Bronze*. There exists moreover a portrait of Byron painted by G. Sanders when the poet was nineteen years of age. This portrait was engraved by Finden and was widely circulated after 1812. It depicts him landing from a boat in some Scottish loch amid storms and precipices of Ossianic mist and turbulence. The face of the youth, even his nose, bears a startling likeness to the features of Chateaubriand, and his tie and hair are depicted as blown sideways in a French *coup de vent*. I have often suspected that Byron read *René* on leaving Harrow, was profoundly impressed by the sorrows of that hero, and that, fearing lest he might be accused of imitation, he thereafter dismissed to the vast recesses of his subconscious the name of Chateaubriand and its creative associations.

In his boyhood Byron was undoubtedly cursed by several of the misfortunes, internal and external, which form the malcontent. He was born a cripple; his father was a scamp who had created much scandal by eloping with the wife of

Lord Carmarthen; his mother was an obese and vulgar woman, addicted to drink and violent bursts of temper; his nurse, Mary Gray, was a drunkard of lax morals who frightened him continuously; his father, whom he never knew, had dissipated his mother's fortune and he was brought up in conditions of penury at Aberdeen on his mother's remaining pittance of £150 a year. Then most unexpectedly he succeeded at the age of ten to the title and estates of his granduncle. Yet in spite of Harrow and Cambridge it took him many years to rid himself of his Scottish accent or the memories of his raffish childhood. He never managed to take for granted this reversal of fortune or to adapt himself without self-consciousness to the position that he had so surprisingly inherited. Although perhaps too persistently aware that he was a member of the aristocratic order, he never succeeded in adjusting himself to the manners or behaviour of that order. He remained an outsider, and in many ways a vulgar outsider, until the end.

In the first two Cantos of *Childe Harold* he sought to compensate for this failure of adjustment by expressing contempt for those social values which he had been unable to imitate or absorb, and by indentifying himself with an imaginary hero who repudiated the world and all its ways. Childe Harold had felt "the fulness of satiety"; "with pleasure drugged, he almost longed for woe"; he was lust's "palled victim"; and upon his brow was stamped "a settled ceaseless gloom." Even after 1812, when he had become the famous and spoilt darling of Whig society, there would come moments when Byron remembered that he was expected to be melancholy: he would suddenly lean against the wall and allow the dancers to circle past him while spasms of scornful misery could be seen to twitch across his pallid face. Yet although *Childe Harold* was a momentary and perfectly sincere gesture of escape from a sense of failure, it was not a mood that survived triumphant success or one which was in fact representative of his temperament. "I would not," he said once, "be such a fellow as I have made my hero for all the world." But, until the publication of *Don Juan* and the *Letters and Journals*, it was as Childe Harold that the world misrepresented him. He became the idol and exemplar of all scattered selves, of all the young men and women who enjoyed the pageant of their bleeding hearts, of all those who lacked the will-power either to integrate their own personalities or to struggle against external circumstance.

I shall not take Byron as one of my specimens, since the essential Byron was not in the very least like that. He certainly possessed and relished a sense of sin and doom and expressed it strikingly in *Manfred* and other important poems. In spite of energetic efforts to appear so, he was not in any sense a daemonic character. He was an easygoing, self-indulgent man, who was wonderfully kind to all manner of men and women, with the exception of those who had the misfortune to fall in love with him. He frequently surrendered to his homosexual tendencies, but he was never the passive, self-reproachful, or effeminate type of invert; he belonged to the category which the French have nimbly defined as *"pédérastie heroïque."* Above all, he was far too virile, vivacious, witty, and humourous to be durably bored with life. He was an optimistic person, high-spirited and eupeptic. Even when he lay dying at Missolonghi he refused to surrender to self-pity, which he regarded as a flabby indulgence:

I seek no sympathies, nor need—
The thorns which I have reaped are of the tree
I planted; they have torn me, and I bleed.
I should have known what fruit would spring from such a seed.

If Byron teaches us anything about causeless melancholy it is that even the most resounding disasters can be mastered by reason, manliness, and humour; and that he was himself one of the least Byronic persons that have ever lived. No, I shall not choose Byron as a specimen.

4

Tuesday, January 29

A specially pleasant bathe before breakfast, when I am able to enjoy to the full what Novalis calls "the delight of movement in water"—*"die Wollust der Wasserberührung."* There is nobody else present since a heavy swell deters the elderly from fear of being dashed against the tiles. But as I am sitting in the sun afterwards a shy, somewhat desiccated Englishman appears. His name, I think is Clitheroe, and I have noticed but not addressed him before. He wears a gold ring with a lapis stone set in it. He has shapely hands which he tends with care. He says that it is a lovely morning and I agree that it is. He says that it seems rather rough in the bath and I also agree. He then climbs with great caution down the little ladder and flings himself on his back. I notice that he has not taken off his ring to bathe. He is a silent man, approaching thirty-seven I should say, with a sensitive expression and meagre limbs.

He strikes me as a melancholy character. If I get the opportunity I shall ask him whether his melancholy is causeless.

At 8.20 A.M. we pass our sister ship, the *Orange* of the Rotterdam Lloyd. I had been told that on the occasion of a similar encounter in mid-ocean a few years ago the two ships were so pleased to see each other that they got too close. They waved and shouted in fervent friendship and then some curious suction drew them together until the *Willem Ruys* bumped her sister and the steering gear of the *Orange* was dislocated. The accident was not, it seems, very serious, but the *Orange* had to stop two days at Suez to have her rudder repaired. Captain de Jonge, whom I ask to give me details of this collision, is reserved. He evidently does not wish either to diminish my confidence in Dutch seamanship or to cast aspersions on his predecessor. This morning therefore the two liners remain at a safe distance apart. We fly flags; we hoot happily; and from the deck of the *Orange* come faint songs of praise. But there is no collision, and V. and I return happily to our cabins, admiring the skill with which two large liners can pass each other neatly and punctually upon the unvintaged sea.

The log tells us that we are now southeast of Durban, and by the afternoon the swell has gone down and the Indian Ocean assumes that satin look which V. had observed on a voyage to Bombay and of which she had often told me. We stand there and stare and stare at the blue water. When the surface is thus wholly unruffled, one can see how difficult it is for the flying fish to become air-borne; as they flit across the surface they leave little scratches with their keels, exactly like the lad-ders left on nylon stockings by barbed wire. We stand there watching them "scuttling across the floors of silent seas."

I am disappointed not to find upon this boat the variety of puddings to which I had looked forward. One of the to me more distressing manifestations of the changing world in which I live is that the fashion for puddings has almost wholly faded. As a child, when staying at Clandeboye or Shanganagh, there were always two different puddings at every meal. We were offered College Pudding, Bachelor's Pudding, Hasty Pudding, Tipsy Pudding, Treacle Pudding, Lemon Sponge, Pancakes, Junket, Coconut Custard, Marmalade Pie, Roly Poly, Suet Pudding, Toffee Pudding, Almond Sponge, Cherry Whirl, Coffee Honeycomb, Apple Charlotte, Macaroon Hasties, Meringues, Marshmallows, Smyrna Mould, and all manner of tarts and creams. Moreover, before the first war, a "luncheon cake" was always handed round with the cheese. V. does not herself care for sweet dishes and prefers those sour concoctions which are called "savouries" although they so seldom are. In fact I feel that she regards my passion for puddings as effeminate, or perhaps Scottish, or perhaps middle class. Although at Sissinghurst I am pampered with the best tarts that I have ever known, I am not offered these delicacies at my club. Day after day, luncheon after luncheon, dinner after dinner, does the menu bear the single word "semolina," and although ices are also provided I happen to hate ice. When once I dared to suggest to our secretary (who although a generous man does not enjoy pandering to any form of decadence) that I might have a soufflé for dinner, his face fell abruptly and in contempt. "But that," he said sharply, "would mean getting in another chef." I did not have the courage to pursue the theme.

I had hoped none the less that the *Willem Ruys*, with her long Teutonic tradition of puddings, and considering the lavish variety of fish, meat, and game that she provides, would at least give me the pudding opportunity that I have, since the age of fourteen, been denied. I was thus delighted when I saw on the menu such suggestive varieties as "Malakoff Pudding," "Rubane Pudding," "Harlekin Pudding," and "Noga Ijs." But when I called for these delicacies night after night, I discovered that they were in fact what in British restaurant cars are called "shape," being little dabs the size and form of a child's sand pie and differing from each other solely owing to the fact that some contained specks of angelica and some bits of orange or ginger. I must therefore resign myself in future to the fact that the puddings of my childhood have, even as four-wheelers, passed from circulation.

The quarter of an hour in the smoking room before dinner is always hilarious. The young men sit in rows on the high stools that line the bar, and the band plays jolly tunes. The band consists of a man who plays the piano, a man who walks about playing the fiddle, and a man who plays a large violoncello. The latter is gifted with a Neapolitan voice, and in moments of ecstasy he will burst into *"O sole mio"* very loud. *"Sto fronte a te"* he will yell, gazing with embarrassing fixity at the man who serves cocktails behind the bar. I note that this orchestra does not adopt the dreamy rhythm which is so popular in the lounges of our English resorts, but that it follows the more emphatic and staccato spasms of the German mode. This imparts even to a love song the scansion of a marching tune and strikes me as manly. It explains why, when

I was in the Ministry of Information during the war, we were receiving constant complaints that the B.B.C. was too "languid" and that the men preferred to listen to the more martial pantings of the German *Rundfunk*. The orchestra in the *Willem Ruys* plays, not "Lili Marlene" and *"Que serà serà"* only, but also "Roll Out the Barrel" and the *Lambeth Walk*. The latter is justly popular with the passengers and I noticed this evening to my dismay that even the Indonesian diplomatist, who is on his way back from some post abroad, will at the incitation of this melody abandon his passive dignity and shout "Oi!"— an exclamation that strikes me as out of character. After dinner we talk to Leonora Hubrecht, who is as gentle as a moth; humourous, artistic, and well read.

Wednesday, January 30

It became rough during the night and when I come on deck before breakfast I find attached to the swimming pool the sad words *"Bad Gesloten"* which means that the splashing is too fierce. All but some six foot of the water has been emptied out of the bath, and what remains twists and writhes like some sea monster out of Jules Verne. We are now south-west of Madagascar and there is a strong wind, which Boumphrey tells me is the tail end of the monsoon. We work all day in our cabins which are quiet and cool.

In the evening there is a variety entertainment in the saloon which they call a "Sex-A-Pool." We are given a paper with a list of twelve qualities, such as courage, table manners, neatness, accuracy, and so on. The Dutch for accuracy is *Nauwgezetheid,* a fact of which I was hitherto unaware. We are expected to mark against these qualities those in which women or men excel. Then male and female members of the audience are called up to prove or disprove the comparative prowess of the sexes in these twelve virtues. The proceedings are amusing and well directed. The men and women are made to blow up balloons and then to sit upon them as a test of courage. They are then required to hang clothes on two washing lines, to give farmyard imitations, and to eat spaghetti blindfold. I am again astounded by the skill with which the Dutch games instructor with his assistant direct these proceedings in Dutch and English. I do not see a steward in a P & O liner behaving with equal dexterity; in the first place he would be ignorant of any language other than his own: in the second place he would develop self-consciousness, feeling that he was making a fool of himself and that in any case it was not part of his job.

Thursday, January 31

A dull grey morning with the monsoon blowing sideways at us and a heavy swell. I go up on deck but the bathing pool is again closed and I return disconsolate. We are off Madagascar and the captain tells me that this is generally a rough patch. We read and work all day. In the evening there is a cocktail party given in the smoking room by Mr. Ruys of the Rotterdam Lloyd, the cousin of our eponym. It is in honour of

Princess Beatrix and we drink her health, stand while the Netherlands anthem is played, and have Beatrix Gebak for dinner. Afterwards there is dancing in the second class where the decks are illumined by red and green lights. But the wind howls round us and there is a slight drizzle and the hatchways are slippery. We return to the saloon and talk to a distinguished old couple, Mr. and Mrs. Gibson. She is chairman of the League of Remembrance and a woman of strength and humour. He is over eighty, but hale for his years. He walks about all day carrying with him the *Daily Telegraph* book of crossword puzzles, at which he glances occasionally but with marked distaste. They have a flat in London but every winter they go on some cruise or other. Their favourite liner is the *Reina del Pacifico,* in which for two years running they have cruised through the Panama Canal and down the western coast of South America. Mrs. Gibson says that the swimming bath in the *Reina del Pacifico* is preferable to that in the *Willem Ruys* since it is entirely enclosed and therefore less embarrassing to persons of mature age. I do not understand this argument but I do not pursue it.

Friday, February 1

Coming up after breakfast, we observe, some miles away and on our port side, the hills and meadows of Mauritius. Through my binoculars I can make out the corrugated iron roofs of sugar refineries upon which the sun beats reverberatingly, and also a few white cottages, similar to those in which, a hundred and seventy years ago, the adolescent Paul made love to the virgin Virginie. I have always disliked that romance, feeling it to have been one of the more unfortunate effects of the persuasive powers of Jean Jacques Rousseau. How far more interesting it would have been had we sailed along the coast of the adjacent Ile Bourbon, where the founder of the Parnassian movement was born and lived for many years. *"J'entends toujours,"* wrote Leconte de Lisle:

> *J'entends toujours, au fond de mon passé confus,*
> *Le cri désespéré de vos douleurs sauvages.*

One of V.'s many advantages is that she never scoffs at my rather silly taste for literary associations. She agrees with me that it was inconsiderate of Captain de Jonge to coast the shore of Mauritius when he could equally well have taken us along the more fabled, to me, beaches of the Ile Bourbon. She goes further. She says that Mauritius is a smug-looking island and indistinguishable from the Isle of Wight. Jan Hubrecht consoles her by explaining that the meadows we see are in fact groves of sugar cane, that the dark woods are forests of coconut palms and that the distant blue mountains are volcanoes, not all of which can be guaranteed to be extinct. Moreover the surf that breaks white and high upon the shores of Mauritius is in fact breaking on the encircling coral reef— the very reef on which Virginie, being in her charming modesty unwilling to take off her skirt and swim ashore, was drowned. The outline of Mauritius sinks behind us and we go downstairs to work.

In the afternoon I have a talk with Neumayer. I ask him whether he can provide me with a perfect specimen of *Welt-*

schmerz, indicating that I do not admit the claims of the young *Werther.* Being a sensible man, he agrees with this contention, saying that foreigners are often apt to confuse the *Sturm und Drang* movement with the later wave of German romanticism, and that in any case Goethe was an Olympian, who soared above the dust of the classic versus romantic controversy. He thinks I should examine Novalis, and above all Hölderlin. I have read Novalis, mainly because Gerald Berners insisted upon my doing so. But I shall have to wait until I get home before examining Hölderlin. I ask him whether the latter's melancholy was causeless: he makes an ambivalent gesture with his hand.

The table next to ours in the dining saloon is occupied by English people, forming a covey of young married couples going out to the Far East. There are Dr. O'Malley and his wife; he is a young Irish surgeon of splendid appearance who has got an appointment in Malaya. There are Mr. and Mrs. Emmett. He has the air of a Bloomsbury intellectual and I derive the mistaken impression that he is going out as an inspector of British Council schools and institutes in southeast Asia. I discover later that in fact he is one of the world's leading experts upon the planting and marketing of tea. Mrs. Emmett is a vivacious and engaging young woman who wears a different frock every evening; she must have been told when a girl that she possessed a musical laugh, since her gusts of merriment are frequent and prolonged. She is, I suspect, an example of causeless exhilaration, and as such does not come within the scope of my particular enquiry. There are two or three other young people at their table and their laughter echoes continuously upon the ceiling of the saloon. At dinner this evening they are ominously hushed, and when we come upstairs later we are told that all dances and entertainments have been cancelled. It seems that this morning, when we were all gazing at Mauritius, a flying officer travelling second class with his wife and child to Singapore fell overboard. It took his distraught wife some three hours before she was certain that he had disappeared and before she told the captain. We were by then some hundred miles from the scene of the misfortune and there was nothing that Captain de Jonge could do beyond sending a wireless to the governor of Mauritius and warning the RAF at Colombo. We are sobered by this occurrence; the orchestra refrains from playing *"Que serà serà"* and the great ship plunges imperviously onward through the night.

V. INDIAN OCEAN

1

Saturday, February 2

On thinking it over I have come to the conclusion that not even Novalis furnishes me with the pure and perfect specimen for which I am seeking. It is true that he suffered often from atrocious melancholy and that he spent many hours of the day weeping upon the tomb of his dead love. But his melancholy was not either causeless or uniform. He experienced, as so often happens with the victims of tuberculosis, bouts of exaltation, nor was he by nature a pessimistic or a gloomy man. In fact Tieck, who often visited him when he was dying, describes him as being "as mirthful as a child." Yet Novalis, who, had he lived, would certainly have become one of the leaders of the German romantic movement, is an impressive person and a man who inspires, not pity merely, but affection.

Fritz von Hardenberg, who is known to literature under his pseudonym of Novalis, was born at Wiederstedt in 1772 and died at the age of twenty-nine. His father was an un-affectionate man of the pietist sect founded by Graf von Zinzendorf. His mother was a colourless woman who suffered much from sadness. Five of his brothers and four of his sisters died of tuberculosis before they reached the age of twenty-five. At twenty-three Novalis fell in love with Sophie von Kühn, and they became engaged. She was only fifteen years old at the time, was almost totally illiterate, and was in fact little more than a vivacious child. Before they could be married she died of a tumour on the liver, and he spent most of the next eight months sobbing on her tomb in the graveyard at Grün-ingen. He then became engaged to Julie von Charpentier, but himself died of tuberculosis before they could be married. The external circumstances of his life were exceptionally in-auspicious.

Many of the familiar symptoms of melancholia can of course be found in the writings of Novalis. He suffered much from apprehension, from what he called *"diese ängstliche Beklem-mung"*—"this terrifying sense of oppression." After Sophie's death he became doubtful regarding his own identity and con-vinced that he no longer belonged to reality. As a student he had been much influenced by the splenetic pessimism of F. Schlegel and sought to find in the world of imagination the satisfaction, spiritual and emotional, which the external world denied him. He obtained much personal pleasure from his un-happiness and indulged in what Krafft-Ebing has called *"ein gewisses Kokettieren mit dem Leid und Weh"*—"a certain flirtatious attitude towards pain and sorrow." He evolved the theory that illness, misfortune, and death could be rendered sources of delight. Good health rendered a man insensitive to suffering. It was unhappiness alone that could teach him the true relationship between himself and the external world. Even death should be welcomed since it was the sublimation of life, a state in which alone man could find the ultimate harmony, the final synthesis of love.

Novalis was a mystic sensualist. As an adolescent he had been much impressed by Jean Paul Richter's *Die unsichtbare Loge*. He came to believe that the visible world was a mere illusion and that it was the invisible world which constituted the reality. Even as a child his constant playmate had been, not his many brothers and sisters, but an imaginary cherub who would sit beside him at night and during the day accompany him on his woodland walks. "The visible," he wrote, "is but the surface of the invisible." He even held the theory that we possessed, or could produce, hidden organs of sensation which were superior to our apparent organs and which, if carefully cultivated, could bring us in touch with the transcendental and even endow us with the gift of divination. It was the physical body which, as an opaque substance, impeded this transcendence. The true poet should break through this barrier of flesh and regard death as his vocation and fulfilment. "Life," he wrote in his philosophical fragments, "is the beginning of death. Life is accorded us for the purpose of death. Death is both a beginning and an end; it is both a dispersal and a concentration." He contended that one day the visible world would dissolve into an invisible absolute in which man would at last find "the blue flower"—*die blaue Blume*—of perfect love and union.

What is stimulating about Novalis is that, in spite of terrible misfortunes, he never surrendered to pessimism. He fought his own fears with combative lust. "Fear," he wrote, "comes to us from the Devil, courage and happiness come to us from God." He admits that it would be a relief to him if he could convince himself that his own anxieties derived solely from physical weakness. Yet he refused to capitulate. *"Fröhlich,"* he wrote in one magnificent phrase, *"fröhlich, wie ein jünger Dichter, will ich sterben"*—"I shall die gaily as a young poet should." So far from regarding this world as fundamentally evil and meaningless, he believed that evil itself was one of man's illusions, even as life upon earth was but a magnificent illusion, "a grandiose spectacle." So far from contending, as F. Schlegel contended, that life was in fact not worth living, Novalis agreed with Fichte that the superior man could become the centre of his own universe and raise himself above the miseries of this transitory world. "All the circumstances of our life," he wrote, "furnish a material from which we can construct what we will. A man of intelligence can make much of his life. Every chance encounter, every incident however fortuitous, can by the superior man be rendered the first step in an unending romance." "At the very root of my being," he wrote, "is the faith and the confidence that I repose in all within me and all around me. Our life may be but a dream, but if so we should strive to render it ever more dreamlike." Novalis is thus, as a specimen, the very opposite to the type of causeless melancholy. Few men have been subject to so many misfortunes and disasters, few men have had such cause for melancholy; yet, strong in his faith in life and death, he refused to capitulate or to escape. I do not understand how Thomas Carlyle should have attacked Novalis for lack of courage and resolution, for his "vaporous lucubrations," or for being a sort of oriental gymnosophist who surrendered abstractedly to misfortune. I can scarcely believe that Carlyle read Novalis with any attention; or it may be that, when contemplating the optimism of a man who could triumph over such repeated blows of ill fortune, he himself felt ashamed of his own intemperate surrender to causeless vexation.

2

I have a lovely bathe this morning; the water is lukewarm, although pumped in at sunrise direct from the sea. There is still a heavy swell and the waves in the bath splash crossly. There is an English major by the swimming pool who insists upon his little son of seven or eight plunging into the angry water. I can see that the child is frightened, and all that I have read about fixations and inhibitions persuades me to protest. "Surely," I say to the man, "you are not going to throw that little shrimp into the pool?" He becomes even redder in the face and throws me an angry look. "Boy must learn to swim," he mutters. Who am I at my age to fight with English majors who ill-treat their sons? I give a sharp twitch to the belt of my dressing gown and walk back with measured tread, along the promenade deck.

It becomes hot as the morning passes, and at luncheon people appear in very few clothes. The Dutch matron who, at Waterloo Station, had seemed so formidable in her astrakhan coat, her golden amulets, and her tidy hair, appears in the saloon in shorts. Her thighs are wide rather than long and are the colour of porphyry. There is also an elderly Englishman who dresses in a beach shirt with very short pants. I am outraged by this insensitiveness. How right Homer was to say that, although it was agreeable to witness the nakedness of the young, old men should always cover themselves up carefully. Twenty-six hundred years at least have passed since Homer made this comment, yet men and women continue to display their persons regardless of their age. I am so indignant that I want to circle round the dining saloon with a large soup ladle slapping thighs. What, I ask myself, would Kingsley have thought of such indecency?

I talk to Boumphrey, the Singapore civil servant, who is always interesting. He says that Marshall, although an excellent criminal lawyer, lacks experience as a politician. Lim-Yew-Hock is more of a statesman, and Boumphrey expects that when negotiations are resumed with the Colonial Office some agreed settlement will be worked out. The new constitution would then come into force in January. He himself has agreed to stay on. I suggest that he may find the administration of the audit department rather more complicated under a nationalist government. He answers: "That may well be. But I feel it is my duty to remain and to do what I can to help." He said this so naturally, sincerely, and modestly that I was impressed.

It is still rough all afternoon. The captain says this is due to the conflict of two winds and that it will subside before long. At 6.00 there is a lovely sunset and I rout V. out of her cabin. We see the new moon like a very thin sickle but turned the other way round. As we watch it, the sea, as the captain predicted, suddenly becomes oily calm. We go to the stern and watch our wake sparkling in the sunset. It is one of the most beautiful evenings that I have known.

Thereafter Mrs. Gill, who is leaving us at Colombo, gives a

cocktail party in the smoking room. She is full of useful information and advice as to what we should see and where we should go during our short stop in Colombo. Her other guests include Mrs. Smith, who has the de luxe cabin and wears wonderful aquamarine jewels. There is Mr. F. Hyams, who is a power in the film world, and whose wife spends her afternoons and evenings playing bridge. Mr. J. Ruys and his wife are there and so are Mr. and Mrs. Emmett. I look about for my melancholy friend Clitheroe but he is one of those who shun society. Dinner this evening is supposed to celebrate the feast of Bacchus and we are expected to wear what they call "Riviera clothes." Considering that people have been wearing nothing else since we left Cape Town there is not much scope for innovation. But the captain, who enters into the spirit of everything, appears as an ordinary passenger in a tartan shirt. Some of the more enthusiastic passengers wear false noses. As one by one these revellers descend the steps into the dining saloon they are loudly applauded by the other passengers. I had always supposed that the Dutch were an undemonstrative and solemn race: but not in the least; on suitable occasions they enjoy noise.

After dinner the wine feast is continued on the Lido deck beyond the swimming pool. Bacchus appears astride a wine cask, paunchy and of an advanced age. I think they had confused him with Silenus. There had been a limerick competition during the day and a mermaid then appears *ex machina* to distribute prizes to those of the passengers whose poems were considered the best. Leonora Hubrecht wins one of the prizes and Mrs. Gill another. V. and I, while enjoying the sight, lean over the taffrail and gaze at Magellan's Clouds. She wears a scarf round her hair, which always suits her so well. Then dancing begins under the red and green and yellow electric bulbs. Jan Hubrecht, who is seventy-three, dances like a two-year-old. One of the young Englishmen, disguised for the occasion in the shirt and pants of a centre-half, tells me that the wireless operator has promised to give him "the latest reports from Murray Field." I register interest.

Sunday, February 3

On going up on deck before breakfast this morning in my dressing gown, I see that the small library that opens out of the main saloon has been turned into a chapel for the celebration of Mass. This transformation is contrived with the usual taste and efficiency of the Rotterdam Lloyd. The back wall, which normally consists of bookshelves behind a wire lattice, is completely concealed by a huge white screen or triptych bearing in the centre a sacred diagram or symbol, and on each of the side panels the life-size figure of a saint, one of whom is St. Nicholas. A small altar stands in front of the triptych and the service is conducted by a priest in white and attended by the monks and nuns from the second class, all equally dressed in white. They are kneeling with their hands joined in prayer. I slip back hurriedly, burrow below decks, and eventually come up again by a forward gangway. But in my short glimpse of the service I had recognised Mr. Clitheroe praying with closed eyes. I am so affected by this spectacle that I feel it would be irreverent to bathe, so I return to my cabin by an underground route.

I feel that on this pious morning I must accomplish a good deed. There is a Dutch girl on board of the awkward age of thirteen or fourteen; she is very plain, poor girl, having no eyebrows to speak of, two sad little pigtails hanging behind, an ugly green frock which is far too small for her, stout red arms and hands, and a figure which must be a lasting sorrow to her parents. I therefore stop and address this monster with words of amity and encouragement. She stares back at me in cowlike incomprehension. I am disappointed that my gesture of compassion should have thus been flung back at me. But V. says that I had no need to feel compassionate; she is in fact a horrid girl who bullies the children in their playing room and throws her weight about, which is indeed considerable. V. had even seen her pinching one of the Indonesian babies on the behind. Mine was a good deed none the less.

In the afternoon we come in sight of the island of Diego Garcia, in the Chagos Archipelago, of which I had never heard before. On consulting the atlas in the smoking room we find that it is marked "Br," which means that it is one of our few remaining possessions. The captain tells us that it possesses five hundred inhabitants who support themselves by exporting copra. We go up to the bridge in order to see it better. It is a dull sight. All we can see is a thin strip of land covered with coconut palms. That is a disappointment, but the storm that follows is not. We see it ahead, looming like a waterspout, and as we approach nearer the sea around us turns the colour of pewter. Then suddenly we are in the middle of it and the tropical rain flings itself upon the ship. The captain tells us that it was what the Dutch navigators call "a sailor's trousers storm," since the rain descends as if being pumped through a hawser shaped like wide naval breeches. This seems to me a farfetched analogy. But when we get out of the storm and the sky and sea are clear and blue again, an enormous fish leaps high into the air in front of us; not as a porpoise jumps, but sideways, showing us the flash of its white sides and stomach like a salmon. Stedall, who is less ignorant than most of us, says that it was certainly not a porpoise; he doubts even whether it was a shark; it must have been a very agile whale. Anyhow the flying fish panic all around us, like tin clockwork toys.

We have a quiet evening for once, talking to the Stedalls after dinner and going to bed before ten.

Monday, February 4

V. goes up on deck at 5.00 A.M. to see the sunrise, which she says was superb. She had looked into my cabin hoping I should accompany her but I was asleep. I work hard all day and also write letters to be posted tomorrow at Colombo.

I am sitting reading on deck when a man comes and sits beside me, saying, "I hope I do not interrupt." It is the melancholy Clitheroe, whose name, I have since discovered, is not Clitheroe at all, but Sidney Culpeper, a descendant I assume of the astrologist and herbalist, and of all the other Culpepers who lie buried in the Goudhurst tombs. "May I ask," he continues with dry politeness, "what it is you are reading with such absorption?" "I am reading *Obermann*," I answer. At this he sighs deeply. "Ah yes," he sighs. "Matthew Arnold's friend." Then without a word he gets up and walks away. I must talk to him again.

An Indonesian from the second class comes to see me. His name is Syed Hussein Alatas, and he is editor of a periodical entitled *Progressive Islam*, which is published in Djakarta. He is of the Arab rather than of the Indonesian type and speaks fluent English. He asks me what are my views regarding the present tension between Java and Sumatra. I say that never having visited either of these two islands before I have no material on which to form an opinion. He is disappointed by this and leaves me with a curt but gracious little bow. Then a nice American by the name of Charles Lyons comes to talk to us. He was in the American Embassy at Cairo during our invasion of Egypt and was charged with the evacuation of the American colony. He got them as far as the Cairo aerodrome when we started to bomb it and all flights were cancelled. He then took them in cars and buses by road to Alexandria, and on their passage past other aerodromes the bombs fell thick and fast around them. Eventually he embarked them on board American ships in Alexandria harbour without any casualties. But it was a close thing and he said he would not go through it again for ten million dollars. He was a charming man and I am sorry that he leaves us at Colombo. We go to bed early.

3

Tuesday, February 5

Generally when we are at breakfast the loud-speaker relays from the purser's office in the Dutch and English languages the instructions and announcements for the day. It tells us, for instance, that no washing will be handed in until after we have left Colombo, that the clocks will be put forward another hour at midnight, that the final of the deck-quoits competition will be held on the second class sports deck at two-thirty, and will Captain Chapman, Mr. Coker, and Mevrouw van den Broek be so kind as to call this morning at the chief steward's office. Yet for some reason which I cannot fathom the authorities are extremely cagey about the times of our arrival in harbour. V. is convinced that it is because the captain has lost his way and hesitates to admit it; I suggest that it is due to superstition—a defect common among mariners—and that they are unwilling to provoke the wrath of Poseidon by stating in advance that passengers will disembark at Colombo at 3.25 that afternoon. The fact remains that we are not told when exactly we reach Colombo and the news is only broken to us gradually in the course of the morning.

Half an hour after noon we see a low line of coast in front of us and shortly afterwards the houses of Colombo rise from the surface of the sea, even as the houses of Alexandria emerge suddenly upright, like Aphrodite, from the Mediterranean horizon. We have a quick luncheon and at 1.20 the pilot climbs on board and we slide slowly into the harbour. The

like Venus(gr)

silhouette of Colombo is unexciting; there is the Catholic cathedral with its aluminium domes; there are warehouses with bright tin roofs; and there are two Protestant churches, the spire of one recalling that in Onslow Gardens, the spire of the other being square and rural as if at Dorking. We do not tie up at a wharf but anchor in the inner basin while little launches and sampans circle around us.

We had been expecting to be met by Carl Harper, a friend of Richard Rumbold, who is an official in the harbour administration or something of that sort. I scan the little boats and launches around us in the hope of identifying him. Meanwhile the mail has been brought on board by the pilot and is being distributed by the deck steward in the smoking room. We are waiting to get our letters when I am told that "an Indian lady" is asking for me in my cabin. I go downstairs and find a charming Ceylonese lady of the name of Mrs. Vere de Mel. She explains that Harper is unable to get away from his office and has asked her to look after us in his place. I talk to her for a bit while V. can be seen in her cabin across the passage with the door wide open hastily going through the many letters which she has obtained upstairs. Then arrives a gentleman in a neat white suit who represents the *Times* of Ceylon and wishes for an interview. I utter some harmless platitudes to satisfy him. Then we climb down into a tug and are taken across the harbour to the Ocean Terminal, which is white and cool and excellently arranged; there are no formalities for British subjects, and we pass through immediately and out into the glare beyond. The journalists take photographs of V. and me blinking in the sun. There is a little crowd of loiterers outside the terminal, including two Buddhist priests in saffron togas and some women in saris. I remark to a journalist how elegant they seem. He replies deprecatingly, *"Tamils!"* I ask Mrs. de Mel what was the significance of that remark and she merely says, "He could not have understood." I am left bewildered by these cross-purposes.

Most of the other passengers who have come on shore with us from the *Willem Ruys* are going in a coach together to the hotel at Mount Lavinia. I had been warned by Richard Rumbold, who has lived in Ceylon, that we should find this boring and had been advised by him, if we had only a few hours to stay in Colombo, to go to the Buddhist temple at Kelaniya some seven miles outside the town. Mrs. de Mel has provided a car for us with a driver who speaks good English and, after visiting a bookshop and a chemist, we drive out there in the hot and dusty afternoon.

For me it is all very like what I had imagined India to be. Crowded streets, old gentlemen with white beards and turbans, hooded carts drawn by small humped oxen, and rows of little shacks selling fruit and vegetables. As we get beyond the town there are groves of untidy palm trees leaning at different angles, a few scattered villas with deserted gardens and plaster peeling from the walls, and now and then a magenta or pink splash of bougainvillea or hibiscus. We cross a wide slow river and shortly afterwards we reach the temple.

It consists of a compound approached by steps leading to a wide white arch. Outside the compound there are little booths at which one can buy lotus buds and frangipani flowers and little earthenware pots and bowls in which to put them. We climb the steps, pass under the arch, and find ourselves in the precincts. There is a low white range of buildings for the monks and students, the temple itself, and beside it a white-washed mausoleum, or dagoba, shaped like a high beehive, and containing, we are told, a relic of the Buddha. A little shuffling guide propels us towards the temple; we take off our shoes at the entrance; inside there are some oldish murals and others of quite modern date. In the central room there is a golden figure of the Buddha, seated in the lotus position, and in a side aisle bowls of flowers in front of a further image and the scent of frangipani flowers strewn in front of it. We creep out and put on our shoes again. In the compound there is a huge bho-tree hung with votive strips. It is said to have been grown from a cutting taken from the original tree under which the Buddha received his revelation. This cutting, with others, was sent to Ceylon by King Asoka in the third century before Christ and, if this be a correct account, then the tree at Kelaniya must be nearly twenty-three hundred years old. It certainly looks venerable.

As we pass this tree we see a woman kneel in front of it with her two children beside her. They close their eyes and place the palms of their hands together in supplication. To whom, I wonder, and for what, are these three praying under that old old tree? *Caelo supinas si tuleris manus*—the attitude of worship is always beautiful.

We leave the temple, feeling grateful to Richard for having advised us to go there, and drive back to Colombo, past the cinnamon gardens, and to the Eighty Club, where Mrs. Vere de Mel had arranged to meet us. We are introduced to her husband and to a Miss Rankine, who teaches at the university or secondary school. We sit in the garden under an enormous tree and are offered iced beer and delicious cheese biscuits.

We watch the crescent moon rising in what remains of a sunset sky; the evening breeze stirs the tree above us and we hear the keelbirds scritching; the air is scented and we succumb to the magic of Taprobane.

At 6.50 we drive back to the Ocean Terminal and find the tug packed with passengers. Mrs. de Mel tells us, just as we are about to step into the tug, that her daughter this term has been reading *The Land* as her set book in class. Would V. kindly autograph her copy? Diffidently she takes from her bag a somewhat battered copy of that poem, which V. signs on a table under the arc lights of the customs shed. I am pleased by this incident. We say good-bye to Mrs. de Mel who had indeed been kind and helpful. We climb on board the tug.

The evening breeze has by then risen to a stiff wind and there are cross little waves in the harbour. We visit other ships, including the *Oronsay* swaying gracefully under many lights. When we reach the *Willem Ruys* we find that our tug rises and falls alarmingly in the rough waves beside the placid gangway of the great liner. V. is encumbered with the pots and flowers we had bought at the temple and I, with my sciatica, my weak heart, my high blood pressure, am as usual dreadfully unhelpful and incompetent. Luckily Boumphrey, who is there, leaps onto the gangway and pulls us both on board. After the whirl and rattle of the tug, the *Willem Ruys* seems as silent and sedate as a cathedral.

We read our letters. Nigel is quite cheerful about his prospects in Bournemouth East. Now that the Committee are aware that many local Conservatives, to say nothing of outside opinion, regard the Executive's "repudiation" of Nigel as intemperate and unfair, he can scarcely proceed, as they threatened, to adopt another candidate to replace Nigel at the next election. Nobody seems as yet to have received the many letters we sent back by air from Cape Town. We suspect that the mailbags were delayed in Egypt.

We go on deck and watch the lights of Colombo slide past us as we steam out of the harbour. The lights of even the most exotic ports in these days appear identical——a line of bright electric standards along the quays, warehouses, and boulevards, and the red lights of Coca-Cola and other advertisements flashing above the town. The air is warm and scented and V. again discovers a quotation from *The Lusiads*:

"Ceylon, the noble island, long famous as Taprobane, whose cinnamon groves fill it today with sovereign pride, will pay tribute of that same fragrant spice to the might and glory of the Portuguese flag as it flutters triumphant from the fortress of Colombo."

Camoens evidently did not foresee the revolt of the external proletariat.

4

Wednesday, February 6

We both wake up refreshed and contented after our hot and somewhat rushed hours in Ceylon. I have a bathe. The little boy who I feared was being bullied by a brutal father now swims from end to end of the bath bravely and uproariously by himself. "Daddy," he shouts, "may I now try swimming on my back?" All this shows me that the Rousseau-Montessori theory of education is fallacious and that Alain was right in saying that the essence of education is *"la difficulté vaincue."* What we all need is, not brains, but character. And—my word!—in this ship we have got it.

I finish *Obermann*, as the confessions of Sénancour are called. I have been reading him, not in the original two volumes of 1804, but in the more convenient version edited by G. Michaut in 1912. The inconsiderate egoism of Sénancour is emphasised by the fact that the book consists of letters addressed to a friend of his own age. It would have been better if he had cast his work in the form of a diary, or memoirs, or even of a novel, since the attention of the reader is continually being diverted away from the varied miseries of Obermann towards the person of his correspondent, who had, after all, his own life to live, and who must have been wearied by this avalanche of self-pity and lament.

The letters, none the less, provide a useful specimen or exhibit of a typical malcontent of the early nineteenth century. Obermann was cursed from the outset with the melancholic humour. "I was born," he writes in his irritating way, "to suffer." He is aware that he lacks resolution and possesses no faculty for objective decision. "It saddens me," he writes, "to feel that I ought to possess some will-power and at the same time to realise that I have no idea at all on what it should be based." He is conscious that he is ill-adjusted to his environment and envies those whose occupation is in harmony with their temperament. "A person," he writes, "who has passed his whole existence in a situation attuned to his own character can be said to have truly lived." "To how great an extent," he writes, "is our unhappiness due to the fact that we are unable to adjust ourselves to the external order." He regrets, as so many malcontents have regretted, that he has been born middle-aged and has never experienced the exaltations of adolescence. "I have had the misfortune," he informs his friend, "never to feel young." "I am," he writes again, "not yet twenty-one years of age; I was born sensitive and passionate; but I have never known what happiness is. . . . Accustomed as I am to see all the flowers of this life wither under my sterile foot, I am like an old man who has abandoned all interest in existence."

This *taedium vitae* leads inevitably to the conclusion that reality, or the external world, is no more than a handful of dust. He is driven to distraction by the purposelessness of creation, by the "intolerable void that I find all around me." Those who possess religious faith or can derive comfort from philosophy may be able to solace themselves for the hollowness of life. Yet he himself can foresee no possible future, except perhaps that one day this world will be dead as the moon and that nothing whatsoever will survive of all human effort and suffering. "What utter loneliness," he writes, "assails us! All faiths and philosophies are but successive shapes of illusion! The only science that we can believe in," he adds insanely, "is perhaps that of numerology." "I shall," he informs his long-suffering friend, "discard even the idea of a better world." He is assailed "by disgust of men, of things, in fact of all human life." "What you call 'the social structure' is no more than a heap of disguised wretchedness, error and deception." There are moments even when he begins to doubt the truth of his own identity. "I am fated," he complains, "to remain somebody who has never existed. I fear that my habit of never identifying myself with the external world has culminated in my not being able to identify myself with myself."

Inevitably a man afflicted with so subjective a temperament, a man of such irritable self-absorption, suffers much from states of anxiety. "Why," he asks his friend, "should I spend my day either assailed by spasms of anxiety or shadowed by long bouts of boredom? . . . There are moments when I despair of mastering the disquiet that distracts me . . . A man who is afraid of life, rather than confident in life, remains for ever more or less sundered from his kind."

What is so insufferable about Obermann, as indeed about most malcontents, is that he derives complacent pleasure from his own misery. "How comes it," he writes, "that a man should be accorded that most durable of old sentimental enjoyments, a delicious melancholy? It possesses a charm rich in secrets, which enables him to feed upon his sorrows and to love himself even at those moments when he is most aware of his own inadequacy and failure."

The only solution of this atrocious problem is that of surrender and acceptance. "Inside ourselves there exists an element of aversion, coldness and indifference. Sometimes I ask myself to what end I shall be led by these doubts which shackle me to indifference and to that apathy from which I shall never be able to escape." Is it not better to accept apathy as a path towards contentment, or at least tranquility? Yet the solitary, the escapist, "the isolated man" is incapable of achieving, not happiness only, but the practice of virtue. No outsider even begins to understand what it is to be good. Yet if we are to share with some other being our sufferings and our self-distrust, that being must be both similar to ourselves and yet wholly different. How can this saving duality be discovered? Only, concludes Obermann (in a commonplace that might well have occurred to him earlier in the correspondence), by ceasing to love oneself solely and by trying hard to love someone else as well.

I ought I suppose to be grateful to Obermann, since he does provide an example of causeless melancholy. There was no compelling external misfortune which explains the acute depression from which Sénancour suffered. His father was cold to him, but he had a kind and adoring mother. He escaped the trials of the French Revolution by being absent all those years in Switzerland. At the age of twenty he married a nice Swiss girl by whom he had two children. It may well have been irksome to so indolent a man to have to support a young family by undertaking work that was not specially congenial. But his penury was never atrocious, the trials that he faced were not intolerable, and to the end of his life he insisted that he did not mind in the least his lack of literary success and the denial of all contemporary fame. In fact his later work, the *Libres Méditations*, indicated that he mastered his adolescent misery and in the end achieved a state of tranquil resignation.

The internal disadvantages from which Sénancour suffered are fully described in the pages of *Obermann*. He was overwhelmed by sadness and self-reproach when confronted, either with the immense indifference of nature, or with the activity of more virile characters. Sainte-Beuve was perfectly correct in saying that Obermann furnishes a truer specimen of the illness of the century than the more dramatic and less authentic René. When confronted with the glaciers of the alpine scenery or the sudden glories of the Napoleonic epic he felt himself to be lone and small, and much afraid. Sainte-Beuve contends that in this he was typical of many of his less well-adjusted or practical contemporaries, that his ennui was illustrative of the impotence felt by many weak characters in face of the sensational achievements of others, and that he should be acclaimed as an example of all those who, in periods of rapid transition, feel that their character, as distinct from their talents, is not solid enough to cope with such large events. In one of those sudden concise phrases which render Sainte-Beuve so illuminating, he describes Obermann as the comforter and companion of all "*génies gauches,*" of all those gifted men who have failed, either to give full expression to their own talents or to fit in with the movement of their times. I quite see that Sainte-Beuve, who was always obsessed by the fact that his will power was weaker than his brain, should have seen in *Obermann* a masterpiece which has never been accorded adequate recognition.

It is less easy to understand how a man like Matthew Arnold can also have fallen under the spell of this plangent egoist. He refers to Sénancour as "the master of my wandering youth." "I leave," he adds excessively, "half of my life with you." To him Obermann was a man shattered by "the hopeless tangle of our age." "O unstrung will!" he exclaims. "O broken heart!" This was the "Dover Beach" Matthew Arnold, the man who envied his father's undimmed faith, the man who found comfort in the "sad intensity" of Maurice de Guérin, and in Eugénie de Guérin's "sense of forlorn and dejected weariness." It was not the Arnold of *Sohrab* or *Friendship's Garland*.

Twenty years later, when he had become an esteemed civil servant, when he had been shallowed by the optimism of the eighteen sixties, he revisited Les Avants and wrote *Obermann*

Once More. I regret this poem and I suspect that Lionel Trilling, who admires Arnold as much as I do and understands him more thoroughly, regrets it too. It was surely an error to drag Sénancour from his quiet tomb at Sèvres in order that the inspector of schools might be reassured that God was in his heaven, that all was for the best in the best of worlds, that the expansion of international commerce would ensure eternal peace, that science would minister to domestic happiness, and that education when extended to the masses would render democracy unselfish and sane. I do not care for Sénancour or Obermann, but I love the early forlorn Matthew Arnold and regret the later dogskin gloves.

I shall lend my copy of *Obermann* to Sidney Culpeper, since I am sure he would enjoy it. But he is a shy bird and difficult to find.

In the evening we have a farewell dinner, since so many passengers will be leaving us at Sumatra and Singapore. It begins with elaborate hors d'oeuvres which are accompanied by champagne. The speeches then follow immediately, before the main meal begins. This seems to me an excellent arrangement and one which might with advantage be adopted at our public dinners at home. The captain moves to the foot of the staircase that leads into the dining saloon; a microphone glistens in front of him. He begins by saying that our minds will be clouded by the thought of "our missing passenger," meaning thereby the RAF officer who fell overboard. "We should remember," he says, "that God watches over the sea as well as over the land." It is so simply said that it is impressive. The captain then continues in a lighter tone. When he has finished, Jan Hubrecht makes a speech in Dutch and English. He appeals for peace and friendship between East and West. The Indonesians present do not applaud this passage; although suave enough, they do not seem to possess the magnanimity of the Indians. Then O'Malley, the Irish surgeon, makes a good speech conveying thanks on behalf of the English-speaking passengers. Then we have an excellent banquet.

We go back on deck. It is a balmy night. We talk to Mr. and Mrs. Gibson and then go to bed.

VI. MALACCA STRAIT

1

Thursday, February 7

When I reach the bathing pool this morning I am greeted by a boyish voice ringing gaily in the sparkling air. "Look at me, sir," it calls, "I can swim on my back." It is the little boy whom, only five days ago, I tried to rescue from a bullying father. He does the back stroke perfectly; between his cherub puffs his little jolly face is wreathed in smiles. His father gazes down on him in affectionate and perfectly pardonable pride. "How quickly," I say to the major, "your son has learnt to swim." He is a generous sahib and does not remind me that I strove, five days ago, to obstruct and even to prevent the experiment. "Yes," he says, "but of course he has taken lessons from the swimming instructor as well."

Now why, if it be so easy to learn swimming, was V. never taught the art? To me movement in water is among the four or five most exquisite physical sensations with which Nature has endowed mankind. But V. cannot swim, because her parents imagined that, like learning Greek or going to the university, it was not the sort of thing which debutantes needed to do. When I think of the regiment of French, German, and Italian governesses who descended upon Knole, of all those dancing classes and music lessons, of the finishing establishment of the formidable Miss Woolf, I am enraged that this simple exercise, in which she would have taken as much pleasure as did Undine, was denied to her. The Edwardians assuredly did not know how to bring up girls.

I ascend to the wireless cabin since I wish to send a message to Vernon Bartlett, warning him of our impending arrival at Singapore. I address the telegram to him c/o the Straits *Times*, but the wireless operator tells me that under the existing regulations I must give a more precise address, inserting the street and number. I assure him that the Straits *Times* is a most important newspaper, that Vernon Bartlett is a most distinguished member of the editorial staff, and that it is as absurd to insist that I should insert the street and number as it would be were I to send a cable to the editor of the *Algemeen Handelsblad* in Amsterdam. He agrees with this but says that regulations, however absurd, are regulations and that telegrams which violate them are apt not to arrive. Besides, he adds wisely (counting the meagre words that I have addressed to Vernon Bartlett), my wireless message would cost me £2.10.0. Would it not be more economical to wait until we are docked at Singapore when I can telephone to my friend direct? I agree with him and return thanks for his opportune advice.

While taking my walk round the deck this afternoon I see Sidney Culpeper sitting alone on a teak bench. He is dressed in a neat grey suit made of some tropical material and he wears a panama hat. Nobody on board, I have observed, ever wears a hat, since the promenade deck is covered by the deck above and there is plenty of shade. In fact I have been surprised to see that in the tropics the officials, the tea planters, and the oil magnates do not, as I had imagined, wear topees, puggrees, or sun helmets, but ordinary felt hats or no hats at all. Having in my youth resided frequently in hot climates, I had been taught that if, without a pith helmet, one ventured out of doors ("even when the sun is hidden behind clouds") between the hours of sunrise and sunset one would instantly be stricken by sunstroke or heatstroke or else become permanently blind. In fact one of my favourite novels, *The Four Feathers,* had been concerned with that very theme. The topee of an ardent young subaltern had been blown from his fair head by a sudden gust of wind and tumbled down the hill from which he had been observing the movements of distant dervishes. It took him but six minutes at most to recover his helmet but in those six minutes, such was the might of the Sudanese sun, his eyes had shrivelled in his head, with unfortunate consequences for all concerned. Thus when, before the second war, I had been in Persia and in central Africa I had always worn my topee. In fact before embarking on this journey V. and I had rummaged in a cupboard and extracted therefrom two khaki sun helmets which we had worn when in the Persian Gulf. Luckily Richard Rumbold had warned me in time that nobody nowadays, unless he be a Eurasian, wears a sun helmet and that, were we to don these coverings at Colombo, we should be exposing ourselves to ridicule and contempt. It seemed odd to me therefore that Culpeper should be wearing a panama hat when in the shade of the promenade deck. I had already realised that he was an eccentric and, since I like eccentrics, I paused in my afternoon walk and sat down beside him on the teak bench.

He possesses a plaintive voice, and when his thin lips part in a smile of politeness they close quickly again, restoring the pattern of a discontented mouth. I am not sure as yet whether the droop of his mouth is due to asceticism, ill-health, some secret sorrow, the denial of love, or just contempt for such as me. He is evidently an austere man and indeed I doubt whether, in the course of his forty-odd years, he has ever experienced, in his heart, his muscles, or his arteries, the throbs of sweet lust. I have met such male virgins before and they arouse in me mixed feelings of esteem, pity, and irritation. I respect their virtue as I pity their incompleteness. But I am annoyed by their combination of pride and penury. Although diffident and almost humble in the company of others, they will, when alone, prance exultantly along the public street. When they descend from a taxi they will enquire the precise fare and then extract from a purse of pigskin leather two shillings, a sixpence, and one of those odious polygons which have replaced the gay little threepenny bits of my youth. In later age the fingers of their hands, as with very avaricious men or women, are apt to assume a clawlike poise, as if, in their dread of expenditure, they were clutching continually at their own self-control.

So I sit down beside him. "Good afternoon!" I say. I have a book in my hand, and he asks me what it is. I say it is *Le Journal d'Amiel*. He says: "What odd books you read! Two days ago it was *Obermann* and now it is Amiel." "Well, you see," I answer, grasping at the opportunity, "I am on this journey examining the subject of causeless melancholy." He does not respond to this gambit and I feel checked. "Allow me," he says, and takes the book from me, turning the pages idly in his slim fingers. "Do you always mark your books?" he asks, and I detect reproof in his question. "Of course I always mark my books unless they be library books." "It makes such a mess," he sighs. A pause follows.

"I know all about you," he begins suddenly. "We have common friends—the warden of All Souls, for instance, and Roderick Meiklejohn." I make a mental note to ask John Sparrow and Meiklejohn about Culpeper when I get home. We talk for a while about these two eminent acquaintances, and he tells me that what he relishes so much about them is "their scholarly attitude towards life." "They are serious people," he remarks irrelevantly, "without ever being bores." Again—or was it my sensibility?—I detect a hint of criticism. "Besides," he adds with a roguish note, "I have read many of your books—woo-hoo!" I am always embarrassed when people mention my books, so I recover the *Journal d'Amiel*, rise from the bench, and say cheerfully, "Well, I must now resume my constitutional!"

As I resume my round (slip-slap-slip-slap go my tennis shoes upon the wooden deck) I reflect upon the significance of that odd exclamation, "Woo-hoo!" It had been uttered without any marked change of intonation, as if he had said "Besides, I have read many of your books, my word!" Even had he used the expression, "My word!" I should still have been perplexed as to whether it was employed with contempt, levity, coyness, or appreciation. He might have wished to express respect for the twenty-odd volumes—some grave, some gay—which I have published over the years. Yet had this been so, he would have employed some other term and not have uttered so ambiguous a sound as "Woo-hoo!" I am disquieted by his exclamation and tell V. about it later. She says, "But he is such a dry stick. Why worry about it?" "Dry sticks kindle easily," I reply sententiously. On reflection, I am positive that his "Woo-hoo!" was intended to convey disapproval. Culpeper is evidently an interesting man.

After dinner the captain invites us up to the bridge and shows us the first lighthouses of the Indonesian Archipelago winking ahead. We have entered the Malacca Strait.

2

Friday, February 8

We are wakened early by the jabbering of the Indonesian stewards, excited at approaching their native islands. We go on deck. From the atlas we had supposed that the Malayan Archipelago was a congested area and that we should pass between thousands of small islands clustering together, each with its native village and its fringe of palms. But we find that the Malacca Strait is as wide as the English Channel and that, at first at least, no land whatsoever can be seen. Then in the course of the early morning we reach Belawan Roads, where passengers are to disembark on tenders for Medan in Sumatra. The coast is flat and it is only when the early mist clears that we can see a distant outline of volcanoes. Meanwhile we lean over the side and watch the little boats put out to meet us. Great cinnamon-coloured hawks wheel round the ship slowly and there are herons also with long dangling legs. The tugs or tenders come out flying the Indonesian flag—a red and white horizontal bar. If I had just achieved my independence I should have chosen a less conventional and more flamboyant design. The launches nozzle up along side the large gangway of the *Willem Ruys* and Indonesian customs officials and security police clamber on board. They instal themselves in the saloon, smoke many cigarettes, and stamp with sullen apathy the landing cards of those passengers who are disembarking in Sumatra. While they are thus engaged on the upper deck, the crew of the launch which has brought them out to our ship are snatching through the portholes of three decks below the boxes of cigarettes which their compatriots are handing out to them. Having taken in as much contrabrand as they can prudently manage, the crew start fishing. They throw out an immense length of line, and after a long and lethargic pause they give a sudden tug at the line and start to pull it in with much shouting and wide swinging of the arms. When after all this movement a tiny little smelt appears at the end of the line an anticlimax is created. It is an excellent instance of what Herbert Spencer called "a descending incongruity." I had expected a heterodontus in the very least.

At 11.30 we steam away from Belawan Roads and I read Hume's *Treatise of Human Nature*. It is a relief after all these self-pityers to find oneself in the company of a Scottish mind. We pass after luncheon an isolated island, the shape of St. Michael's Mount, and quite obviously difficult of approach. V. looks at it longingly, feeling that if she lived there alone she would be out of reach of the telephone, friendly neighbours, plumbers, and amateur gardeners who want to know the names of her paeony hybrids. As night descends there are more lighthouses winking at us from unknown shores; but what is strange is that, unlike Morocco or even Corsica, the Spice Islands send no breath of nutmeg or cinnamon or other aromatic shrub across the waves towards us. We pound onwards in the moist but scentless night towards Singapore. "Woo-hoo" the huge brown hawks whisper to me in my dreams.

I understand why Sidney Culpeper should disapprove of me personally. He sees in me a well-fed, plump, flabby, complacent survival from Edwardian England, who has been accorded advantages and opportunities which he has done nothing to justify or deserve. My curiosity about life, my senile zest, must seem to him no more than a shallow euphory, based upon insensitiveness to the fears of this hydrogenic age, indifference to the wickedness and cruelty of the world around me, and a lack of any even rudimentary sense of original sin. I understand why my personality and my books should grate on his nerves. But why on earth should he extend this disapproval to the *Journal Intime* of Amiel, surely one of the most distinguished confessions that have ever been written? His attitude of disapproval spreads beyond myself and my works to embrace the books that he had noticed me reading on the boat.

It has, in fact, been with ever increasing admiration and respect that I have been rereading the *Journal Intime* in the two volumes edited by Amiel's friend, Edmond Schérer. It is not only because I enjoy his cool calm prose, but also because I recognise in him a man of fastidious and even saintly character. Here was no blubbering egoist, delighting in self-exposure and prepared with relish to impose upon his contemporaries the narrative of his sufferings. During his lifetime he never divulged his disappointments and dissatisfactions: his diary was first published in 1882, a year after his death. It was with astonishment that his friends realised posthumously that this most competent scholar had in fact been tortured by self-distrust.

Amiel was not a morbid or an abnormal man. Although his childhood may have been clouded, he thoroughly enjoyed the six years of youth when he was a student at Bonn, at Heidelberg, and in Berlin. He was still a young man when he secured a professorship at the University of Geneva and he remained there for the rest of his life. He was in no sense a solitary, but enjoyed going on excursions on Sundays to the Mont Salève, when he would laugh loudly with his companions and munch sandwiches with glee. He lived with his sister and was devoted to his nephews and nieces. He never inflicted his melancholy upon others; it was at nighttime, in the solitude of his candlelit bedroom, that he would confide to his diary the pangs of unfulfilment by which he was obsessed.

Amiel was no weakling; he possessed a muscular intellect and a remarkable gift for analysis and prevision. No man has better analysed the defects and merits of our English "gentleman conception" or more accurately forecast the effect upon European culture of American egalitarianism. I quote the following prophecy as an illustration of his acuteness:

What terrifying tyrants would the Russians become if they were ever able to spread the darkness of their domination over the peoples of the south! It would be a polar despotism, a tyranny such as the world has never yet experienced. Silent as the shadows, incisive as ice, impenetrable as bronze, their tyranny would be veiled by a surface amiability and the cold glitter of snow. They would bring with them slavery without mitigation and without compensation. Yet it is probable that, in the course of time, they themselves will lose both the faults and the virtues of their present half-barbaric state.

Amiel was devoid of the arrogance of the introvert, his detachment and pessimism being softened by a graceful modesty, which had about it the humility of holiness. Nor did he approve of the selfishness inherent in a character that shrinks from positive action. He was no escapist:

I can understand [he wrote] the mystic delights of Buddhism, the ecstasies of the Sufis, the kief of the Turks, the spiritual absorption of the East. At the same time I feel that this form of pleasure can only bring death with it: such indulgence, like the abuse of opium or hashish, is in fact a gradual suicide. How inferior are these methods of escaping from reality to the joy of energetic action, to the sweetness of love, to the beauty of enthusiasm, to the sacred savour of duty accomplished!

That so virile a man should have suffered, and recorded, the symptoms of a malcontent renders his *Journal Intime* all the more memorable and instructive. As so many of the unfulfilled, he found it difficult to feel young. "At thirty-seven," he recorded, "I am left without will, desire or talent. The fireworks of my youth are today no more than a pinch of ashes." He reproached himself for indolence, for "this frightful vice of procrastination," and realised that his daily habits of punctuality and order were but excuses for a lack of concentration on essentials. He too felt that he was ill-adjusted to society. "Fundamentally," he wrote, "I cannot fit into the existing order of things." He reproached himself bitterly for his lack of creative activity, for his failure to give expression to the genius that he felt he possessed. What did his work amount to? Some courses of lectures delivered to indifferent audiences, a few translations from German and English, some incidental pamphlets, some articles in philological magazines. It was not for these that he had been endowed with so acute a mind.

He was subject to renewed and almost causeless bouts of anxiety. "I am haunted," he wrote, "by a sort of sacred terror, not for myself only, but for all mankind. . . . In us, the children of this age, eternity inspires hateful anxiety and infinity a mysterious terror." "Alas!" he confessed, "it is my nature to be always a little frightened of what gives me pleasure." The only remedy he could find against these bouts of disillusion was a categorical sense of duty.

He was too acute and honest not to realise that fundamentally the dissatisfaction of the sterile genius comes from lack of objective will power. "My great sin," he confessed, "is to have been too readily discouraged." "The cup," he wrote, "that I should wish to be for ever removed from my lips is the necessity of willing something, the obligation of having to make a decision, to resolve on something, to take action." Activity implied moral responsibility and he was alarmed by moral responsibility. "Every one of our actions," he reflected, "is a hostage which we hand over to a vindictive destiny. . . . Every hope is an egg from which may be hatched either a dove or a serpent." He was for ever haunted by "an unquiet and corrosive sentiment of doubt, which renders living impossible and grins sardonically at all our desires."

The tragedy of Henri-Frédéric Amiel was that he was too

fastidious to compromise with reality and too idealistic to content himself with the second best. His friends, admiring the brilliance of his mind and the width of his erudition, believed that one day he would publish a work of genius. They never foresaw that he would be rendered immortal by a confession of his own insufficiency. He was in fact too fine a soul to adapt himself to ordinary life, and his faith was not sufficiently insistent to render him a mystic. "What is real in life," he wrote, "fills me with repulsion and the ideal can never be achieved." Yet he clung fiercely to his own ideals. "To betray an ideal," he wrote, "is the most irreparable of all acts of violation; it is the rape of one's own conscience."

Unlike so many malcontents, Amiel is life-enhancing, not life-denying. He does not depress, he invigorates. Surely he must have been, not a great stylist merely, but a very superior man.

3

Saturday, February 9

At 6.30 in the morning we are wakened by the steward playing his temple tune on the gong. We are annoyed by this since 6.30 today means 5.30 yesterday and 4.30 the day before. I stay in bed till 7.30 and then dress and go on deck. We are sliding slowly into Singapore Harbour. It is a grey morning and the decks are wet after a tropical rainstorm during the night. Boumphrey, who with his wife is preparing to disembark, says that this is an excellent thing as it will mean a cool day for the visits he had prescribed for us. I am sorry they are leaving the ship. The Stedalls are also leaving us and are visiting their daughter at Kuala Lumpur. But they will be rejoining the ship for the return voyage.

The first impression of Singapore as we slide in is that it is about the greenest place that I have ever seen. It is like entering Dartmouth on a muggy August afternoon. As we get inside the harbour there are bungalows, some in Tudor style and some with loggias as in Florence, and flagstaffs, and signalling stations, and a wireless mast. We sidle up to a long quay on which the rain of last night has left enormous puddles. There are coolies standing about in dirty white ducks, and a few Europeans come to meet their families and friends. They stare up at our huge ship as it edges alongside the quay. Suddenly, as they catch sight of their relations, they are galvanised into spasms of recognition: fingers point, arms wave, and parasols are agitated. When these mimetic signals are exhausted they stand gazing up at the boat and its burden with a fixed smile of welcome. It is a difficult expression to retain for long. Then the gangway is lowered, communications are established, and the greeters pour on board to clasp the greeted in their arms.

I go down to V.'s cabin and knock at her door. Having been wakened at 6.30, which she insists is really 4.30, she had gone to sleep again and was still in her bunk. But she dresses hurriedly and we go down to breakfast. Thereafter the mail is distributed.

I get an airmail letter-card from Colin Fenton dated February 3 in which he tells me that on returning to the flat in order to pick up his suitcase for the weekend he found the contents of the suitcase scattered over the floor of the hall. For a moment he supposed that somebody had been playing a joke on him, but on entering the sitting room he found that all the drawers had been turned upside down and that the carpet was strewn with typing paper, carbon paper, writing paper, envelopes, steel clips, cigarettes, and bootlaces. On entering John Sparrow's bedroom and my own little cabin, he was confronted with similar chaos. Being quick at the uptake, he then realised that the flat had been visited by housebreakers. His own cigar case had been taken, my possessions had been rifled, and they had stolen the enamel and diamond watch which had once belonged to Richard Rumbold's great-grandfather, a most prosperous nabob. So Colin, abandoning all hope of getting to the country that afternoon, had telephoned for the police.

The theory was that the thieves had been incited to this act of depredation owing to the chance that, two days before my departure, there had been a feature on television depicting the Albany and some of its tenants. The impression conveyed was that of elderly bachelors residing in lonely opulence, and therefore offering fair game. I do not myself believe this was the direct cause of the visitation, since before the television display I had several times been rung up on the telephone and the receiver had been banged down the moment I answered. I had assumed that this was due to the fact that one of Colin's lady friends had telephoned, hoping that he would reply, and had rung off in irritation at the sound of my bronchial voice. I had in fact asked Colin to suggest to them that it was unkind thus suddenly to sever communication and that I should have enjoyed a little friendly chat. But I now see that it was burglars planning to pounce and seeking first to assure themselves that the flat was empty. In any case, I possess practically no jewelry and there was not much, beyond a cigarette case or two, and Lord Curzon's links, for them to find. It seems that the thieves had gained admittance by forcing the basement bolt. Miss Macmillan, before she left for the afternoon, had fortunately concealed the teapot, the milk jug, and the sugar basin in a box in her kitchen. Captain Adams, the secretary of the Albany, was justifiably annoyed by this occurrence. Having small sense of possesssion, I was just amused.

4

We are still reading our letters when a young Chinese and his wife appear shyly at the cabin door, carrying an enormous bouquet of orchids and gardenias. They are Mr. and Mrs. Hsin-Chang Chang. They had been told to meet us by V.'s friend, Su-Hua, an artist and a writer, who had unfortunately gone off to Hong Kong for a short visit. I leave them to talk to V. while I make a bad attempt to get hold of Vernon Bartlett on the ship telephone which has been connected with the main exchange at Singapore. The connection does not seem to be a good one, since those who stand in front of me in the queue behind the ship's intercom are manifesting impatience verging on hysteria. They wiggle and waggle at the machine and shout desperately, "Halloa!" at the receiver. I abandon the project and return to the cabin. I find that a note has arrived from the commissioner-general asking us to luncheon, and thereafter to go to the races. I reply by the A.D.C. that we shall be delighted to come to luncheon but that race meetings are not up our street. Mr. and Mrs. Hsin-Chang Chang then accompany us on shore where they have a car waiting. We drive into the town.

We pass the customs sheds, and at the gate in the steel fence that encloses the dock area we show our passports to an extremely neat sergeant of the native police. We then pass the railway station, which displays the word "Singapore" in large white letters as unself-consciously as if it had been "Tonbridge." What, I reflect, had this romantic name hitherto conveyed to me? A prolonged political controversy on the theme of "the Singapore base" and a feeling of shattered surprise when this assumedly impregnable fortress fell so quickly to the Japanese. But now it all seems prosperous and undamaged. We drive along Anson Road and Robinson Road and Collyer Quay to the Esplanade. We stop at Cavenagh Bridge and look at the junks anchored along the wharf of the Singapore River. We enter a huge cool bank where I again try in vain to get into contact with Vernon Bartlett. We then go to a huge cool post office where I send a telegram to the ambassador at Djakarta and am treated with politeness and skill. We had learnt that the airmail letters which we sent from Cape Town to be flown to Rotterdam had, owing to some oversight on the part of the postal officials, been put on board a ship returning to Europe and not into the KLM aeroplane. This means that the letters we now post by air from Singapore will probably arrive sooner than those we sent from the Cape a fortnight ago. This is disquieting and it is for this reason that we stop at the nice cool post office in Singapore. We then visit a poor bookshop where I fail to find a copy of Hölderlin and then go to the majestic emporium of Whiteaways. I try on a neat Saigon jacket, since I am feeling the heat. I am aware that it is too tight for me and am about to ask for a larger size when our fellow passenger, Mr. Hyams, who happens also to be buying tropical clothing, remarks brightly: "Too narrow across the shoulders." Now Mr. Hyams may know everything about the film industry, but he knows nothing about my figure. So I buy the coat immediately, although I know in my soul that it does not fit me and that, like all tropical coats, it is deficient in pockets.

We then drive to the house of the commissioner-general, Sir Robert Scott. It is a nice cool house set in a wide green garden. The grass of the lawns is not our sort of grass but a sort of camomile which, when mown, looks firm and green and compact. We are taken up to a large wide loggia on the first floor, where there are huge bamboo armchairs with chintz cushions. We are greeted by Lady Scott, the wife of the commissioner-general, whose family I used to know in distant Constantinople days. We are given iced drinks and then taken to wash and brush up. Then other guests arrive for luncheon, among them Mr. and Mrs. Lane. He is something of a botanist and V. extracts from him much curious and useful information. I observe that the men, on arrival, take off their coats and that their shirts show long damp patches on the back. I refuse to take off my coat. V. thinks that my modesty is due to the fact that I am wearing braces which might look bourgeois if revealed. The others probably suppose that my hesitation is due to the fact that I am suffering from some skin eruption on the forearms. But the truth is that I consider it incorrect to take off one's coat when lunching at a government house. When later I confess this to V., she snorts. She does not share my reverence for protocol.

After luncheon we take a stroll in the garden. There is a

circular orchid bed in which the plants are grown on sticks like sweet peas at home, only that the beds are raised on bricks so as to protect them from damp. There is a magnificent clump of sealing-wax palms. There are also baskets of orchids hanging from the trees and great gardenia bushes in full flower. We meet the head gardener, a polite Tamil and one of the slimmest men that I have ever seen. He is naked to the waist and, although in no sense scraggy or starved-looking, is so beautifully made that my hands could meet round his torso.

I have a talk with Sir Robert Scott, who is an elegant but enlightened man. He thinks very highly of Lim-Yew-Hock and is optimistic about the negotiations about to take place in London between him and the Colonial Office. He has an affection for Marshall, but regards him as "unpredictable." He tells me that the Chinese in Singapore are divided into two camps, not exactly "right" and "left," but according to their age groups. The older generation desire stability, are afraid of being dominated by Communist China, and would be glad if the Governor retained reserved powers, enabling him to suspend the Constitution in the event of disturbances or an emergency. The younger generation are for the most part nationalist; they revere Mao Tse-tung, not so much because he is a Communist, but because they see in him a nationalist leader who has liberated China from exploitation by the foreigner. They are anti-colonial rather than pro-Soviet or pro-Marx. His Excellency is soberly optimistic about the future.

The Changs then pick us up in their car and we drive to the botanical gardens where we are met by the curator. He takes us into the laboratory building, where there are many thousands of orchid seedlings arranged in sealed flasks upon racks. Each flask contains a jelly composed from algar seaweed, and when the baby orchids have developed sufficient roots they are planted out in pans with a mixture of powdered brick, charcoal, and liquid manure. The curator calls these seedlings his "test-tube babies."

We are then taken to the orchid enclosure in the gardens outside. It is encircled by a high fence of steel mesh, which is electrified, partly in order to protect the orchids from the ravages of monkeys, but also to protect them against interference by the public or seizure by the professional orchid thieves who rob the gardens of their rarest plants and sell them to collectors in Miami and elsewhere. V. and I are not interested in orchids, which seem to us exotic and sparsely flowering vegetables, for the most part scentless, and only rarely more beautiful in colour or markings than the reticulata irises or the bearded irises that grow so lavishly at home. The curator tells us that they used to train monkeys to climb up the trees and bring down the orchids from their summits. These monkeys were of a specially intelligent breed called Berok monkeys and the leader of the troupe, Merah, could understand as many as eighteen Malayan words of command. These monkeys have died off and the only way that they can collect new orchids nowadays is to wait until the trees are felled. There are, he believes, many undiscovered orchids still in Malaya, but the habit of this shy plant is to hide itself and its seedlings on the summits of such trees as cannot be climbed by man. The gardens themselves are magnificent with flowering trees and the great sealing-wax palms in which the monkeys swing and jabber. We fear that we have been a disappointment to the curator, since our ignorance was evident. But it was rather like being shown emerald tiaras by M. Jacques Cartier in the rue de la Paix.

The Changs then take us to the aquarium in Victoria Park. It is air-conditioned and delightfully cool. In the dim hall we meet Mrs. Ault, who introduces us to her husband who has come down from Kuala Lumpur to meet his family: he is a very handsome man with the polite yet reserved bearing of a Foreign Office official. It is an excellent aquarium and V. and I as always gaze in fascination at the sea horses, which are the most heraldic of all beasts. We also admire the Monodactylus Argenteus, and above all the dragonfish, or Pterois Volitans. I say to Patricia Ault: "See there! That is the Pterois Volitans." "Oo-er!" she answers.

Then off we go in search of pottery, which is one of V.'s abiding passions. But everything in the shops seems to be Japanese in taste and we buy nothing.

5

The Changs then take us for a short rest in their flat in the university compound. It is a nice flat on the ground floor, with lattice blinds let down to keep out the heat, and a wide tiled floor which shines with wax. The children of the faculty play together under the trees outside; we can hear their voices and their laughter as we talk together in the quiet room.

Mr. and Mrs. Chang are delightful people. He was educated at Cambridge and pronounces English with so perfect a Cambridge accent that it might be Dadie Rylands speaking, or the provost of King's. He was professor of Chinese at London University and is now professor of English at the university at

Singapore. His wife is also a highly educated woman who teaches.

Mr. Chang, when in London, had criticised me on the B.B.C. for the disparaging things I had said about Chinese manners in *Good Behaviour*. I had seen his talk in *The Listener*, but all I remember of it was that it was polite and amusing. It did not induce me to reverse my opinion that formal manners, once they become a ritual, entail unnatural conduct and a wastage of time. He has published a book which he gave me on *Allegory and Courtesy in Spenser*. I love courtesy, but I hate allegory and find *The Faerie Queene* most wearisome to read. But I admire Edmund Spenser as a poet, have visited the ruined tower at Kilcolman where he "struggled through dark ways," and was so impressed with the charm of Mr. Chang and the alertness of his mind that I shall read his work with attention.

I assured Mr. Chang, as I sipped his delicate tea, scented with jasmine, that no sensible person could make light of the Confucian system, if only because it had dominated Chinese thought for some twenty-five hundred years. In fact, I accepted with reverence and belief six of the seven rules that K'ung Ch'iu, whom we call Confucius, had defined as the paths which a superior man should follow in his ascent towards virtue. I agreed that we must all cultivate and develop such qualities as wisdom, righteousness, altruism, compassion, sincerity, and faithfulness to oneself and others. All that I had said in *Good Behaviour* was that his insistence upon the seventh path or quality, namely *Li*, or "propriety" or "etiquette," appeared to me to attribute ethical importance to a matter of custom. Mr. Chang was far too polite to assail my invincible ignorance, and merely sat there smiling courteously. I must however have let slip some expression such as "escapist philosophies," since he told me that Confucius himself was not an escapist but a man who struggled hard to reform administration. After all, he had been minister of crime and for a while deputy prime minister, and had sought to convince the authorities that good government should be based upon paternal administration and should inculcate the precepts of filial piety towards the state. It was only when he found from experience that no despot could be rendered actively benevolent that he abandoned politics for reflection. Like so many Englishmen who had devoted but little study to the subject I seemed to him inclined to confuse Confucianism with Taoism, the system advocated by "old big-ear" Lao-tse. It was the Taoists who advocated quietism, the return to nature, the female principle, and the doctrine that "by doing nothing, everything is accomplished." Nor was I right in taking it for granted that the *Analects*, which were collected and edited many years later, in fact represented the sum of Confucius' teaching. When I return to London I shall read them again with a less impatient mind.

We then drive back, through Raffles Place and along Collyer Quay, to the dock area. We persuade the Changs to come on board with us and we give them a drink in the smoking room. V. mentions that I had received an airmail letter-card that morning telling me that my flat in the Albany had been entered by burglars and an unspecified number of my possessions taken away. Mr. Chang smiles at this, pulls out his pocketbook, and hands me a cutting from this morning's newspaper. Since it is printed in the Chinese language I ask him to translate it for me. It reported that I had recently been shown on television seated at a writing table "in my palatial flat in London." Tempted by the opulence of my surroundings and appearance, some determined thieves had broken into my flat and taken away much jewelry, many valued possessions, and "all the stars of the many orders which this eminent writer possesses." Mr. Chang explained that he had refrained, until told that I was already aware of this outrage, from informing me that the robbery had been reported in the local newspaper since "he did not wish to be the first bearer of bad news." Never again shall I write disrespectfully of Chinese manners.

We see Mr. and Mrs. Hsin-Chang Chang down to the gangway and return to finish reading our correspondence. Colin Fenton's letter-card is open on the table beside me and V., in stretching forward to read it again, upsets my full glass of martini over it. It had been written with a biro pen and on receiving the martini it explodes like the advertisement for Stephens ink. I have never seen any communication become so suddenly incommunicable.

The captain comes to talk to us. He tells us that he had been on the bridge all night when approaching Singapore, since the Chinese junks are inclined to go fishing without lights. Poor man, his troubles never cease, but he confronts the accidents of earth and sea with a clear blue eye. One of the Javanese stewards that afternoon had gone on shore where he had been entertained by some compatriots. They had given him rice brandy, or *arak*. Being as a Moslem unused to alcoholic liquor, and the drink being one of great potency, he had collapsed. His friends had bundled him in a taxi, telling the driver to take him back to the ship. On arrival at the dock gate, however, the police discovered that the man was dead. So when we return to Singapore the poor captain will have to spend the whole day attending a coroner's inquest.

Sunday, February 10

It is a grey morning with no islands to be seen. We again cross the Equator. I go up to the saloon and have our passports stamped by the Indonesian officials who have remained in the boat since we left Sumatra. They are seated in a row at a long table, and when I hand them our passports they give me a gilt-edged grin. They are perfectly polite but somewhat indifferent; they seem to lack powers of concentration.

There is a following wind and it is sultry and sticky. In the afternoon we pass the island of Billiton, the tin island, from which my old friend Baron Michiels van Verduynen of the Netherlands Embassy in London derived his very substantial income. There is a menacing maroon-coloured sunset, and we lean over the side talking to the Hubrechts who will part from us tomorrow at Djakarta. A lighthouse begins its heartbeats in the dusk. On the surface of the sea are streams of a brown and yellow mixture. Jan Hubrecht tells me that it is fish spawn and that the sea in this area is packed tight with fish. The Americans, realising that the exploitation of these fisheries might provide food and employment for the overpopulated islands, presented the Indonesian Government with a fleet of up-to-date trawlers. The result was that the local fishermen, instead of working five days in the week, only worked for three. I notice that Jan Hubrecht, who has a real affection for the Indonesians, very rarely mentions their faults.

After dinner we go to our cabins and pack the things we shall need for a week's sojourn in Java.

VII. JAVA

1

Monday, February 11

We slow down during the night so as not to arrive too early at Tandjongpriok. We get into the harbour at 8.00 and tie up at the dock at 9.45. We lean over the side watching a mixed but impressive delegation of Indians who have come down to welcome their new ambassador, a handsome man who joined the *Willem Ruys* at Colombo. They climb up the gangway and the ambassador receives them in the library. How often in the past have I witnessed and attended similar ceremonies! I notice that both the reception committee and the ambassador are wreathed in exactly the same false smiles as are adopted by Europeans on similar occasions. The Russians are the only people who, when welcoming delegations or being met by reception committees, do not even pretend to register pleasure. They will pass along the line, barely touching the hands outstretched in welcome and averting their gaze from the faces of those to whom those hands belong. French cabinet ministers sometimes adopt a similar procedure: it is called *la poignée de main parlementaire*.

We introduced ourselves three days ago on the boat to Mr. and Mrs. Jackson, for whom we had a letter of introduction from Lindsay Mackie. Jackson is chairman and managing director of "The Anglo-Indonesian Plantations," who own a vast estate in the interior of Java called "P. & T. Lands." He was interned by the Japanese during their occupation of the island, and his wife was also thrown into a concentration camp. For three and a half years they remained in durance vile, each unable to ascertain what had happened to the other, and exposed to the humiliations inflicted on prisoners of war by *Bushido,* the Japanese doctrine of chivalry. They do not seem to have suffered physically or mentally from this ordeal, which must indeed have been a test of self-respect. They are now going out for a three months' inspection of the properties. They invite us to visit their plantations during our stay in Java and we accept with delight. We shall spend two nights in the house of the local representative or manager, Mr. Shaw. He and his wife have come down to the harbour to meet them, and we arrange that we shall go up there for Tuesday and Wednesday nights. We bid a sad farewell to the Hubrechts, who are off to Surabaya. They have been met by their son, a tall man with a manner that is enterprising and gay.

The ambassador at Djakarta, Dermot MacDermot, then comes on board to greet us. He is a man of distinguished appearance, arrayed in an immaculate white suit and possessing to the full the courtesy, consideration, and reserve inculcated in its rising members by the service in which I was born and bred. He tells us that unfortunately he will not for the moment be able to ask us to stay at the embassy, since his niece has been taken ill and his spare bedroom is occupied by a night nurse. So we arrange to lunch and spend the day at the embassy and to return on board for the night.

We then walk down the gangway and set foot on Javanese soil. The Rotterdam Lloyd have an army of porters to meet us; they are dressed in blue linen shirts with the initials "R.L." embroidered on their chests. We had been warned that we should not be allowed to bring any money of any sort on shore, since the Indonesian Government are much disturbed by the existing currency situation. It is the first time, since I left school, that I have found myself without a penny in my pocket, but MacDermot assures me that he can provide us with cash once we reach the embassy. He then introduces us to his wife and we pass into the customs shed. We are made to enter two little sentry boxes, marked "Men" and "Women," in which, but for the presence of the ambassador, we should have been searched for contraband notes. But the ambassador shows his diplomatic pass and the official, after staring at it in dumb perplexity for one or two minutes, jerks his thumb towards the exit, signifying "You may go." I did not derive the impression that he meant to be rude but merely that he had not acquired the art of combining authority with politeness. There are two embassy cars drawn up outside and V. enters one of them with Mrs. MacDermot while I and the ambassador follow in the one behind.

It is some six miles from the harbour of Tandjongpriok to the capital, which I have always known as Batavia but which is now renamed Djakarta. We drive out of the dock area and along the flats which are bordered on one side by the lagoons that open from the sea and on the other side by the municipal rubbish dumps that are thick with indigent Javanese picking at the garbage in search of food. I ask the ambassador about the existing political situation which, in so far as I have gathered from the newspapers of Singapore, is momentarily disturbed, owing to a difference of opinion between the central government at Djakarta and the military leaders in the adjoining island of Sumatra. MacDermot is evidently fond of the Indonesians, realises that they are faced with almost insoluble problems, and refrains from any form of criticism. I have not, moreover, come out here to study politics but to examine the nature of causeless melancholy. I therefore do not press my questions and content myself with gazing right and left of me and at the mixed traffic which, as we approach the capital, becomes congested. We are twice held up at level crossings which bisect the road.

We then enter the town of Djakarta, of which the Dutch in former days used to boast as being the cleanest city in Asia. There are wide avenues, a few handsome government buildings, and numerous small houses built by Dutch civil servants or Chinese merchants and surrounded by little gardens which must once have been trim. The embassy is an attractive house, not large, and possessing a well-kept back garden. The ambassador goes off to his work at the chancery, and V. and I are taken by Mrs. MacDermot to visit a shop where they sell batik prints. I buy a tie on which, against a cream background, there is a trelliswork of brown; it costs me 22/- which V. regards as too expensive. We are accompanied on this expedition by the MacDermots' young son, aged about nine or ten. His name is Conor, he is being educated at a local Catholic school preparatory to going on to Downside, and he is one of the most vivacious and alert little boys that I have met. I discover that MacDermot is a cousin of Niall MacDermot, who was with Nigel at Balliol and who is at this moment fighting the by-election in North Lewisham.

We return to the embassy for luncheon. The ambassador brings with him from the chancery the London newspapers which have just arrived by bag. After luncheon the MacDermots retire, as is the custom, for a siesta. V. and I remain in the cool drawing room, glad to enjoy a rest. I seize a copy of the *Daily Telegraph* for February 6 and a few minutes later I regret having done so. It contains a full account of the meeting held on February 5 by the Conservative Association for Bournemouth East and Christchurch. The Executive had decided to reaffirm their repudiation of Nigel, immediately to adopt an alternative candidate for the next general election, and meanwhile to instruct all their branches to have no further dealings with their elected member. He is thus precluded from informing his own constitutents of the reasons which prompted him to abstain from voting with the government on the Suez issue. This is terribly unfair, but I realise that, once patriotic emotions are aroused, few people relish being told by their M.P. that he had striven to abide by his election pledges, or that he regarded the government's violation of their treaties and engagements as dishonourable in itself, as liable to put American and world opinion against us, and as doomed to expose us to serious humiliation. I fear that this means that Nigel has lost the seat which he had won at two elections by a many thousand majority and which he has served so conscientiously and so well. I am shattered by this news and sit there in the drawing room staring in front of me in despair. I am not optimistic about the final issue: *"Mit der Dummheit kämpfen Götter selbst vergebenst.*

After tea we go with Mrs. MacDermot and Conor to the bazaars, where V. finds some lovely batik. The MacDermots urge us to stay to dinner, but we wish to return for our mail to the *Willem Ruys* and I am brooding too bitterly over Bournemouth to face entertainments. So we drive down to Tandjong-priok again and have no difficulty in climbing into the corridors of our friendly boat. But there is no mail for us apart from one post card. The purser explains that the Indonesians insist on dealing with all mail themselves, with the result that, since few of their postal officials can read, the letters are delivered one by one over a protracted period often lasting for weeks. We dine in an almost empty saloon and afterwards sit on deck with the Gibsons, listening to the sounds of the little port.

2

Tuesday, February 12

We have breakfast on board and then prepare to leave in order to catch the train for Bandung. We have difficulty in finding porters to carry our luggage but eventually Van Ruy and a colleague, the Dutch stewards on our deck and that above us, come to our rescue and carry down the cases themselves. We enter the customs and as we do so are greeted by Micklethwaite, the embassy information officer, who had been sent down to see us through. The Indonesian customs official makes me open my typewriter case but then becomes distracted by some other avenue of power, never glances at my customs declaration, and just makes a curt sign of dismissal with his cigarette. We get into the embassy car and drive to the station at Djakarta; it takes us thirty minutes. We find that the train will not be leaving until half an hour after the time announced. We sit down with Micklethwaite and have some beer on the platform. The train comes in and we climb up into the first-class coach, which is air-conditioned and comfortable. Sitting next to us is a Javanese mother with her baby; it is a nice baby, sleeps most of the time, and only starts screaming when offered a bar of chocolate.

The scenery at first is dull—just rice fields stretching over a plain under a grey sky, and small villages with huts under brown-tiled roofs. Then suddenly behind this plain rises a background of volcanoes, table mountains and sugar loafs. It is different from any landscape that we have seen before, and we stare out of the windows in surprise. The lower hills are still terraced as paddy fields, and there are muddy pools in which water buffaloes wallow; we see white ibexes, and children flying primitive kites which become entangled in the telegraph wires and hang there, giving a sad effect of litter and aspiration unfulfilled. At 2.30 we reach the station at Bandung, where we are met by Steve Hodson of P. & T. Lands, a tall and strikingly handsome Irishman with a matted mass of thick white hair. He takes us to the Maison Boghijen, a cool modern restaurant, where we have iced drinks and an excellent tomato omelette. Then off we go towards Subang.

The suburbs of Bandung, of which the Dutch were so proud, are not to V.'s taste or mine. True it is that we notice a fine

Amherstia nobilis in full flower, but we also observe that along the wire fences of the bungalows are trained that most odious of all climbing roses, the Dorothy Perkins. On leaving Bandung we start to climb up into the mountains, and after an hour or so we enter the confines of the P. & T. Lands. We pass quinine plantations, rubber plantations, and acres of tea bushes aligned in rows. We climb higher and higher and cross the pass below the great volcano where the smell of sulphur drifts across the road. Then we drop down into the heat again towards Subang, which we reach at 3.40. We are staying at the house of Mr. and Mrs. Shaw, which is spacious and beautifully cool. We are offered a gin and tonic and then go out into the garden. It has a wide lawn sloping down to the canal and edged with beautiful shrubs and trees—allamanda, gardenia, hibiscus of many varieties, and large frangipani trees. Before dinner Shaw takes us round the compound. He calls it "the village." There are several other neat houses set in green gardens, a clubhouse, and a statue. There are elegant young women in shorts playing golf on the green. We then return, have an excellent shower, and dine. We go to bed early, as we have had a hot and exhausting day.

Mrs. Shaw is a wonderful hostess, and the main living room is bright with pretty chintzes and exotic flowers beautifully arranged in jars. She shows V. to her bedroom, which is in what is called "the Pavilion" and which, although joined to the main house, has a detached look. I hope that V. will not during the night be attacked by bats, panthers, or marauders. Shaw shows me to my own room off the main sitting room. "That," he says, pointing vaguely in the direction of the bed, "is your Dutch wife." I do not understand the purport of this remark, but I giggle politely even as I giggle when John Lawrence tells me one of his city tales.

I have a bath and a cold shower, adjust the electric fan so that it will not play directly upon me, look under the bed and into the cupboard for fear that there might in fact be some Dutch woman lurking, and shut the bolt of my door in case this woman were to intrude upon me during the night. The sense of hospitality possessed by these empire builders, these pioneers, these planters in the Far East, is, I have been told, without stint or limit. Anything that might bring pleasure to a guest—whether it be vegetable, mineral, or animal—is, as a matter of course, provided for him. I am disquieted by this thought. I creep into bed.

I have always prided myself on the circumstance that I can in any conditions drop off into deep sleep. In fact during the war I slept for seven hours lying on the floor of an American aeroplane speeding from Casablanca to some Cornish airport. But tonight I am restless. In the first place, anxiety regarding that Dutch woman fills me with unease; in the second place, my bed is so hard that the floor of the American aeroplane was in comparison a silken mattress stuffed with cygnet feathers. This Subang bed is constructed of a board and above it a thin coverlet of cast iron. At last I drift off to sleep, but dream that I am the fourth side of the Rosetta stone on which that famous palaeontologist (the chairman of the Bournemouth East Conservative Association) is chiselling a long inscription in praise of Eden in the Indonesian language. In my many moments of wakefulness I hear the tropical rain thundering down upon the roofs and the banana leaves; lightning flashes; the electric current fails and my fan ceases to revolve. In my exhaustion I can still feel the chairman chiselling away viciously at my back.

Wednesday, February 13

At 6.00 A.M. a siren howls over the village, and at 6.30, by which time the whole staff are expected to be in their factories or at their office desks, it howls again, but on this occasion more briskly and in a less pleading tone. I rise and dress. In the sitting room I find Mrs. Shaw, who is an effective housewife, going round the flower vases snipping off the dead petals and leaves. It seems that these exotic flowers, magnificent though they be, do not last long in water. V. appears from her pavilion. Mrs. Shaw asks her whether she has slept well and V. answers politely that she was kept awake by rain and thunder. Mrs. Shaw enquires whether we thought the beds hard and explains that these beds are specially designed for the tropics to keep one cool at night. A bolster, she explains, is provided to protect the limbs from being chafed or bruised and to assist the air in circulating. I had noticed a little bolster laid upon my bed but had discarded it; V. had put hers under her pillow, a position which, in her ignorance, she imagined bolsters were intended to assume. "Yes," explains Mrs. Shaw, continuing the while to snip the frangipani blossom, "they are a great help. We call them 'Dutch wives.' "

A stranger comes to breakfast. He is passing through on his way to Djakarta and has been spending the last fortnight in Sumatra. I think he must be a journalist, since he not only possesses much information, but seems anxious to communicate that information to others. He tells me more about the situation in the Federal Republic of Indonesia than I have hitherto ventured to acquire. He says there are as many as three thousand islands in the archipelago, each with its distinct traditions, customs, and even religion, and each resentful of government control. Sumatra, for instance, although not so thickly populated as Java, is far richer in natural resources. The Sumatrans regard themselves as more cultured, more virile, and less incurably indolent than the Javanese and much resent any interference on the part of the central authority at Djakarta. Only recently Colonel Ahmad Hussein, chairman of the Bateng council, had established a dictatorship in central Sumatra, arrested prominent Communist politicians, and fixed his headquarters at Padang. My informant does not see how the central government could cope with these military rebellions. The Javanese army is so unwilling to maintain order in the other islands that hundreds of thousands of people in southern Celebes have been obliged to evacuate their villages for fear of bandits. Even within the vicinity of the capital itself the *Dar-ul-Islam*, or trained fanatics, burn and plunder. The central parliament at Djakarta is composed of twenty-nine separate parties out of two hundred and sixty members; the civil service is untrained and regarded by the population as corrupt; and the government seem to believe that by restricting the import and export of currency and at the same time by printing paper money they can bribe the adjoining islands into submission. All sensible people, my informant assured me, hoped that the President Sukarno, or the popular Vice-President, Dr. Hatta, will realise that the Indonesians are not ripe for self-government or parliamentary institutions and will establish a dictatorship or "governing council" to put an end to what must inevitably culminate in bankruptcy and chaos. I have no means of course of judging how far this itinerant journalist's pessimism is justified. I do not like pressing questions on the ambassador, on Jackson, or on Shaw, since they seem reserved on the subject and I do not wish to intrude on their discretion. And after all, I am for once in my life determined not to take any interest in politics. I was careful not to mention *apartheid* in Cape Town, or to discourse upon minority rights in Colombo and Singapore. I am not going to start being intrusive up here among the tea gardens and the rubber groves.

We are called for in a powerful green and white American car by Steve Hodson, who had offered to take us round a part of the estate. But before I record what we visited and examined, I shall insert here some notes on this plantation which furnishes an example of enterprise such as I deeply admire and enjoy.

3

The history of this vast estate is indeed impressive. I have been reading it in a leaflet lent me by Shaw, which is supplemented by Mr. Wilfrid Daukes's two detailed volumes entitled *The P. & T. Lands*. It is the story of a long battle waged by skilled endurance against the animosity of nature and the envy of man.

When during the Napoleonic Wars the British occupied the Dutch East Indies, when, that is, Stamford Raffles was lieutenant governor and Rollo Gillespie commander in chief, the islands were assailed by what appears to be an endemic

Indonesian malady, namely acute inflation. It was decided that, if the troops were to be paid and labour obtained, drastic measures must be taken. The existing currency was called in by Order in Council and the expenses of the administration were to be met, pending readjustment, by the sale to private individuals or companies of public land. In 1812 the Council, at a meeting from which Rollo Gillespie was absent owing to illness, decided to hold an ostensibly public auction for the disposal of these properties. At this auction the estate known as the "Pamanoekan and Tjiasem Lands," consisting of more than half a million acres and measuring twenty-four miles from west to east and thirty-six miles from north to south, was disposed of to a Major Shrapnell and a Mr. Skelton for the sum of £20,000. It was rumoured at the time that these purchasers were mere men of straw and that the property had in fact been sold at a price below its real value to the lieutenant governor and two of his associates on the Council. When Raffles eventually quarrelled with Gillespie (as he quarrelled with so many of his colleagues, subordinates and superiors), it was whispered in London that the lieutenant governor had used the currency crisis and his own despotic authority for purposes of private gain. Raffles bitterly resented this rumour, but he never succeeded in convincing his critics that the charge was wholly without foundation. The property which in 1812 had been sold for £20,000 was, less than a hundred years later, valued at £3,725,000, which shows what an immense amount of energy and capital had in the interval been devoted to what the French colonial school would call its *mise envaleur.*

Major Shrapnell and Mr. Skelton rapidly disappeared from

the scene, and, after changing hands repeatedly, the property was acquired by a remarkable Dutchman of the name of Peter Hofland. For thirty-two years, from 1840 until his death in 1872, he developed the lands with skill, adaptability, and resolution. At first he concentrated on the production of the spices for which the islands were renowned, on mace and nutmeg and vanilla. He introduced coffee and for years coffee export was the main source of profit. But in the end the soil wearied of coffee production and the ingenious Mr. Hofland then switched to sugar-cane and Peruvian bark, or quinine, and teak. On his death the property went to his sons who had not inherited their father's wisdom or energy. Under the names of Le Comte de Pamanoekan and Le Comte de Tjiasem, these two men dissipated their father's fortune amid the gambling resorts of Europe. Finally a Dutch company was formed to take over and administer the estates. The interests of this company were in 1910 acquired by an English consortium styling itself "The Anglo-Dutch Plantations of Java." During the boom years between 1920 and 1929 the company planted rubber groves and tea gardens. They prospered exceedingly. The profits for the year 1925, for instance, were as much as £700,000, and dividends were paid at the rate of 125 per cent. Yet the lands were not immune to setbacks and vicissitudes. Markets fluctuated; the Dutch authorities expropriated, with handsome compensation, large areas of the original territory; the trees and shrubs were constantly threatened with blight and sickness; and the 75,000 Indonesian labourers were often afflicted with epidemics, or bouts of mass indolence.

In March 1942 the Japanese landed in Java. During the three and a half years of Japanese occupation, when the European staff of the company were languishing in internment camps, the properties declined. The Japanese authorities uprooted many stretches of the tea gardens in order to plant coca. Their purpose was to manufacture immense quantities of cocaine wherewith to drug the population of China into apathy and subservience. In August 1945 the Japanese surrendered, but an unfortunate pause elapsed before any allied forces were available to take control. During this interlude, the Japanese, who had recovered their self-confidence, organised and armed an Indonesian nationalist resistance. When eventually the British, and subsequently the Dutch, forces appeared, they were met with armed rebellion by the Javanese and were unable for some time to establish their authority outside the main ports and towns. It was the Javanese who, during this interlude of chaos, themselves did great damage to the properties. Many square miles of tea gardens were uprooted, seventeen tea and rubber factories were destroyed, most of the office buildings and houses of the company were burnt to the ground, and the hydroelectric installations were shattered. When the company's representatives at last returned to their former headquarters at Subang they found the place in ruins and armed bandits prowling among the jungles and the weeds.

Most men of business would have been daunted by this catastrophe and by the prospect that, once Indonesia obtained her independence from the Netherlands and a nationalist administration was established, conditions might become even more difficult. But the company, having successfully endured so many storms, decided to plough onwards. They adopted the more modern name of "The Anglo-Indonesian Plantations Limited," rebuilt their factories, repaired the damaged plant and buildings, and started to rehabilitate the lands. By 1951 P. & T. Lands was once again one of the most flourishing plantations in the world. The profit for that year was most substantial, the only snag being that, under the currency conditions imposed by the Indonesian Government, the company are unable to transfer to Europe, and to their shareholders, the full amount of their gains.

When I look round me at the splendid lawns, the flourishing gardens, the neat bungalows, the trim offices, the throbbing factories and the many hydroelectric installations of the company, I can scarcely believe that these thriving properties can so recently have been subjected to devastation. The faith, the resolution, the science, and the vital energy displayed by the company and its employees have in truth been rewarded. I cannot understand the thoughts of those who would dismiss as "colonialism" an enterprise which brings prosperity to so wide an area and provides security and gainful employment for 34,000 Javanese, who might otherwise be scavenging among the garbage heaps of Tandjongpriok.

4

I had been told by Dermot MacDermot, himself an Irishman, that Steve Hodson had a fund of stories which he would relate with a remarkable rendering of the Tipperary brogue. I am glad to say he does not this morning indulge in these imitations. Irish stories now depress me miserably, since they remind me of my lost childhood, of a mood that has vanished, and of the years before the Irish had become humourless. He talks to us as he drives his green and white car up into the mountains about the charm of the Javanese, of their childish affections and gaiety, of how sad it is to reflect how many years must pass before they enjoy the true fruits of their independence. He criticises the Dutch for having failed to instruct the Indonesians in the art of self-government; in India we created a large army of trained and self-assured civil servants, who were able to take over the administration with competence and without either bitterness or self-pity. When the Dutch abandoned their rule, they left behind them few Indonesians sufficiently educated or reliant to be able to handle the machine. Much avoidable inefficiency has thus marred the early stages of their self-government. Steve Hodson loves the Javanese. He tells us that they possess no conception of the value of money and are almost incredibly improvident. His own workmen on the estate, although well and regularly paid, are always in debt to moneylenders. The latter are often Chinese or Indians, and the Javanese wonder innocently how it comes that their fellow Asians should be so prosperous, whereas, week by week, they themselves remain continually burdened with debt. The Chinese build handsome bungalows in the cool hills and spend much of the fortunes they acquire by their ingenuity and vigour in summoning doctors to attend to their imaginary illnesses. They will give European doctors large sums to inject them against every form of malady, and at the same time they pay retaining fees to Chinese doctors, who visit them daily to inspect their pulses and their tongues. I had not realised before that the Chinese had become so hypochondriac.

By then we are up in the mountains and are persuaded by Hodson to ascend a gazebo from where, he assures us, one has a marvellous view across the low country and beyond to the Java Sea. All we see is cloud swirling and the plains wrapped impenetrably in a Scottish mist. Around us stretch miles of tea plantations, sturdy-trunked little bushes like gardenias cut down to about three or four feet and planted in long rows. Only the top few fresh leaves of every bush are actually plucked and sent on to the factories. Between the bushes is planted a sort of woodruff, the seed of which Hodson brought out from Ceylon, and which makes an excellent covering plant and mulch. The workers who pluck the delicate leaves, which this morning are still soaking from the night's rain, put them in slung baskets and take them down to huge barns scattered about the plantations. Having dumped there the contents of their baskets, they discard their wet rags, wash themselves at the taps provided, and then stand up stark naked while they wind round their limbs their batik sarongs.

We are then taken to a tea factory. The first stage is that of drying. The fresh leaves are spread on wide slats bearing canvas trays like those used in the hop gardens at home; they are dried sufficiently to remove the surface moisture, but not so thoroughly as to prevent their fermenting during the watches of the night; they are then placed in a truly brutal machine which stamps and rocks and rolls and worries until all the moisture is squeezed and teased out of them; they are then carried into a vast clear barn where women of all ages sort the leaves into different heaps according to quality. In the end we reach a final stage where the heaps of dried leaves are carefully labelled "Pekoe," or other such John Lawrence names; and finally we end up in a little room where there is a table, two chairs, an electric kettle, a teapot, and three blue teacups in a row.

We get into the car again to visit the adjacent volcano of Cancuban Prahu, or such, without much confidence, I believe to be its name. We pass through jungle at first, with great clumps of splendid tree ferns and here and there a sudden cluster of scarlet or yellow flowers on a tree below us; the vegetation thins; a strong smell of sulphur assails us; the mist thickens and forms sliding puddles on the windscreen; and out we pass onto the summit of the mountain, where a flimsy bamboo railing preserves the visitors from tumbling, like Empedocles, into the fumes and fire of the crater. V. grasps me securely by the seat of my trousers. As we expected, the crater is hidden by white cloud, as neat and close as a cup of milk filled to the lip; there is nothing whatsoever to be seen inside.

We come down again, past the tree ferns and the daturas; we pass a neat young rubber plantation with little canisters like messtins hanging on to their trunks to catch the juice. As we reach the lower levels we pass a sacred banyan tree, hung with rags, which makes me suspect that the Indonesian Moslems have retained much of their primaeval animism. And then we get back to Subang.

In the evening we visit the "big house" now tenanted by Mr. Philip Fletcher, the managing director, or what they call "Representative No. 1." He is not in good health, but he rises from his chair and shows V. the hibiscus hybrids which he loves to cultivate. V. and he stroll together among the various bushes, contradicting each other, repeating Latin names to each other, and feeling comradely and horticultural. I sit in a long long chair and have a long long drink. The Jacksons come to dinner. They tell us stories about their imprisonment by the Japanese. It says much for their strength of character that such ordeals should have left them free of hatred or self-pity.

Thursday, February 14

St. Valentine's Day and also the day of the North Lewisham by-election. After breakfast we are taken by Mr. Clavninga, the Dutch director of rubber, to visit his factory. We first see the rubber milk, which we had watched dripping into mess-tins from the scarred trees, coagulating in large zinc vats. It is then, by a process which causes the operating machine to tremble with fury, reduced to long crepe strips; if one twitches off a piece and flings it on the floor it bounces beautifully. The stench is horrible. The crepe is then cut and rammed into squares, sewn up in canvas bales, and the date of gathering and quality of product is then stencilled on the outside.

We return to the Shaws' house, collect our luggage, and drive off to Bandung with Mrs. Shaw. We stop at a shop at No. 15 Tjimanuk Street where we find and buy the best batik material we have yet seen. We lunch at the magnificent Savoy Hotel in Bandung and thereafter start on our long drive back to Djakarta. The ambassador meets us on our arrival at the embassy and we have cool drinks. I eye with hatred the armchair in which I had sat stricken by despair on reading the news that the Bournemouth Association are to adopt another candidate in place of Nigel. We dine and go to bed. We sleep perfectly.

Friday, February 15

We have a delicious breakfast with iced papaya and honey. V. goes off to shop with Mrs. MacDermot and I sit on the terrace and read. The ambassador comes out and hands me a telegram saying that Niall MacDermot has won North Lewisham by a good majority. After luncheon we go to the old town where there is a native market and a decrepit Dutch fort. The encircling lagoon stinks horribly, and to me the market appears squalid and insanitary. V. of course is as happy as she can be, and she and young Conor MacDermot dart about from booth to booth. I have never seen such a collection of junk in my life—shells, coral, stuffed fish, snakes, lizards and alligators hanging from the beams. V. says it recalls for her the description in Garth's "The Dispensary" which is quoted in Aldous Huxley's *The Devils of Loudun*, which she has been reading on the boat:

> *Here mummies lay, most reverently stale,*
> *And there the tortoise hung her coat of mail;*
> *Not far from some large shark's devouring head*
> *The flying fish their filmy pinions spread.*
> *Aloft in rows large poppy heads were strung*
> *And, near, a scaly alligator hung;*
> *In this place, drugs in musty heaps decayed,*
> *In that, dried bladders and drawn teeth were laid.*

It is the last day of the Chinese New Year festival, the Tjap-Go-Me, and as we drive back to the embassy we are met by a procession headed by a long paper serpent or dragon with men's legs appearing underneath it. It wobbles along, turning its angry jaws to right and left and waddling horribly. We call in at the English club, which is an attractive building with a wide encircling verandah opening upon a beautiful playing field. At the time of our invasion of Egypt a Javanese mob broke into the premises and tore down and stamped upon the portrait of the Queen; they then moved on to the British Information Office, which they wrecked, and then to the embassy, where they pulled down the Union Jack and burnt it in the street. MacDermot, I am told, behaved on this occasion with the utmost composure and restraint. Realising that the Indonesian Government were not themselves responsible for the demonstration, which may have been organised and paid for by the Soviet and Chinese embassies, he merely lodged a formal protest and insisted upon payment being made for the damage done. He then drove to the club and replaced the shattered portrait of the Queen by another portrait taken from his own study. Being a loyal monarchist, I was irrationally enraged by this insult inflicted by the Djakarta mob on my beloved sovereign. Much as I deplore the Suez escapade, I fail to see how it can in any way have affected the interests or the emotions of the Indonesian proletariat.

We drink champagne at dinner in celebration of Niall Mac-Dermot's victory at Lewisham. After dinner a sparse young man in flannels appears and I discover that he is the newly appointed vicar of the English church at Djakarta. He says to me: "It is a pleasure to meet you. I have never forgotten as a boy hearing you conduct the massed choirs at the Crystal Palace." In that I am totally unable to distinguish between Puccini and Beethoven, this must have been a case of mistaken identity. He must have confused me with Dr. Nicholson the organist. V. is delighted by this episode.

Saturday, February 16

The ambassador's niece, Miss Christie-Miller, has recovered from her illness and she shows me a vocabulary of the official Indonesian language which is being taught as a *lingua franca* to supersede the many different dialects. This purified tongue is referred to as "the *Behasa*," meaning just "the language." Words signifying the more advanced products of civilisation are rendered by the transliteration and adaptation of Dutch terms. Thus police is *"polis,"* book is *"buku,"* and school is *"sekolah."* Objects moreover are described by their visual appearance rather than from any etymological derivation. Thus a drawing pin is called "an umbrella pin," since it resembles the shape of a Chinese umbrella. Many of the terms, as in basic English, are composed of composite expressions. Thus a bed is called "the container of a sleeping person," a teapot is "a tea container," and an express train a *"kretasombong"* or snob container. They have no word for pink, which they call "young red."

We have an expedition to the botanical gardens at Bogor, which the Dutch and the British used to call "Buitenzorg," on the analogy of Schifanoia or Sans Souci. There is a magnificent white government house, which the Dutch governor built in 1765 and where Raffles resided during his rule over the island. It is now tenanted by President Sukarno, whose yellow presidential flag flies from the summit and whose sentries pace up and down the terrace. The house is surrounded by a fine park and by the gardens, which are rightly regarded as rivalling those of Cape Town, Singapore, and Ceylon. We are met at the entrance by a young Englishman, called Leonard Forman, who works at Kew and has been out here for twelve months collecting specimens. He has taught himself the language, adores the Indonesians, and will be coming home with us on Monday in the *Willem Ruys*. He introduces us to the curator, Soebjana Kassa, who takes us to see his beastly orchids. We then go out into the larger garden, which has superb lawns, rare trees, and impressive clumps of bamboo, palm, and traveller's tree. Through the centre of these groves rushes a muddy torrent visited by exotic birds. The Java sparrow in so far as I can observe is scarcely distinguishable from the sparrows of Sloane Square. In one of the ponds is the great lily with the tea-tray leaves, which caused such a sensation in England when Paxton got it to flower at Chatsworth and named it the *Victoria Regia*. I thought it a boisterous and insensitive sort of plant.

We have a picnic lunch in the porch of the office buildings where Forman and other resident students have their quarters. On a high tree near it hang suspended the flying foxes, or giant bats of Java; they look like old umbrellas hung up to drip, but when they leave their perches they have wings as wide as those of an albatross, and through my binoculars I can see that the wings are ribbed and hooked like those of

Satan. But we have an excellent picnic brought by the Mac-Dermots from Djakarta.

After luncheon Forman takes us to what he calls "the haunted grove," a place which the Javanese shun. It is a damp circle enclosed by towering bamboos and constitutes the grave-yard of former Dutch officials. *"Rust plaats,"* I read on a moss-grown tombstone, *"van D. T. de Eerens, Gouverneur Generaal van Nederlandschindie."* There are also the graves of young English officials and near it a cenotaph, in the form of a pretty little temple, erected by Raffles in the memory of his first wife, Olivia, who died at Buitenzorg. On it Raffles had in-scribed the verses which Olivia had some years before ad-dressed to their mutual friend John Leyden, the scholar and poet.

They are not good verses:

> *Oh thou who ne'er my constant heart*
> *One moment have forgot*
> *Tho' fate severe has bid us part*
> *Yet still forget me not.*

We leave these gloomy precincts for the gaiety of the native market in Bogor. There is a small Chinese temple at the en-trance to what I should have called the bazaars where wor-shippers burn joss sticks and little rolls of paper, like cracker mottoes, in honour of some unknown god. A filthy old man comes up to V. and offers her some strawberries in a basket; they look fresh and very shiny and I suspect him of having spat on them round the corner in order to give them that glistening appearance. I entreat her not to buy them. She re-proves me for lack of "enterprise" and for never having been able to master my civil servant inhibitions. We then drive back to Djakarta and pick up our luggage. The ambassador, with his accustomed courtesy, motors down with us to Tandjong-priok to see us on board. He brings the elf Conor with him. The ship seems empty since most of the other round-trip passengers, including the Neumayers and Sidney Culpeper, have flown for these few nights to Bali. We sit on deck for a bit talking to the Gibsons, who have been staying at the hill station at Putchak. We then retire to our nice soft bunks.

VIII. TURN ROUND

1

Sunday, February 17

The MacDermots had pressed us to stay another night at the embassy, since the boat does not actually sail until tomorrow morning. But we expected to find further letters on board and we wanted a clear day to read, answer, and post them before leaving land. As a matter of fact only three more letters dribble through the congested apparatus of the Indonesian post office and we shall in any case wait till we return to Singapore before we post anything. We have in some strange way lost confidence in Javanese mails.

It is fortunate that we embarked last night, since after breakfast this morning there is a gentle tap on the door of V.'s cabin and the steward enquires when it will be convenient for her to have her things moved. "Moved?" she answers in justifiable bewilderment. "But moved where?" "I am sorry, madam," replies the wretched Van Ruy apologetically, "I thought the purser would have warned you. This cabin has for months been booked for the return journey by a gentleman who comes on board this afternoon. You are to be moved to cabin No. 50 on the deck above."

V., who had last night unpacked and hung all the things she had taken or bought on shore, who has already spread out on her bunk her books and papers preparatory to a long quiet morning with *La Grande Mademoiselle,* is infuriated by this announcement. All the blood of her Andalusian ancestors, of the Dukes of Ossana and the several branches of the Borgia family, seethes within her. In vain does the calm white stewardess appear to assist the terrified Van Ruy and to assure her that it will not take more than fifteen minutes to move her things into the new cabin. V. cannot bear in any case to have her clothes touched by other people and the storm gathers dark, rapid, and menacing, like that which struck the ship after passing Diego Garcia. I hurry off to the purser's office in the hope of diverting or at least modifying this typhoon. The purser explains that the gentleman who has engaged V.'s cabin did so many months ahead; that it is the cabin in which he had travelled out to Java four years before; that he has a personal affection for it; and that we had been warned before we left London that for the return journey one of our two cabins would in any case have to be changed. I am discussing the affair quite blandly with the purser when V. arrives in a "give *me* the dagger" mood. The purser turns pale and his hands shake. He asks us to go back to our cabins for the moment and he will see what can be done. Macbeth has never been among my favourite Shakespearean characters, but I now begin to see his point of view.

We return to our cabins and V., foreseeing that the battle

would be lost, begins in fury to cast the manuscript pages of *La Grande Mademoiselle* and her attendant reference books into a suitcase. When the mild stewardess offers to take her dresses off the hangers and to pack them she tells her, with true Borgia ferocity, to desist. The purser then comes along and with trembling courtesy proposes a compromise. He offers us adjoining cabins on the upper deck, communicating with each other through a private bathroom. I think this an excellent sop: V. refuses to regard it as a sop at all. Van Ruy and his colleague Cavallé from the deck above then pull out the drawers of my dressing table and gather together the suits hanging in my cupboard, and in five minutes there they are hanging quietly in the cupboard, or dispersed peacefully in the identical drawers, of cabin No. 52. The whole operation does not take long to complete and within twenty minutes there I am again seated at my new desk in my new cabin typing away peacefully. With V. however the process is prolonged, since she will not allow anyone to touch her belongings but insists on repacking them herself in her suitcase. When at last she is settled in her new cabin, which is in fact identical with the one from which she was expelled, I point out to her how nice it is to be on the upper deck, only one landing below the main saloon, and how convenient to have a bathroom adjoining through which we can communicate with ease. She casts upon me a glance of contempt and my sympathy for Macbeth is much increased. "I shall *never* forgive them," she says, "never!" I return to my gentle little typewriter and during the rest of the morning I can hear the click of the hangers as she replaces them indignantly upon the rail in her new cupboard. The storm with which she has been shaken subsides in the course of the afternoon; but the thunder continues to rumble in the distant mountains.

In the evening the captain gives a party to those of the passengers who have made the journey out to Java and are now about to make the journey back to Southampton. He tells us that the Indonesians have become most trade-union conscious and that there are two separate unions among his own Indonesian crew which compete against each other. They are sympathetic to the Javanese dock unions and the union of lighter-men, and their sympathy for each other is always liable to delay proceedings and to complicate the times of departure. He hopes, however, to cast off early tomorrow morning. He also tells us that on the journey out, when we were abreast of Mauritius, he had warning of an approaching cyclone and diverted his course. I am angry about this, since I should have liked to experience a cyclone from the safety of this strong and stable ship. Yet, for today at least, I have had enough cyclonic disturbance.

Monday, February 18

When we lived on the deck below, in cabins Nos. 122 and 123, we regarded the *Willem Ruys* as a silent ship. It is true that when we woke in the morning we had noticed how varied, vivacious, and matutinal are the noises that a liner can make. There were the cries of children who had been turned out into the passage while their parents dressed and who, when bored or lonely, would shout "Mama!" or "Mummie!" through the cabin doors. Then at 7.15 came the sound of our fellow passengers summoning food or drink. There are, I am glad to say, no electric bells in the ship, and when one presses the bunk-side push a hooter hoots gently, like distant freight barges on the Hudson River, and a little light goes on in the passage outside. Then comes the quick patter of Indonesian feet, followed by restrained jabbering, the opening and shutting of cabin doors, and I am glad to feel that Mrs. Hyams has received her early-morning orange juice.

But in our new cabins, Nos. 50 and 52, while we were still tied to the dock at Tandjongpriok, we were kept awake last night by the sound of merchandise being placed on board. I quite see that, in that our new cabins are close to the hold, we must expect, the night before sailing, to be kept awake by the whine of cranes and the clatter of bales of rubber, cases of tea, and sacks of tapioca being lowered and securely packed into the bowels of the ship. I agree also that once the loading has been completed it is necessary to render the hold water-tight and shipshape by lowering the several sections of the lid upon it and by attaching these sections to the rim of the hold and to each other by bolts and wedges which have to be driven home by muscular blows. What puzzles me more are the other sounds, the purport of which I am not able to identify. There is the sound of pianos being dragged across my ceiling; the sound of whippet tanks falling down escalators; the sound of enormous hollow boilers being repeatedly scraped and struck by sickles and hammers. Even more perplexing are the smaller sounds. There is a sound of fidgeting and nestling, like that of blackbirds in April under the eaves at home. There is the sound of shoe trees being taken out and dropped one by one upon the deck above my head. And there is the sound of Dutch quartermasters giving orders in undertones. I am a good sleeper and after an hour or so these noises of the night cease to disturb me. But V. is a bad sleeper and I fear that she rested ill last night. "It all comes," she said this morning at breakfast, "from their having turned us out of our nice cabins and put us in the stern." "Prow," I corrected. "Well anyhow next to the hold." And I admit that our present position is more exposed than were our previous quarters amidships to the noise of nautical manoeuvres.

Those of our fellow passengers who are making the round trip and have spent their six days in Java in various ways returned late last night on board. Several of them, including the Neumayers, the Carters, and Sidney Culpeper, had flown to Bali. The Neumayers had enjoyed their visit immensely; they had stayed with a sultan or rajah in his house and had witnessed native dancers circling by the light of torches, a performance which they had admired as both beautiful and authentic. They had brought back with them and showed me with pride some of the neat little objects which the Balinese carve out of native wood. I find Culpeper leaning over the side and gazing at the morning activity of Tandjongpriok. "I hope," I say to him, "that you enjoyed your visit to Bali." "It was," he answers, "one of the nastiest experiences that I have ever endured. The aeroplane in which we were sent was utterly unfit for service; it poured with rain the whole time and the filthy pathways of the villages were glutinous with mud. I was made to sleep at night in the hut of the headman of a village who, the tourist agency assured me, was a sultan who would be only too glad to offer me hospitality. I was made to share a bedroom with a complete stranger; my bed was little more than a mat; I was kept awake by the sound of rats scuttling all around me; and the food was utterly nauseating." "But at least," I say, "you saw the natives dance?" His lips assume the line of discontent. "I always knew," he says, "that I should loathe that tourist posturing. And then the village headman, or sultan, charged me much for his hospitality and tried to sell me some of those horrible little wood carvings which are turned out on lathes at Djakarta and are disposed of to tourists as native work. I have seldom enjoyed myself less." "Do you never enjoy yourself?" I ask him. "Woo-hoo!" he answers. I move away, reflective.

2

We cast off from the dock side at Tandjongpriok at 11.00 A.M. precisely. Friends and relations of the departing passengers are packed along the quay and people throw paper streamers at each other which tauten and then snap as the gap between us widens. Mrs. Gibson, who is leaving no friend behind her at Tandjongpriok, or in fact any where in the East Indies, but who has a gift for sport, buys many rolls of streamers and hurls them violently at the people on shore. As we start moving, the crowd on the quay cheers and waves and the wireless on board plays a sturdy record of the *Chant du Départ*. The tall steel cranes on the dock side become draped with fluttering ticker tape and so do the lifeboats in the ship. As we slide out beyond the breakwater the tugs hoot and shrill farewell, to which the *Willem Ruys* replies with a deep dignified bellow. As we gather speed and face the ocean, the wind jerks and tugs at the remains of the strips of paper hanging on the lifeboats; they twist and turn for a bit and then snap and sail away into the Java Sea. The low land of the lagoon fades behind us into a grey mist. The sun comes out again and the waves turn blue.

We go down to luncheon and scan with interest the faces of the new passengers who have embarked at Tandjongpriok for the journey home. They consist almost entirely of Dutch civil servants and businessmen accompanied by their wives and families. We look out for Leonard Forman, the young botanist from Kew whom we met at Bogor, but we cannot find him; we discover afterwards that, as his ticket is being paid for by the Indonesian authorities and not by Kew, he is travelling second class. We are sorry about this as V. had looked forward to discussing with him his plant-hunting expeditions in Borneo and the habits of anonaceous trees.

By the afternoon, life on board resumes its normal rhythm. Tea and biscuits are handed round the decks; passengers affix labels on the chairs that they have hired for the journey; Mrs. Hyams is seated at her bridge table, and the orchestra plays "Lili Marlene." I had hoped that we should pass close, and in daylight, to the Sunda Strait, which separates Java from Sumatra and which was in 1883 the site of a volcanic explosion more terrible even than that of Mont Pelée in Martinique in 1902. In the spring of that year it was observed that an unusual amount of smoke, steam, and mud was issuing from the crater of Krakatoa. Nobody took much notice until on August 27 the mountain exploded. When three days later the smoke and ash had cleared it was found that the island, which had before risen some fourteen hundred feet above the sea, had entirely disappeared and that a gulf had been opened on the floor of the ocean a thousand feet below sea level. This eruption created a tidal wave which caused the death of many thousand islanders, which spread round the Cape, round the Horn, and was even observed swaying along the English Channel. The roar of the explosion was, we are credibly informed, heard three thousand miles away in Australia and Madagascar, and the volcanic dust hung in the stratosphere for the next twelve months producing the most magnificent sunsets. In 1922 a new but smaller volcano arose in place of Krakatoa and was named by the Indonesians "Anak Krakatoa," or "Krakatoa's Baby." I was sorry not to be able to see this baby, but it is either too dark or we are too far out in the strait. All we see is the lighthouse on the tip of Java blinking farewell.

The captain, with whom I discuss topography and ocean travel, is, I believe and hope, pleased by my interest in my surroundings. He tells me that passengers are often irritatingly ignorant of, and indifferent to, the wonders of the deep. He told me that once on a glorious spring evening the vessel was passing close to Crete, when the snow mountains were flushing scarlet in the sunset. An American woman on board was furious with her fellow players because they insisted in breaking off their game of bridge to dash on deck and catch a hurried glimpse of the astonishing spectacle. He also told me that, crossing the Pacific a few years ago, he stopped to speak to a passenger who was reading Miss Rachel Carson's admirable work on *The Sea Around Us*. "Captain," this moron complained, tapping the book upon his knee, "this book tells me that the Pacific is one of the largest sheets of water on the earth's surface, but to me it seems just the same size as the other seas." He says that a lifetime spent on the ocean wave has taught him that ordinary landsmen have no sense whatsoever of proportion or distance. "How far, for instance," he asks me, "do you think we now are from Tandjongpriok?" "About two hundred and fifty miles," I answer. He looks at me with a kind expression in his nice blue eyes. "Two hundred and ten," he says. I did not feel that my sense of distance was so much at fault. I asked him of what the cargo consisted which had so lustily been placed on board during the watches of the night. He said there had been much rubber, many cases of tea, a little teak, and a large quantity of tapioca. I was surprised about the tapioca, since my experience at my club has taught me that the taste for milk puddings has declined. I have never cared very much for that glutinous root, and when I was offered it as a child I was apt to whimper and protest. I can remember even that my uncle Dufferin, who shared my aversion, was sympathetic to me on the subject. "When," he said, "you have been viceroy of India you can refuse to be given tapioca ever again." He was always a comforting man. But when I remarked to the captain that it seemed strange that there should be any profit to be made by growing and exporting a substance needed for the manufacture of unwanted milk pudding for English children, he told me that tapioca was used for all manner of other things. It was tapioca for instance that provided the gum, starch, or oil which imparts so bright an aspect to glossy magazines. I had never known this fact before and, as always, I welcomed the information that he gave me with gratitude.

I have hitherto supposed and proclaimed that I enjoy great

heat. It is true that in Persia, when others complained, I rejoiced in the dry oven air. But here in the tropics I find the sticky heat oppressive and am glad to get down to my cabin where the air is conditioned to a very tolerable temperature. I found at Djakarta and Subang that when writing in shirt sleeves the blotting paper was liable to adhere to my flesh and that when I raised my hand to lift the cigarette from my lips the blotting paper accompanied the gesture. Moreover I have a suspicion that in the tropics my deafness becomes more stultifying. V. continues to insist that I am not deaf in the very least and that my frequent inability to interpret the words spoken to me by others is due solely to the fact that I do not "know what to listen for." Is it that with strangers I have by now mastered so completely the technique of pretending to follow what they say that they are unaware of my deafness and do not for that reason trouble to raise their voices? Or is it that they do in fact raise their voices but that I have become too deaf to notice this added volume? I can hear well enough when talking to an ordinary individual, but my hearing becomes blurred when there are other noises, such as general conversation or an echo in the room. I am beginning also to become aware that the pleasure that I take in the company of my friends is sometimes conditioned by whether they speak high or low. I can always hear what V. says, or what Hugh Dalton says, or what Colonel Buxton says, or what Colin Fenton says: but I cannot hear what Violet Trefusis says, and this is a sadness to me. But I console myself with the reflection that I am not dependent for my happiness on sound; only on sight.

3

Tuesday, February 19

I have a bathe in the morning; the pool is empty and calm. Our morning is interrupted by boat drill which is conducted for the benefit of those passengers who have recently come on board. Now that we have adjoining cabins, V. and I share the same lifeboat; thus if Krakatoa again explodes we shall breast the tidal wave together. We steam all morning along the distant coast of Sumatra, which shows a line of blue hills backed by splendid volcanoes. V., who has developed an unexpected liking for volcanoes, in that she assumes that they are uninhabited, feels that we have not visited a sufficient number of them on this Indonesian journey. I assure her that volcanoes are invariably thickly populated because of the fertility of volcanic soil.

After luncheon we slide once again into the green harbour of Singapore. The mail is delivered and distributed. There is a long letter from Ben saying that Luisa is off to Florence for a few days in order to submit to Berenson the layout of the twelve hundred plates of his catalogue on which she has been working for months so hard. He also tells us that Philip Toynbee is organising a pilgrimage across Europe to express the sympathy of young England for the plight of the Hungarian liberals and the proletariat of Port Said. I shall send him a scallop shell if I can find one in Singapore: and also a small hard pea. There is also a letter from Nigel who had been much impressed by a speech delivered to the Party by Harold Macmillan, in which he had drawn a distinction between pride and vanity and their several associations and permutations. Nigel is not optimistic about his future relations with his local committee who, feeling doubtless that they have behaved inequitably, have stifled such pangs of conscience as they may experience by smothering them under the fixed idea that he has been unpatriotic in criticising the Suez fiasco. But he is heartened by the sympathy and encouragement of his fellow Members of both parties who urge him not to capitulate. The Members of the House of Commons are always lavish in their sympathy for stricken deer, but rare indeed are those among them who will translate that sympathy into either action or overt words. They remain aloof while the deer is being mauled and battered by the herd, congratulating themselves inwardly that their own local committees are less ignorant and malicious. In a few months they will have forgotten the circumstances of the case and will remember only that a politician, on those occasions when his thought and knowledge are at variance with the emotions of his constituents, must be very careful not to be idealistic. V. just snorts contemptuously when I make these realistic comments, remarking that she has always hated politics in any case. But whereas the Conservative Association of Bournemouth East regard Nigel as a traitor and a renegade, the House of Commons admires his integrity and courage. *Intabescantque relicta*.

We are engaged in this discussion when V.'s Chinese friend, Su-Hua, is observed climbing diffidently up the gangway. V. greets her with affection. Su-Hua is an artist and a writer; her book which was published in England under the title *Ancient Melodies* possessed much charm; she was at one time teacher of calligraphy in Peking University, is intensely patriotic, and regards the passing of the old order with a rather impressive mixture of regret and pride. We give her tea on board and thereafter we go with her into the town in search of books. I want to buy Wurtzburg's life of Raffles, and V. wants to buy a book on Malayan flora and fauna. Su-Hua, being a poet and an artist, and residing in a college some miles from Singapore itself, does not with any confidence know her way about the town, but recalls vaguely that the best bookshop is somewhere in the vicinity of Raffles Place. So round and round we walk as dusk descends, and in the end we find a shop where they produce a very elementary book on Malayan flowers and where I obtain a battered copy of Wurtzburg's biography with a large inkstain upon the dustcover.

Su-Hua then suggests that she should take us to a Chinese restaurant. V. is entranced by this proposal, expecting that we shall be conducted down some alley in the Chinese quarter, that we shall step into some dark kitchen-cellar where no white foot has ever stepped before, and that we shall be met by the smell of opium and the sight of Chinese stripped to the waist stirring a cauldron in which simmer birds'-nests, shark fins, and hedgehogs. I venture to suggest that we have had our luncheon, that we have just had some tea, and that we must be back on board for dinner. I should have learnt by now that it is a mistake, when the river of romance is in spate, to intrude into it with my galoshes, my timetables, and my predilection for regular meals. So off we go to the Chinese restaurant. Su-Hua is not quite sure where the restaurant is but she explains the idea to the driver who astutely grasps her intention. We drive off into the residential part of the town, past lawns and villas, and (since the street lamps have just been lighted) I note how exotic are the shadows cast upon the pavement by banana leaves. We draw up at a large, recently constructed apartment building, on the top floor of which I see a neon sign proclaiming the words, "Peking Restaurant," to the harbour and the outer sea. We enter a chromium lift and hum upwards. There is a long large dining hall set with numerous neat tables, each one arrayed with plates, glasses, and napkins as neatly folded as are those of the more fashionable hotels at Ilfracombe. Beside each place, in addition to the expected cutlery, is a sheaf of tissue paper containing two chopsticks of bone. V., who I fear is manifesting slight depression, cheers up at the sight of these chopsticks. We order soup and bamboo shoots, which I eat sadly with a spoon; Su-Hua to our delight uses the chopsticks with that dexterity which can be acquired only after forty years' unbroken residence in China. There are a few solids floating in the soup, resembling worm casts in shape and having the consistency of chewing gum. I refrain from considering whether they came from newly born puppies, or cuttlefish, or cormorants.

Wishing as always to extend the frontiers of my knowledge, I tell Su-Hua how at Bogor we had visited a small Chinese temple and had observed the devout buying little spills of paper with inscriptions on them and burning these spills in the incinerator in the courtyard. I ask her in whose honour and for what form of supplication these spills were being burnt. "In temper?" she asks me. I reply that, in so far as I could see, the charms were chosen and then incinerated with the utmost equanimity and with due reverence. "I think," V. murmurs to me, "that when she said 'temper' she meant 'temple.'"

"Yes," I persist brightly, "it was in the temple. Can you tell me to whom these offerings were made?" "To God," she says. "But what God?" I ask. "To Buddha," she replies. "But it was not a Buddhist temple," I persist, "and in any case Buddha wasn't a god." "Chinese people think so," she replies quite sharply. "That is for what the tempers are." So I give it up and munch my bamboo shoots in silent nausea.

Su-Hua has been given for her soup course a little china scoop or ladle which V. feels would make admirable Christmas presents for those of her friends who use bath salts at home. She asks Su-Hua if, after our meal, the shops in the Chinese quarter will still be open and if she can buy some of these ladles before returning to the boat. So we pay our bill, descend in the chromium lift, enter the car, and drive round and round the Chinese streets seeking some booth where one can buy little porcelain spoons suitable for scooping up bath salts. I enjoy that part of the expedition. The shops and booths are gay with lights, the jostling crowds on the pavement are extremely Chinese, and the hawkers upon the pavements utter Asian cries. I ask Su-Hua what they were calling. "They speak the Fukien language," she answers, so once again my thirst for information goes unassuaged. But from a vendor I buy a serpent with a rat in its mouth which, when wound up with a key, writhes upon the floor and beats its victim upon the stones. There are no ladles to be found. We drive back to the ship and V. casts her arms around dear little Su-Hua and bids her a loving farewell.

We are glad to meet our friend Boumphrey in the saloon. He has come on board to revisit the *Willem Ruys* and to greet his former fellow passengers before they turn home. He has brought with him a little Chinese blue and white bowl which he presents to V. He tells us that his wife's ankle has not mended itself and that she is now in hospital and may have to have an operation. We are sorry about this. A messenger arrives bearing an enormous bunch of orchids for V., which have been picked for her by Lady Scott, the wife of the commissioner-general. We are touched by this act of courtesy. The Stedalls have rejoined the boat, having spent a week at Kuala Lumpur. Their daughter and son-in-law have come down to see them off, and I regret that two such attractive people should not be coming back with us to Southampton. Mrs. Stedall tells me that her daughter, in expectation of their visit, had planted a moon flower in her garden and that, during the full moon of last week, it had blossomed outrageously arousing curiosity and pleasure. Then we go down to our cabins, and V. arranges Lady Scott's orchids in the pots she bought at Bandung. I do not eat much dinner, since the soup at the Peking Restaurant has made me feel sick inside. I, who used to be able to eat anything without the slightest reaction! Such are the penalties of old age.

4

Wednesday, February 20

A lovely hot morning. We stop at Belawan Roads again and a tug comes out with passengers leaving Sumatra for Europe. The cinnamon-coloured hawks again circle around the boat but the heat haze has obscured the distant mountains. V. and I do not really appreciate the occasions when the *Willem Ruys* insists on stopping at harbours or roadsteads. What we love are the long empty days at sea, when we can go down to our cabins and read and read and work all morning and all afternoon. Those are indeed periods of blessed void repose, when the sun blazes down upon us and the sea is so calm that the porpoises make wide circles as they plunge and the halcyons lay their eggs upon the waves.

I shall cease for the moment reading about my malcontents, since in the aggregate I find them irritating. I shall read about those who, in that they regarded the aim of life to be the pursuit of pleasure and the avoidance of pain, sought to escape from the ambitions and disillusions of the material world. I shall begin with Epicurus. It is not that I admire that philosopher, but that I do admire Lucretius profoundly. If that great poet derived from the doctrines of Epicurus such authentic intellectual and spiritual solace one is obliged, when considering escapes from melancholy, to approach his theories with attention and respect. Yet I remain perplexed, and in a sense disquieted, when I find a man of Lucretius' muscular intelligence eulogising Epicurus as the mighty liberator, as the almost divine revealer of truth.

Even in the account given by Diogenes Laërtius, who strikes me as a perfectly objective biographer, Epicurus appears as a sort of Dr. Buchman, or popular revivalist. His father owned a small private school at Samos and the Athenian intellectuals —to whom for some extraordinary reason the profession of schoolmaster appeared degrading—would often reproach him for having himself taught little boys to read and write. His mother, Chairestate, was a local sorceress who would stump round the villages of Samos, selling philtres and charms. He was the pert type of schoolboy who would show off to the class by asking his teachers bright, embarrassing questions. He moved to the island of Teos, where he studied under Nausiphanes, a follower of Democritus and Pyrrho. Having acquired from him the outlines of the atomic theory and the doctrine that pleasure, which was the aim of life, could only be achieved by the avoidance of disturbing desires, he turned against his master and in fact assailed him with virulent abuse. He accused him of debauching his pupils and called him an "impostor," a "prostitute," and even a *pleumon,* or lungfish. He then retired to Mitylene, where he frequented the gymnasium and earned notoriety by attacking all existing philosophic theories and educational systems. He derided the followers of Plato for their "fancy notions," for their belief that knowledge was the road to virtue, for their assertion that such a thing as absolute justice did in fact exist, and for their faith in immanent ideas. He was equally contemptuous of the physicists for their doctrine of Necessity and the Theophrasteans for their belief in Fortune. He quoted Homer to prove that pleasure was the only aim in life and that the gods were utterly indifferent to the sufferings of mankind. He also derided rhetoric, dialectic, mathematics and astronomy. He argued that the sun was no larger than it appeared to the human eye and was in fact the size of a large orange. His criticisms and his conceit enraged the Mitylenians, who rose in their fury and battered on his door. He was obliged to escape by night from the menace of the mob and sailed for Lampsacus in the Sea of Marmora, where he established himself by toadying Mithres, the Syrian steward of Lysimachus, thereby earning the reproach of "flattering a barbarian."

In 306 B.C. he moved to Athens where he remained until his death some thirty-five years later. After his experience in Mitylene, he felt it would be wiser not to give public lectures, and he therefore gathered his disciples together in a garden outside the Diploon gate. This garden was still in existence when Cicero and Atticus were undergraduates at Athens in 78 B.C. The community which Epicurus there gathered around him was based on the principle of mutual admiration. He himself was venerated as "the leader," or "the father," his birthday was celebrated as a religious festival, and his pupils were encouraged to carry with them little clay images of the master concealed in their vests. His assistants were called "the guides"; he established something in the nature of a publishing business, employing several slaves as copyists; and he admitted women to his courses, among them the courtesan Leontion, who was the Aspasia of her age. Although he preached austerity, and although the general standard of living in his garden-suburb was sparse and low, there would, on the twentieth of each month, be held a communal feast, which created much scandal and which gave to the early Epicureans the abusive nickname of "the twentiers."

It is difficult to resist the impression that Epicurus—although, without the slightest acknowledgement, he had cribbed most of his ideas from previous philosophers—possessed an outstanding gift for publicity, organisation, discipline, and the presentation of doctrine in popular form. To the Athenians of the third century the idealism of the divine Plato may have seemed esoteric and abstruse, whereas the mumbo jumbo preached by Epicurus was easy to understand and perfectly delightful to practise. Yet I repeat, it remains a mystery to me how so virile a person as Lucretius can have discovered in the escapism of Epicurus an element of *vivida vis* or *élan vital*.

I admit of course that Epicurus has been unfairly traduced by his opponents. The Stoics, the early fathers, and the puritans denounced him as the prophet of profligacy, as "the father of lusts." Origen was horrified by the worship accorded to his images, and Macaulay in our own age condemned Epicureanism as "the silliest and meanest of all systems of natural philosophy." The denial of life, the retreat from temptation, can create the very highest spiritual values, but it can also lead to subhuman behaviour, such as that of the cynic Diogenes, who began as a *faux monnayeur* and ended by living in a barrel and defecating publicly in the painted Stoa, the National Gallery of Athens.

Yet it would be an error to suppose that Epicurus preached hedonism; he realised that pleasure was but a rare occurrence and that suffering could be "permanent, obscure, and dark." The aim of man, he contended, during his brief passage from birth to extinction, was the avoidance of pain and therefore the elimination of all unnecessary desires:

Happiness [he wrote] has nothing to do with wealth, or power, or public office, but with painlessness. Let us therefore rid ourselves of all false cravings, of the appetite for transitory enjoyments and render ourselves supreme masters of our nature.

He thus argued that the superior man could be happy, even when undergoing torture on the rack, and could remain consistently himself "even when asleep." Such a man would avoid marriage or falling in love, would not indulge in politics, would cultivate his friends, manage his property reasonably, be kind to his servants, secure the protection of the powerful, and "take more delight than other people in State festivals."

Much as I myself fear pain and dislike mental distress, I refuse to believe that the good life can be founded upon any escapist philosophy. I believe with Aristotle that "happiness is action," or, in other words, self-fulfilment. Only extremely religious people can achieve happiness by running away. Nor do I believe in the hedonistic paradox. The wise man avoids those pleasures which may end in pain and chooses the pains from which pleasure may result. For if, as dear Socrates remarked, "if the good and the pleasant be identical then why are some pleasures felt instinctively to be evil?" The hedonist can find no answer to this pertinent question.

I am seated on deck, reading my Loeb edition of Diogenes Laërtius and marking those passages that I regard as relevant, when Sidney Culpeper relapses with a sigh into the chair beside me. "Oh, it's Greek this time!" he remarks, taking my book from me. "You do show off, don't you—hee, hee!" "But it's a crib that I am reading," I answer defensively. "I am reading about Epicurus. I suppose that, as a Catholic, you despise Epicurus." "But I'm not a Catholic," he answers. "I saw you the other morning attending Mass." "Oh yes! You see, I love worship, and I indulge in it whenever opportunity occurs." "Would you pray," I ask, "to a tree in a temple compound?" "Of course I should," he answers, "I believe in everything, even in animism. You see, I happen to be a very sincere person. Hee-hee!" I turn upon him a gaze of scrutiny.

"But what do you do in life?" I ask him. "I collect jade," he answers. "You must be very rich?" "I *am* very rich," and in saying this he sighs as deeply as Nicodemus.

"I do not believe," I begin, "in these escapist philosophies. I agree that the aim of life should be the pursuit of happiness, but I do not believe that this entails the escape from pain. 'Happiness' admittedly is a meaningless word, since if it exists at all it exists only in sudden moments of transitory elation and can never be defined as a condition. But satisfaction, or contentment, can be regarded as a condition or a state of mind. Of course I agree that content or discontent are largely dependent on external conditions, such as health, environment, love, friendships, and a favourable economic and social background. But they also depend on opportunities for self-fulfilment, self-expression, and self-integration. One should notice, for instance, how small are the occasions for satisfaction or dissatisfaction. Thus if, on rising from my writing table, I upset my typewriting paper upon the floor and fail from indolence or hurry to pick it up and stack it tidily again beside my typewriter, I experience a definite sense of failure, of inadequacy, or even perhaps the pang of self-reproach. This causes me sadness and apprehension, as when one sucks in a breath of cold air and there follows a small stab in a tooth. The avoidance or postponement of effort, however small, invariably leaves behind it this tiny despair, this minute sense of incompleteness. I am beginning to feel that the essential occasion of causeless melancholy is the recurrence of unfulfilment, of uncompleted action, however trivial such action may be. I am referring to minor acts of volition. Let me take another example. You have some task to perform which, although unimportant, may be momentarily displeasing, such as answering a disagreeable letter, or reading an article which has been sent to you and which it rather bores you to read. If you grasp such nettles immediately, before passing on to the more agreeable tasks of life, you experience a feeling of satisfaction, even of triumph. But if you postpone accomplishing this disagreeable necessity, you are afflicted thereafter with a sense of guilt, the unpleasantness of the required action being prolonged and therefore intensified by the fact that it is unfulfilled. Thus I regard sloth as the major cause of melancholy, in that it provokes a sense of inadequacy, and therefore of self-reproach, and therefore of guilt, and finally of fear. I have an idea that melancholy is caused less by the failure to achieve great ambitions or desires than by the diurnal inability to perform small necessary acts. Thus, to take a further minor instance, punctuality when successfully observed creates satisfaction; unpunctuality, even among extremely lax and selfish people, creates discontent, since it implies a lack of decision and an inability to consider the convenience of others. Do you think I am wrong in all this?"

Culpeper hands back to me my copy of Diogenes Laërtius. "You do," he exclaims, "enjoy hearing yourself talk, don't you? Hee-hee!" "Well, as a matter of fact," I answer, feeling inquisitive rather than wounded, "I don't think I do." He rises and leaves me, since it is time for his tea.

IX. TEMPLA SERENA

1

Thursday, February 21

V. went on deck early today to see the sunrise. To the right, below our horizon, lay Penang, the Singapore of the eighteenth century, the base from which so much power spread. On the portside, quite close to us for once, the volcanoes of Sumatra stood up above Medan. There, hiding itself behind the precipices of Tapanuli, slumbers the great lake of Toba, which to V. suggests all manner of inaccessible things, such as the purple euphorbia, the giant dipterocarp, isolation, and the lily of Malud.

A young airman, who had also come on deck in his dressing gown, pointed out to her the island of Sabang at the northwest tip of Sumatra which, with its sister islands of Breuëh and Punasu, forms the roadstead known as the Bengalen Passage. "It was there," he said to her, "in that little haven, that the *Prince of Wales* and the *Repulse* were sunk by Japanese bombs." Remembering my interest in the beauties of nature and in historical sites, V. decided that the moment had come to rouse me from my bunk. I accompanied her sleepily to the deck. It was indeed a superb spectacle, and as I looked through my binoculars at the Bengalen Passage I recalled the shattered horror with which I had read the telegram announcing the loss of these mighty ships, a disaster which, as we all knew, presaged the fall of Singapore. I lowered my glasses and remarked that it had not been there that the ships had been bombed, but in the Gulf of Siam, the other side of the peninsula and some five hundred miles and more to the east. I have noticed that V. is inclined to attach greater credence to the information supplied by casual acquaintances than she is to the solid and indisputable facts furnished to her by her immediate family. "But," she protested, "this officer knows the area intimately. He tells me that, when based on Singapore, his squadron used frequently to fly over the strait and that they would always pick up that little island in order then to swerve to the east and to avoid the volcanoes." I glanced at the young airman and saw that, since my arrival, he had become slipfaced. Why on earth, I reflected, in an Indonesian sunrise, should he enjoy making false statements? Was it to increase his self-importance or merely to provide interest? I am puzzled always by the devices of the mythomaniac.

After breakfast I return to my cabin and spend a happy morning reading Lucretius and losing myself in the *templa serena* of his transcendent style. As usual, at 12.45 we come upstairs again, look at the log, and have a drink in the smoking room with Mr. and Mrs. Gibson. This has now become a regular ritual. V. always orders a "gimlet" and has acquired the embarrassing habit of scooping out the ice shavings from her glass, using, not a spoon as would be delicate, but her own fingers. The table manners of Edwardian debutantes have always made me blush. Mrs. Gibson has a tomato juice and Mr. Gibson and I have a "not-yet" each, one of the most recurrent and stimulating cocktails that I have yet encountered. I take the opportunity to ask Mrs. Gibson, who is humorous and shrewd, what she thinks of Sidney Culpeper. The following dialogue ensues:

MRS. G.   What? That thin dry man?

H.N.   He is certainly thin, but I do not think he is dry.

MRS. G.   He ends his sentences with a silly giggle—hee! hee! [Mrs. Gibson's imitation of Culpeper's little self-protective sounds is not a good imitation.]

H.N.   Sometimes he says, "Woo-hoo."

MRS. G.   I think that's very foolish, besides it's rude.

H.N.   No, not rude, exactly. It's something else.

MRS. G.   What do you mean by "something else"?

H.N.   I wish I knew. I suppose I mean impertinence.

MRS. G.   But do you enjoy impertinence? I hate it.

H.N.   Well, I like being treated with respect by my own generation, but I don't really like being treated with meaningless respect by the younger generation. I find it an ageing attitude and one that precludes easy conversation. You see, when a man who is young enough to be my son treats me with conventional respect, I am quite sure that he fails to understand me. But when he mocks at me, I become inquisitive and exhilarated. What I enjoy about Culpeper is that his manner towards me is that of a kind assistant master at a private school towards a promising little boy in one of the lower forms. I relish that. It is like seeing oneself in the mirror of the future.

MRS. G.　Nonsense! I see him as a dull and ill-mannered man, who gives me the creeps. And what does he do in life?

H.N.　He collects jade.

MRS. G.　He would.

At that the gong rings and we all go down to luncheon. I have a delicious luncheon, consisting of Stamppot van Boerenkool. After luncheon I go to the barber's shop, since my hair has grown so long in the past few weeks that it becomes entangled with my shoe laces. Of all the minor ills that flesh is heir to the process of having my hair cut has for long been for me the most atrocious. It combines four of the things that I most dislike: sitting still, the sound of steel snipping, being touched by puggy fingers, and being breathed on or tickled down the back of the neck. When I get to the shop I find that there is already a customer of oriental race seated in the chair. There is in addition a Dutchman reading an illustrated paper and waiting his turn, which I realise with disgust is prior to mine. For once I have not got a book in my pocket and sit there fuming with impatience. The barber is a conscientious worker and, like Mozart, seems unable to let well alone. He keeps on returning to the same area of the Oriental's head, snipping each black hair separately. Then he brushes the hair backwards and applies to it Dr. Dralle's Berkenhaarwater. I hope that this means that he is reaching the end of his performance, but not a bit of it. Slowly he strops a razor and then proceeds to trim the verges of the Asian's hair with irritating pedantry. At last the towels are untucked from the man's brown neck. He rises, pays the bill, and leaves the shop. His place is taken by the Dutchman. I notice that he is a man of languid habit and I dread lest his lethargy may communicate itself to the movements of the barber. He has thick towy hair, and to my relief the barber deals with it brusquely. At last it is finished. The Dutchman rises, stretches out his arms with the fists closed, yawns vastly. The barber turns upside down the leather cushion on which his late customer has been seated and signs to me to take my place. I forbid him to dawdle, refuse to have my verges trimmed, and accept only a slight dash of Dr. Dralle's Berkenhaarwater. At last I am liberated and leave the shop free, elated, cropped, but *tonsus inequali tonsore.* V., when I join her, is so horrified by my appearance that she refuses to come on deck with me. I rumple my hair violently and she relents. Crowned with the smell of bay, laurel, and heartsease, I accompany her to the saloon, where we observe a curious sight.

Seated at a table near to us, also engaged in having tea and cake, is a man clad in a saffron shirt and aged in the middle forties. I notice that there is something odd about him, since his face is puckered and his shoulders heave. I assume at first that he is afflicted by a prolonged bout of sneezing, but closer watchfulness discloses that, like Jean Jacques Rousseau, he is in floods of tears. His mouth is distorted, his stout round shoulders persist in shaking, and his eyelids spill water over his crumpled cheeks. I draw V.'s attention to this phenomenon. "What an astonishing exhibition!" she says. "I hope he is not English." Then her abiding compassion reasserts itself. "He has probably," she explains, "left his wife and babies at Sumatra while he journeys home in quest of some new job. The thought has struck him that they, in the verandah at Medan, are at this moment seated round the bamboo table also drinking tea. This thought has been too much for his self-control. Poor man!" "There," I remark, "are his young barbarians all at play, and he their sire. . . ." By then the man has extracted an off-white handkerchief from his trouser pocket and tries, in vain, to stem or dry his tears. We then notice that he is reading something propped upon his knee. "It must," V. whispers, "be a letter from his fiancée confessing that she loves another." Not wishing to intrude on private misery, we rise and walk away. As we pass his chair, we see that it is not a letter that he has been reading, but a book from the ship's library. "It must be *Misunderstood*," V. says to me, "or perhaps *Black Beauty*." Out we step onto the deck and into the sound of the Indian Ocean seething; the mystery remains unsolved. "No Englishman," V. comments, "would have sobbed like that in public, not even Nelson." "Probably," I add, "he has been for the last years living alone up country and is not used to being noticed when he cries. I wonder what Joseph Conrad would have thought of him. Certainly not *Tuan* Jim." "Poor man!" sighs V. "He must be very susceptible."

As a matter of fact, we have noticed that on this return journey the passengers seem to lack the gaiety and exuberance of those who sailed with us from Southampton to the East. No longer does the young laughter of Mrs. Emmett echo against the ceiling of the dining saloon; no longer do the boys from Uppingham get slightly tipsy in the smoking room; no longer does the band play *"Que serà, serà"* with its former enthusiasm. The captain tells me that there are two reasons for this lowered temperature. In the first place, the younger people when their leave has expired like to postpone their return to their jobs in Malaya, Singapore, or Java by taking a few weeks at sea. On the other hand, when going home for their holidays they generally go by air so as to return as quickly as possible. In the second place the boat on this voyage back to Europe is filled with elderly Dutch civil servants, businessmen, and planters, who have given up their jobs in Indonesia and are many of them uncertain as to what jobs they will manage to find at home. They are therefore both elderly and sad.

We are steaming west towards Ceylon and have covered more than four hundred miles since Belawan Roads. I sit on deck all evening reading Lucretius. V. goes down to her cabin and grapples with *La Grande Mademoiselle*. There is a cocktail party given to passengers by the captain and the officers. This is surely the most hospitable line on which I have ever travelled. After dinner they all dance horribly. V. and I go to the stern where we gaze over our wake at the surrounding stars. I can still distinguish Aldebaran, my guiding star. There is the Southern Cross looking cockeyed and feeble. V. regards it with contempt and infinitely prefers the firm wide tread of our own constellations.

We put the clocks back an hour and go to bed.

2

I have always loved Lucretius, ever since the days when— half a century ago—Cyril Bailey, in his offhand Balliol manner, first indicated to me that here was a majestic poet whose writings did not form part of the usual curriculum at school. In those days it was the poetry of Lucretius, rather than his personality or ideas, that impressed me. I was awed by the eagle sweep and hover of his dark wings. Since then, having mastered my childish indolence, having read Masson and Cyril Bailey's own monumental edition, I have become fascinated by the character of the man, by the problem of his purpose, by the nervous, even neurotic, tension which renders the *De Rerum Natura* so insistent and taut. It was most agreeable to sit there reading the poem again and watching the vast swell of the Indian Ocean bearing us along *sauve mari magno*.

Who was Lucretius? Was he in fact a patrician whose culture was wide and deep? Was he, as some have asserted, a native of Naples? Or was he a Celtic freedman serving the family of the Lucretii, who allowed him to adopt their name, even as the princes of the House of Loewenstein permitted their Jewish bailiffs to call themselves Loewenstein rather than to be saddled with comic names, such as "Verdigris," or "Beer-tree," or "Threefoot"? All we know is that he was a little younger than Julius Caesar and a little older than Catullus. Cicero certainly read his poem, since he remarks in a letter to Quintus that it contained passages of genius. It has been stated even that it was Cicero who prepared the *De Rerum Natura*

for the press and, if this be true, it may to some extent account
for the reticence which the Augustan poets displayed. It would
have been ill-regarded at court to refer to anything associated
with Cicero or indeed with the Epicurean doctrine. Catullus,
who must have known Lucretius personally, reveals his influence, but does not mention his name; Horace was quick to treat
Epicureanism as a joke; Ovid mentions him once but with the
conventional epithets of "immortal and sublime"; Statius calls
him "passionate and learned"; and Virgil, who was a schoolboy
at Cremona when the poem was published, also avoids men-
tioning him directly, but in the second Georgic devotes to him
five lovely lines:

> *Felix qui potuit rerum cognoscere causas*
> *Atque metus omnis et inexorabile fatum*
> *Subjecit pedibus strepitumque Acherontis avari!*
> *Fortunatus et ille deos qui novit agrestes,*
> *Panaque Silvanumque senem Nymphasque sorores.*

In a gloss written by Jerome on the *Chronicle* of Eusebius
occurs the statement that Lucretius was rendered insane by a
love potion administered to him by his wife and that he died
by his own hand. It is difficult to believe that a poet who could
give to so wildly imaginative a theme such logical, almost Eu-
clidean, precision can have suffered from mental derangement.
But I agree with Cyril Bailey that the passages dealing with
the plague at Athens and the use of wild beasts in warfare do
suggest morbidity and even hallucination.

Tennyson, whose discreet but salacious mind was always
attracted by conjugal abnormality, seized on the Jerome story
with avidity. He tells us how "Lucilia, wedded to Lucretius,

found her master cold"; instead of paying her the attention that she expected and deserved, he would retreat into moods of melancholy abstraction, when he would brood upon Epicurus or upon "the rise and the long roll of the hexameter." Lucilia therefore visits a sorceress who provides her with a love philtre. This drug has a deplorable effect upon her husband, who begins to suffer from nightmares—"storms, and what dreams, ye holy gods, what dreams!" In the end, he can bear it no longer and thrusts a sword between his ribs; hearing him fall, Lucilia runs into the room and is profoundly distressed; she:

> *Beat breast, tore hair, cried out upon herself*
> *As having failed in duty to him, shriek'd.*

I am always shocked by the lack of taste, and even humour, manifested by Tennyson in his domestic idylls. But his poem on Lucretius is memorable for a lucid exposition of the Epicurean doctrine and for three magnificent lines:

> *I thought I lived securely as yourselves—*
> *No lewdness, narrowing envy, monkey-spite,*
> *No madness of ambition, avarice, none;*
> *No larger feast than under plane or pine*
> *With neighbours laid along the grass, to take*
> *Only such cups as left us friendly warm,*
> *Affirming each his own philosophy—*
> *Nothing to mar the sober majesties*
> *Of settled, sweet, Epicurean life . . .*

But then occurred Lucilia's love potion and the wind of the wings of madness comes to shake his mind:

> *I saw the flaring atom-streams*
> *And torrents of her myriad universe*
> *Ruining along the illimitable inane.*

I am quite prepared to believe that Lucretius did not get on with his wife and ended by going stark staring mad.

He suffered much from ennui, or the *taedium vitae;* was frequently assailed by indefinable apprehensions and by a sense of guilt; was morbidly interested in the slow movements of the moon; and was clearly a victim of dread and melancholy. He may also have been afflicted by sexual impotence, and there is a passage in his fourth book (lines 1233–48) which certainly suggests this misfortune. A vivid sentence in the same book (line 1140), in which he speaks of the smile that lingers on a woman's lips after she has exchanged glances with her lover, suggests that Lucilia was not exacting merely but also unfaithful. In any case, he seems to have hated women, sneering at them bitterly with the words *"veneres nostras."* It is preferable, he contends, for a man to indulge his passions quickly and promiscuously, rather than to disturb his equanimity by the process known as "falling in love." In any case:

> *Ex hominis vero facie pulchroque colore*
> *Nil datur in corpus praeter simulacra fruendum*
> *Tenvia; quae vento spes raptat saepe misella.*

[*But from the beauty and fair complexion of a man nothing in fact enters our body, unless it be the enjoyment of thin images, which lovesick hope grasps in the empty air.*]

The relevance of Lucretius to my theme is that he also was afflicted by the *maladie du siècle*, that he also was terrified by the dissolution of all previous certainties, habits, conventions, and beliefs. But instead of reacting to his universal decay with the abstracted melancholy of Werther or René, he reacted to it, as Mr. John Osborne has reacted, with passionate rage, with *saeva indignatio*. As a boy he had witnessed the decline in human values brought about under the tyranny of Sulla. The old religion had turned into a nightmare of horrid superstitions; the old Roman virtue had become the object of schoolboy jokes; the army was today the instrument of dictatorship; the senate was composed of corrupt and frightened millionaires. He became so obsessed by corruption that he persuaded himself that even the soil of Italy had been poisoned and was no longer capable of giving birth to wheat and vine. The actual terror which this caused him produced a passionate desire to escape and to help others to escape. The only solace was to expect no solace; the only comfort lay in blind unawareness and acceptance. To him Epicurus became the divine liberator, the mighty Prometheus, the guide whose intellectual vitality had enabled him to pass beyond "the flaming bastions of this earth," and whose genius "had quenched all other lights even as the sun subdues the stars." Here was the prophet who had come to liberate mankind from fear. Nay, he was more than a prophet, he was in himself a god—*Deus ille fuit*.

It was Epicurus who taught us that only by natural philosophy could man master his fear of life and death. The gods, even if they exist, are utterly indifferent to human suffering; the sequence of the seasons, the majestic rhythm of the stars are not due to divine ordering but to natural causes; pleasure, or the avoidance of pain and fear, is the true guide to life—*dux vitae diva voluptas*: the wise man will not sadden himself by nurturing unattainable desires; he will imitate the gods, who live in quietude, "smiling secretly." Above all, he will not allow his tranquility to be disturbed by superstitious nonsense regarding future penalties or rewards; when a man dies, he becomes nonexistent and therefore death should mean nothing more to him than a dreamless sleep. This splendid quietude can be achieved by a study of natural philosophy, by belief in the atoms "ruining along the illimitable inane," and by the exercise of reason. Fear was an inevitable affliction for the superstitious man. "Through every wood," he writes, "throughout the vast mountains and the deep forests, terror creeps with shaking limbs." The superior man can be liberated from guilt and fear. "The faults," he writes, "that reason is unable to subjugate are so trivial that nothing should prevent us from living a life of tranquility like that of the immortal gods."

Yet Lucretius, in spite of his persistent wish to rid himself and others from the oppressions of guilt and fear, was not wholly an escapist. He contended that a man should make the best of his own opportunities for productive living—*vitaque mancipio nulli datur: omnibus usu*. A magnificently unhappy man was Lucretius, and his fierce poetry should render us ashamed of our contentment. But how wonderful it is to communicate again with the vigour of such conviction and to allow his mighty line to linger in the ear, while seated on the deck of the M. V. *Willem Ruys*, gazing out on the angry sea, *turbantibus aequora ventis*.

3

Friday, February 22

In my spare moments, which are few, I have been reading C. E. Wurtzburg's massive work on Stamford Raffles. He was certainly a man of powerful vision, courage, and resolve; I suppose also that he must have possessed compelling charm and that Dr. Jacks was correct when he wrote of his "Promethean touch." But he was also rather vapidly optimistic, vain, insubordinate, quarrelsome, and often vindictive and tricky. I prefer his doughty antagonist, Rollo Gillespie, of whom Bill Wakeham wrote so vivid a biography. Raffles was certainly a great naturalist; he founded the Bogor gardens as well as the London zoo, and he discovered many unknown plants and trees. He must also have been one of the most unlucky men that ever lived. His idealism was misinterpreted, and his progressive principles were derided as visionary and sentimental. Everything seemed to go wrong with him; his children died one by one; his wife Olivia succumbed to the Java climate; and on his return to England with his collections and his ruined career the ship *Fame* on which he travelled burst into flames and he had to escape in a small boat with his second wife and baby, watching all his possessions sink into the water in a cloud of steam. In the end he was found dead on the back stairs of his London house at the age of forty-five. The enmity he aroused was contemporary, his fame posthumous.

I had often heard that passengers on board a ship are prone, such is the uniform tenour of their days, to spread and to believe all manner of rumours. I have heard it whispered that, owing to the Suez Canal misfortune and the indolence of the dockhands in Java, we are running out of fuel and that, if we ever reach Colombo, we shall have to remain there for several days in order to replenish our empty tanks. I have heard it whispered that, since being exposed to Communist propaganda in their home villages at Madura, the Indonesian section of the crew are in a state of mutiny and that we may at any moment be exposed to a night of the short knives. I am consoled by the thought that:

> *Whatever happens, we have got*
> *The Maxim gun. And they have not.*

But today I was asked by two people separately to tell them what exactly happened to V. and myself when we were attacked by a panther that night when we slept in the jungle. They are hurt and disappointed when I assure them that we never slept in the jungle and that we never even saw a panther. How can this rumour have originated? Neither of us has made any allusion, however remote, to such an adventure. I have come to disbelieve everything that I am told.

A giant boarded our ship at Singapore. I think he is an American and he must be almost seven feet high. I first became aware of him when I returned from my bathe yesterday morning. The water in the swimming pool splashes over the edge with the movement of the ship, creating a wet area immediately round the bath and thereafter comes a dry area where the deck planks have dried in the sun. Passing this morning from the wet to the dry area, I observed imprinted on the latter the footstep of a giant man. It was like the fossil footmark of a dinosaur. Then I identified its author leaving the *Eetsalon* after luncheon. He is a magnificent young man and has to stoop to avoid striking the ceiling of the saloon. V. suggests that he must possess a radar apparatus similar to that owned by bats which warn him of the approach of solids. Being quite good at science, and possessing an imagination which expands rapidly, she suggests that in the atmospheric conditions prevailing around the Equator this apparatus may cease to function adequately. The young man, as he moves through the decks and the saloons, may with his head strike the lever which operates the sprinkling system in case of fire. Our cabins, when we return to them, may be found cowering in a rainstorm and *La Grande Mademoiselle* and my own diary, which are spread upon the bunk, will be drenched and become illegible.

We arrange with the Stedalls about sharing a car tomorrow when we reach Colombo. I go down to the second class to find Leonard Forman and to ask him to join us. But he is hiding somewhere as is his wont (he does not really care for his fellow Europeans) and I leave a note on his bunk. I then go to the purser's office to get some Ceylonese money and there I meet Sidney Culpeper, wearing his absurd panama hat. As I expected, he is, like all rich people, careful about money and, like all virgins, he carries with him, not merely a wallet for bank notes, but also a little pigskin purse for small change. "Are you coming up to Kandy tomorrow?" I ask him. "Woohoo," he answers. "Not on your life. I hate the place and the road is dangerous, what with cobras and strayed elephants and such bends, my dear, you have no conception! No, I shall visit a friend of mine in Colombo. He has made a fortune in hair oil and has a superb collection of celadon and some quite happy pieces of jade." "Jade," I reply sententiously perhaps, "is seldom happy. It is the saddest of all the hard stones." "Woo-hoo—you *are* pompous, aren't you?" I move away, irritated. I do not like being called "my dear" by comparative strangers. I am glad he is not coming to Kandy.

4

Saturday, February 23

We are wakened early by the whining of the cranes which raise the top-covers from the hold. We pass the Colombo breakwater at 6.30 and have breakfast at 7.00. We collect the Stedalls and enter the launch which is to take us ashore. I surrender my seat to an Indonesian lady and Stedall does the same with his: the younger men remain seated, amused doubtless by these gestures of archaic courtesy. As I swing there, clinging to a handrail affixed to the roof of the cabin, I read an advertisement which is opposite me; it says that Dal's Oriental Bazaar enjoys the patronage of Mr. Menzies and Sir Godfrey Thomas. I am entertained by a sudden picture of an identical Benares brass pot adorning the chimney piece in the spare bedroom at Canberra and St. James's Palace. It is calm this time in the Colombo basin and we glide across to the landing place that leads to the terminal. The sea hawks, which Stedall calls the "white-headed Brahminy kites," circle slowly above us. It is all blue and hot.

On landing we are conducted by the representative of a travel agency towards a neat little car driven by a Ceylonese driver. Remembering what Culpeper has said about the bends, the cobras, and the rogue elephants, I tell the driver that I suffer acutely from phlebitis and that he must drive slowly: as a result we creep at about twenty miles an hour the whole thirty-five miles up to Kandy and back. The driver speaks English in a high and rapid monotone, which is exactly like an imitation by Peter Ustinov of a Ceylonese chauffeur who speaks English. He is a horrible man. I sit in front next to this monster, and V. and the two Stedalls sit in the back. At the last moment Leonard Forman appears, but the driver insists that it is against the law for him to take more than four passengers. He rejects Forman firmly. This is the first of many instances of his sullen resolve to prevent us doing what we want to do. We drive away from the terminal at Colombo at 8.30.

On leaving the ship V. had been handed a note brought on board by the pilot. It was from that nice Mrs. Vere de Mel who had looked after us on our former visit to Colombo. She says that she has arranged with John Gibson, a friend of Richard Rumbold, to pick us up just outside Kandy. On reaching the village of Kadugannawa we must telephone to him from the local post office. He will then join us, escort us round the botanical gardens at Peradeniya, give us luncheon in his house, take us to see Kandy, and ensure that we have plenty of time to get back to Colombo before the boat sails.

We creep through the suburbs of Colombo and pass the bridge which we had crossed on our former visit on the way to the Buddhist temple. The driver, in his high monotone, seeks to draw my attention to the beauties of his island. "On right," he chants, "is calico plantation; on left is school and dispensary; beyond, you will see paddy fields, where plenty rice." At 9.15 we meet our first elephant, slouching along with a child on his back and plunged in deep meditation. At the base of the coconut palms are heaped the litter of empty shells, looking like some sacked ossuary. The driver stops and despatches a village boy to pick for us some cannon-ball blossom —a waxy, highly scented, magnolia-like cluster of pink and orange petals. As with most tropical flowers, the tangle from which they burst is dried and disorderly: rare and distant do they bloom from a thicket of dead wood.

We stop at a village called "Little Paris," where the driver takes a long drink from a king coconut—the first agreeable action that I have seen him perform. Then on we drive through the green vivacious morning, skirting foothills warily and meeting other elephants sunk in gloom. The naked torsoes of the young men are muscular and graceful; the white hair and beards of the old men stand out against their black nakedness, conveying the impression of a photographic negative. When twenty miles from Kandy we begin to climb, and the monotony of the coconuts is at last varied by gracefulness. We pass the Viper Rock, perched high on a peak, and the driver starts telling me a long high-pitched story about a Ceylonese Robin Hood, who lived in a cave under this precipice and who, although he plundered the rich daily, was wonderfully kind to the poor. I am unable to conceal my boredom at his legend.

At 11.00 we reach Kadugannawa and I tell the driver to stop at the post office as I must telephone to a friend. "No time telephone friend," he answers. I explain that I must telephone to him since he will join us here and that we are lunching at his house. "No time lunch friend," he says. "Lunch

Queen's Hotel." I reply with some asperity that we do not intend to lunch at the Queen's Hotel, and I enter the post office in anger. I had been rather dreading the "press button A" business in a Ceylonese village post office and the fuss about inserting the correct coin. But when I tell the clerk that I wish to speak to Mr. Gibson he at once dials a number and immediately hands me the receiver. John Gibson is on the line and says he will be down in four minutes. The clerk in the post office refuses to let me pay for my call and I am impressed by his promptitude and smile.

In a few minutes John Gibson turns up. He is a thin man with a small beard, considerable knowledge, and an amusing turn of mind. He squeezes in between me and the driver, and the latter regards him with unconcealed distaste. They talk to each other in the local dialect and with great fluency. Gibson explains that the driver is pledged to get us back to Colombo by a certain hour; that he is afraid it may rain and that the roads will then become so slippery that he will be unable to drive at more than eight miles an hour; that he may be correct in this apprehension; and that therefore, after visiting the gardens, we had better after all lunch at the Queen's Hotel in Kandy and then start back to the boat. The driver makes no effort at all to hide his triumph at my discomfiture. He is a dreadful man, conceited and devoid of compassion.

So on we go and after a mile or so we enter the Peradeniya gardens and drive round them. They are situated on the banks of the Mahaweli Ganga, which slides brown and luscious below magnificent trees and lawns. There is a fine avenue of cabbage palms, many clumps of splendid bamboos, and a variety of flowering trees and shrubs, such as the *Dolichan-*

drone spathacea and the *Acanthus ilicifolius,* by which V. is fascinated and impressed. At one point across the river has been flung a bright new Bailey bridge. Gibson explains to us that it has been erected by an American company who are doing a film version of Pierre Boulle's excellent novel *Le Pont de la Rivière Kwai.* For the needs of their own public the company have felt obliged to turn the British Intelligence Service into the American Intelligence Service, thereby missing the whole point of the story. The Americans, with all their virtues, do not possess a sensitive regard for fact; they have, like Mr. Ford, been educated to despise history and to prefer legend. I regret this, since it leads to misunderstanding.

The driver by then is suffering such agonies of impatience that we are forced into the car again and I feel guilty about V., who wanted to explore these gardens thoroughly and had no desire at all to see Buddha's tooth. So on we drive to Kandy, which is exactly what I had imagined Simla to be, complete with viceregal lodge in the shape of the Queen's Hotel. We sit in the lounge for a bit, drink excellent Carlsberg beer, and wait for a table to be free in the dining room. I slip out into the hall where I had observed a jeweler's stall and where I buy a topaz as a birthday present for V. It may be just a piece of glass but it shines beautifully and the jeweler put it into a tiny little envelope of basketwork which the Ceylonese women use as receptacle for betel nut. We lunch in a wide cool dining room and are given excellent butterfish. The windows look out on the terrace constructed above the lake, and we watch the priests in their saffron robes passing leisurely along.

After luncheon we drive quickly round the lake, past the

ugly little temple in which the tooth of the Buddha is pre-
served, past an attractive Bosporus-like pavilion built out into
the water and now used as a library, and down again to
Kadugannawa, where we say good-bye to John Gibson with
regret. He had striven on the way down to induce the driver
to turn up a little road that led to a small temple of great
beauty. The driver had refused with a combination of oiliness
and resolve. John Gibson was amused by my indignation.
"There is something in what he says," he remarks grinning.
"You cannot afford to miss the boat and there may be a storm
on the way down." In any case I refuse to address another
word to the driver for the rest of the day.

I am sorry to have missed the little temple which Gibson
wished to show us, since I prefer small pious temples to those
which are rich and famed. Not that in any case, however
atrociously I might be assailed by fear and melancholy, I should
adopt the Buddhist way of life, whether the *Theravada* or the
Mahayana versions, or the sombre discipline of *Zen*. I am
constantly assured by Richard Rumbold that my invincible
ignorance is due to a materialistic, not to say hedonistic, strain
in my nature. I assure him that it is rather that I refuse to
surrender my own personality to any doctrine, or to abandon
the habit of believing that I am I. Moreover, although I may
agree with him that in some cases it may be both wise and
profitable to abandon desire, I am conscious of a deep dis-
inclination to do anything of the sort. For me desire is the
flame of life. The eight-fold path of meditation, remembrance,
occupation, effort, thought, speech, action, and belief is not a
path designed for my hurried footsteps. I have no wish at all
to pass "beyond the Intellect." I have no hope of ever reach-

ing "the absolute moment of cosmic consciousness." Richard Rumbold tells me, with his gentle affectionate smile, that all this derives from lack of humility, from lack of any sense of the horror of life. "But, Richard," I protest, "I am not a conceited man, and were I to succeed in enucleating all desire I should be left with no energy at all; I should become a magnolia." "Might it not," he whispers softly, "be better to become a magnolia—or to contemplate the jewel in the lotus?" I am sure he is right about all this. I feel ashamed.

Beautiful it is on the way down with superb forest and mountain scenery. I am not surprised that legends have grown up around Taprobane and Serendip as an island paradise. Gibson assures me that if we wished to come back next winter and stay for a few weeks he would easily be able to find us a bungalow and servants. I tell this to V. as I see she is disappointed by not being allowed to remain longer at Peradeniya. My hatred of our driver is increased when I find he has hidden my cine-camera in the boot and when I miss taking what would have been an impressive film of elephants washing in a pool. At 4.45 we are back at the terminal where the launch is waiting. I ask Stedall to pay the driver and do not wish to speak to him again. On walking away from the car, I cast at him a glance of disfavour at which he bows.

By 5.30 we are on board again and get our letters. I hear from Nigel that his Executive have adopted a Major Friend as his successor. In the end, I suppose, most people will realise that the Suez adventure was dishonourable and futile and did our reputation and interests much harm. But the Executive appear to have a fixed idea that it was "unpatriotic" of Nigel to have warned his constituents that the operation was unlikely to prove a success. I doubt whether they had ever heard of the Tripartite Declaration or realized that our overt violation of it, and during the very week of the presidential election, would arouse fury in Washington and lead to threats. I simply do not understand how Anthony Eden could in this way have gone against the principles of his whole policy and career. He must be very ill indeed and the whole fiasco fills me with pity and terror.

After dinner we go on deck and watch the Orient liner, the *Empire Fowey*, slide out sparkling into the night. She was a former German ship, the *Potsdam*, and was used by the Nazis as one of their *Kraft durch Freude* vessels. She is now being employed as a troopship carrying men home from the East. Little *Kraft* about it all, I fear, and no *Freude* at all. We lean over the taffrail as we move out of the basin and watch the lights of Colombo slide away.

We are not so exhausted as we were during our former visit to Ceylon. I suppose we are getting accustomed to the heat. But I do not sleep well as I am worried and angry about Nigel.

X. LEMURIA

1

Sunday, February 24

I am typing away in my cabin when V. bursts in from next door, exclaiming excitedly, "Come quick! Porpoises!" We dash down to the grille two decks below, as from there one gets a wider view of the sea than that provided by a cabin window, and it is closer to the level of the waves. There beside us and quite close is the largest school of porpoises that I have ever seen; hundreds of them frolicking and splashing like American college boys playing water polo. They are pleased with life; they leap at least three feet up into the ringing air; their bodies flash and drip in the sunshine, and, if we could but hear them, they would be calling each to each.

What is the difference, V. asks me, between a porpoise and a dolphin? I tell her that dolphins assumed a prominent part in classical myth, poetry, painting, and sculpture and that, in so far as I can remember, there is not even a word for "porpoise" in the Greek or Latin languages. In the *Odyssey* dolphins figure as the staple food of the ogress Scylla, who sticks out her horrid head from her Sicilian cavern and pounces on the dolphins as they pass and repass through the Straits of Messina. The Pliny family, both uncle and nephew, were much interested in dolphins and relate many facts about them which a modern ichthyologist might deny. According to the elder Pliny, dolphins are peculiarly susceptible to the sound of the lyre and, like so many highly musical people, are apt to fall in love with boys. There was a lad at Naples once, of the name of Hermias, who would walk down to the quay on St. Valentine's Day, then known as the Feast of Lupercalia, and in the sight and hearing of the trippers who had come to the seaside for their spring holiday would summon his dolphin-lover to his presence. "Snubnose!" the boy would shout, and immediately the dolphin would arrive, offer its back to the ingle, and off they would sail together across the bay to Posilippo, where the boy attended school. Then there was another boy, a native of Hippo in Tunisia, who was so deeply loved by a dolphin that Alexander the Great appointed him, in spite of his tender age, high priest of the recently consecrated temple of Poseidon in Assyria. The porpoise, on the other hand, was a smaller member of the cetacean family, had a differently shaped jaw, was not paederastic, and was in fact a normal mammal, the females of the breed producing large families, each baby, after long gestation, being two feet long at birth.

V. is inclined to distrust my scientific knowledge and even my classical illustrations which, I admit, are too often based upon vague memories. She says she will ask the captain, who is the only person in this ship whose word she believes. He tells her that the porpoise is a small and more agile member of the dolphin family; that he lacks the deep groove which, in the dolphin, runs from the base of the mouth to the ear, producing a fine sculptural effect; and that he jumps into the air, not, as Boumphrey told us, in order to rid himself of body lice, but in order to cut off the fleeing shoals of smaller fish. I do not believe this, any more than V. believes my story about the priest of Poseidon or the Neapolitan boy who rode to school across the bay. Yet I assure her that my facts are derived from the elder Pliny, who was a most reliable naturalist, and that the story about the schoolboy is told at least twice in the letters of his nephew, the esteemed governor of Bithynia. She remains unconvinced.

On the gangway after luncheon I meet Culpeper. "Did you see the porpoises?" I ask him. "Horrid wet things," he answers. "Not at all," I reply angrily, "they are symbols of exaltation and delight." "Woo-hoo!" he giggles. Certainly he lacks vivacity and our feelings for each other are what I believe is called "ambivalent." I enjoy entering into conversation with him, but irritation ensues so quickly that we never part as friends. What is worse is that he, with his derisive ejaculations, always seems to get the last sound. I realise that the pleasure that I derive from our brief encounters is not unmixed with what very clever people now call "masochism."

V. takes the occasion to expound to the captain her imaginative idea that the Equator ought to be marked with coloured buoys, similar to those which delimitate the lanes followed by champion swimmers in swimming baths. He is delighted by the idea but points out that the buoys would have to be attached

to something and that this, in mid-ocean, would prove a difficult and costly operation. She suggests that they need not be
attached, since they could be constructed of cork or some
buoyant material and would "just float." All this comes from
having a poetic imagination and having recently been reading
Camoens. There is a charming passage in Canto X of *The*
Lusiads about Sumatra, the Golden Chersonese, and Singapore. I must verify the passage when I get home.

At Singapore an air-commodore of the name of Clouston,
joined the ship for the return journey. He is accompanied by
his wife and debutante daughters. Mrs. Clouston is a very
pretty woman and does not appear to be a year older than
her two girls. The air-commodore is a quarry of information.
I ask him to confirm to V. that I was right in stating that
the *Prince of Wales* and her consort had been sunk, not off
the tip of Sumatra, but in the Gulf of Siam. He draws a sketch
map to indicate the exact latitude. "But," V. protests, "it was
a young airman who told me that they were sunk off Sabang
Island, and he knows the place intimately, having again and
again flown over the Bengalen Passage when his squadron
was stationed at Singapore." "What airman?" asks the air-
commodore menacingly. Wishing to protect the young mythomaniac from reprisals, I add hastily: "But I don't think he was
an airman; he was wearing a dressing gown." "I think I can
guess who it was," says the air-commodore. I regret this episode
since it is sad to get mythomaniacs into trouble with their
superiors.

It is really hot today and even in my air-conditioned cabin
the thermometer climbs to eighty degrees. They dance in the
saloon after dinner and we talk to Major and Mrs. Green.

He is a younger man than I am and yet he is unable to ride or shoot, which until a few years ago were his favourite pastimes. It is a terrible misfortune to be rendered immobile if one depends so much for happiness upon the use of one's limbs. Major Green takes it all with stoic acceptance; he does not grumble or quail; he is a fine example of *gravitas*. I tell him that I have spent the last two days reading Epictetus and that he must agree with me that there is very much to be said for many of the precepts that the Stoics inculcated and which famous Romans, such as Cicero and Seneca, at least pretended to observe. "Don't know much about that sort of stuff," says Major Green, "but I am sure you are right." I am impressed by his courtesy and courage.

2

Does my distrust of all escapist systems, and my contempt for Epicurus personally, lead me to adhere to the seemingly opposite extreme and to proclaim myself a Stoic? My adherence is checked by the thought of Cicero in his most self-satisfied moments, of that awful Seneca, and of Marcus Aurelius. But Epictetus—the impoverished, majestic, and witty cripple—commands both my esteem and my affection. I ought, I suppose, to be less affected by sentimental associations.

I remember an evening in early spring when I was travelling in a small boat from Patras to Corfu. We stopped for an hour or so at Preveza, a mere Epirote village, and no more beautiful in itself than any other of the many *scalas* in the Ionian and Aegean seas. The warm silence of sunset descended upon the little harbour, giving resonance to the small sounds that reached us—the splash of an oar, the laughter of a fisherman, the high note of a gramophone playing in a quayside taverna. I leant over the taffrail (*O! Le crepuscule des petits ports!*) reflecting that here, among the lights that had begun already to twinkle from the village, Epictetus had lived and thought and taught. We turned northwards into the approaching night, passing over the flat seas of Actium, and my thoughts veered round to the great proconsul, to Cleopatra's little yellow body, and to Heredia's memorable lines. How repugnant it is to me that my government, with sullen Tory pride, should have quarrelled with the Greeks, the most natural, apart from the French, of all our allies!

There are many of the Stoic tenets which I respect and share. They believed in a First Cause, to which with delightful inconsistency they would give varied and indeed contradictory names—Zeus, Destiny, the World-Soul, Nature, God, Logos, Reason. They believed, with Virgil and Shelley, that one day this earth and its erring inhabitants would be destroyed by fire and that some more perfectable cycle would begin anew. They accepted the existence of evil, holding that without it there could be no virtue, even as without folly there could be no wisdom. They believed that every human being was endowed with an instinct, or conscience, which obliged him to distinguish between good and bad; this instinct could be fortified by experience and developed by learning. It was the duty of every individual to strive to render himself in harmony with Logos, or Nature, or universal reason. He could thus acquire the four cardinal virtues of wisdom, courage, temperance, and justice. Above all perhaps the Stoics were in this sense at least no escapists, in that they regarded virtue as a positive, and not merely as a negative, capacity.

Yet, as so often with the Greeks, they narrowed the conception of virtue into a self-regarding conception and identified "the good" with "good for me." The Greeks, I regret to say, had but small idea of duty, even as they had but rudimentary instincts of compassion. It was the Romans who elevated the Stoic doctrine of "the suitable" into the imperative of *officium* or duty. It was in this manner that the excellent precept of duty towards oneself was enriched by the wider duty towards one's neighbour. "Reverence the gods," wrote Marcus Aurelius, "and help man." All this was certainly an enlargement of virtue. But the Stoics, like the Epicureans, relied too much upon the pleasure-pain principle, and their teaching was marred by a negative and feminine element. They believed in self-fulfilment, but they also believed that a man would be happier, or at least less miserable, if he refrained from taking avoidable risks.

I dislike the doctrine of "Apathy" and their contention that a man who could by the exercise of reason regulate his desires and aversions was more likely to attain to tranquility than a man who with energy and courage faced the rewards and punishments of life. Tranquility, even if it diminishes dread, appears a feeble aspiration.

But I come back to Epictetus, who was in truth a charming and extremely witty person. He taught that if a man desired contentment he must "make the best of his own faculties and take everything else as it happens to occur." What really matters is not what we do but the way in which we do it. "We should be careful," he said, "how we play the game, but utterly indifferent to the ball itself." If we are to avoid anxieties and disappointments, or what dear Mrs. Carter calls "solicitude," then we must concentrate on internals, which are within the control of our own will and reason, and ignore externals, which are outside our control. What I like about Epictetus is that he disbelieved in pessimism and regarded the "ivory tower" school as something that was contrary to nature. "You were not born," he told his pupils, "to be depressed and unhappy in society; you were born to enjoy yourselves in the company of your fellows." "Solitude," he said, "is the state of a helpless person"; and he contended that a man who shirked all social responsibilities could never develop the valuable virtues of fidelity and honour. Although himself an extremely austere man, he disapproved of the squalor practised by the cynics as by some subsequent ascetics. He insisted that his pupils should blow their noses properly, wash with soap and water, and clean their teeth. His *Encheiridion*, or manual, is replete with shrewd worldly aphorisms, devised for the avoidance of displeasure. It is a mistake to be fussy when one goes to the public baths, or irritated when the maid upsets the oilcan, or concerned with the seat you are allotted at a dinner party, or to laugh too loud, or to listen to authors reading their own works, or to show off in front of less educated people, or to be self-satisfied. "If you really want to be good," he said, "you must begin by convincing yourself that you are bad." "Grasshoppers are musical," he said, "but snails are dumb." "Remember," he said, "that you are an actor in a drama and that it is the author who decides how it will end." "You will prove unconquerable," he said—and this in fact was the essence of his teaching—"if you enter into no contest which you are unlikely to win."

I admit that such precepts are shrewd rather than noble. I do not like the Stoics much more than I like the Epicureans; but I like Epictetus of Prevesa or Nicopolis much more than I like Epicurus of Samos and Mytilene.

3

Monday, February 25

The Indian Ocean this morning is again a satin sheet of Oxford blue. Again we notice that the flying fish, on emerging into the air, make a little scratch across the satin waves. It is only in the last yard or two of their flight that they really rise above the sea; they then drop into it, as I have noticed before, with a little plop like a pebble, creating concentric ripples exactly like those made by a stone when dropped into a pond. V., whose gift of observation is more delicate and precise than my own, says that it is not like a stone being dropped, but like a hard little pea being dropped; it is a tiny fall, and the circles that spread away from it are small and quickly obliterated. Meanwhile the clouds upon the horizon are magnified by their reflection on the oily surface and loom like large white cloths. As we watch the wide waters we see a shark basking on the surface like a hippopotamus or a log. At our approach it turns over lazily, disclosing a triangular fin.

The Carters, who are Kentish neighbours of ours at High Halden, have a charming American woman with them, called

Mrs. Boynton. She is the type of American that I most enjoy, rather like Amey Aldrich, or Mrs. Morrow—educated, sharp, silent, low-voiced, and with a tolerant but incisive sense of the ridiculous. She sits on a deck chair all afternoon, reading a vast book entitled *The Expansion of Christianity*. I take her as a terminal or landmark in my afternoon walks around the deck. Eight times round I have to go, across into the second class, round by the swimming pool, and then out into the wide open air of the sports deck where people are playing deck tennis and quoits. I am often interrupted by fellow passengers or whales and am apt to lose count of my laps. I therefore take Mrs. Boynton and her book as a checking point, and when I reach her I transfer one match from my left-hand trouser pocket and place it in the right-hand pocket; when eight matches have thus been transferred I pause to exchange conversation with Mrs. Boynton before embarking on my second mile. While thus pausing this afternoon we are addressed by an English passenger who has an affable manner but does not appear to me to possess an exceptional personality. "I see you are reading?" he says to Mrs. Boynton. She indicates assent. "Do you enjoy long books?" he asks. I suppose that this was a sensible enquiry, but when he left us Mrs. Boynton and I chuckle gently. Meanwhile V. is down in her cabin scribbling on large sheets of folio paper about the courage, impetuosity, and soft heart of La Grande Mademoiselle.

Leonard Forman comes up before dinner to have a drink with us. We had been feeling guilty about him ever since we had failed, owing to the respect for law manifested by the abominable chauffeur at Colombo, to give him a lift to the botanical gardens. But he bears no resentment and had in fact spent a pleasant afternoon with a friend whom he had known at Bogor. He says he can easily go to Peradeniya on his next visit to the Far East.

V. and he discuss botanical subjects. Forman is so exquisite, so expert, a herbalist that he does not call flowers by their names but only by their genus. This complicates conversation. He tells us that when he was plant-hunting in Borneo he stopped for a week in a Dyak village. Although they have abandoned the practice of head-hunting, reverting to it for only a few years during the Japanese occupation, there was a bunch of skulls hanging like coconuts from the main beam of the hut in which he slept. The women would light herbs below this trophy and the smoke from the fire would twist through the eye sockets of the skulls. He told us that there was a Presbyterian missionary in the district who would impress the Dyaks by playing to them gramophone records of negro spirituals and Christian hymns. They regarded this as the most exciting magic that they had ever witnessed and when, at the end of the performance, the missionary would ask them to testify to this unknown god, they would raise their arms in unison and proclaim their conversion.

For once there is a magnificent sunset, the western sky all green and gold and on the fringe of the horizon a little line of clouds standing out black against the glow, like pine trees at Ravenna.

After dinner there is horse racing in the saloon. It takes hours before the dice are thrown and the horses begin their leaps along the green course. The clocks are put back another hour but we retire to bed at our accustomed time.

Tuesday, February 26

It is very hot but not as calm as yesterday. V. is convinced that the air pumped into her cabin through the orifices of the air-conditioning machine is "unnatural," and that if she opens the window onto the flaming sea she will acquire God's air, which is purer and cooler. She does so, with the result that the thermometer in her cabin rapidly jumps up two degrees. She then closes her cabin window, adjusts the nozzles of the air-conditioning machine, and settles down to *La Grande Mademoiselle*, with her books of reference and her notes spread like a picnic on the bunk beside her.

At 12.55 we go on deck and have our accustomed "not-yets" with the Gibsons. We find that the passengers are sharply divided between those who assert that the fish we saw basking yesterday was a shark and those who contend that it was a whale. I say it was quite certainly a shark, since I had distinctly seen, not its teeth only, but also its dorsal fin. I assert this with sharp conviction, not because I am really positive, but because I hate whales, which are ugly, blubberous, and lazy beasts. Mrs. Gibson, who is aware that I really know nothing at all about marine monsters, laughs silently.

The band, in the hope of stimulating the apathy of the passengers, bursts into preprandial jazz. The captain, who is also saddened by the melancholy of this return shipload, gets them to lift the carpet in the saloon and does a turn with the two Miss Cloustons. He is assuredly a man of formidable energy and possessed of great social talent.

I spend the day reading Ronald Gray's book about Kafka. It is refreshing, after all the rubbish that has been written round *The Castle*, to find someone who seeks to explain rather than to expound.

I have twice read Kafka's *Castle*, since Edward Sackville-West, who disapproved of my materialism, kept on assuring me that I "ought to do so." To me, who dislike allegories, it was incomprehensible and wearisome, as when somebody at breakfast tells one his dream of the night before. The whole drama seemed to be conducted in a fevered atmosphere and recalled those restless occasions when my temperature has risen above 103 and somebody in the top left-hand corner of the ceiling repeats Gertrude Stein sentences at me in a monotone. "You ought, they ought, we ought," the voice insists, and I feel guilty and afraid. In the same way, in Kafka's story, Czech villagers gabble quickly at each other in tavern kitchens, the atmosphere of which is heavy with the steam of wet clothes drying by the stove. Never have I been able to solve the sentences or even to understand what Kafka was writing about.

We are assured by his friends that he was a gay and entrancing companion with merry eyes and a frequent laugh. He was one of those rare malcontents who, like Amiel, have the unselfishness to hide from their companions the sad self-searchings that scorch their souls. One of the odd things about him was that he seems to have derived as much pleasure from his clothes as Sidney Culpeper derives from his. He was always dressed in the latest Prague fashion and his little buttoned boots twinkled with blacking and gaiety. To be extremely well dressed is, I suppose, a form of disguise and a means of self-assurance. Baudelaire also, although his heart had been devoured by wild beasts, dressed like a prosperous accountant on a Sunday afternoon.

I have much enjoyed Ronald Gray's calm, cool, sensitive book on *Kafka's Castle*. He assures me that I need not have expended effort in searching for a clue to the novel's allegory. It would be as arbitrary, he says, to identify the castle with God as it would be to assume that it is intended for a mother-image. Nor need I become unnecessarily irritated by the appalling fecklessness of Kafka's hero, who seems always to be dropping off to sleep at important moments. This trick of sudden slumber may, Gray tells me, imply that Kafka is only truly himself when he can banish self-concern and that it is the unawareness of the sleeping condition that suggests to him that there may after all be some absolutes, some certainties, in life.

What pleased me much about Gray's book was that he persuaded me that my inability to understand Kafka's prose was not wholly due to my own denseness, or to waning powers of concentration, but can be explained by Kafka's deliberate ambiguity. His technique of dual description, it seems, was that of what the Germans call a *Vexierbild*, namely those drawings which provide a double image according as one follows the outline of the objects primarily depicted, or traces the other outline of the space that intervenes. I see what he means, since I can recall old political caricatures in which drawings of the murder of Gordon displayed, if regarded otherwise, the unmistakable profile of Mr. Gladstone. "The mystery," Mr. Gray writes, "that still envelops the scene is of the kind that must accompany any supposed contact with spiritual forces." I quite see that.

Kafka, like most malcontents, is worried by an abiding, if causeless, sense of guilt. He suffers terribly from being unable to determine where his guilt lies, and is inclined to "draw unfavourable deductions from simple facts." That way persecution mania lies. So unquiet does his conscience become that there are moments when he doubts the truth of his own identity. "Am I," he murmurs, "the self I think I am?" This feeling of basic unreality, when a man begins to doubt whether it is in fact his own heart thumping, inevitably leads to distrust "regarding the propriety of one's own existence." The people around him are positive that they really are what they seem to be, namely Josef Sebenik or Frau Schultz. But Kafka, doubting whether he really is Kafka, derives the impression that he is apart from all these folk, peeping into the tavern kitchen through a crack in the door. This adds to his sense of estrangement.

"Man cannot live," writes Kafka in his *Reflections on Sin and Suffering*, "without a permanent trust in something indestructible in himself, although both the indestructible element and the trust may remain permanently hidden from him." In *The Castle* his hero is desperately seeking for some external confirmation which will bring him certainty. In the end he realises that his quest is hopeless and appears to find tranquility, and even satisfaction, in its abandonment. "It is a novel," writes Ronald Gray, "about a man's entry into a state of grace." I am grateful for this explanation.

4

At dinner V. is angry because one of the ship's officers has had his hair cut in a style of which she disapproves. I say that it really ought not to be a matter of distress to her whether a Dutch officer in a Rotterdam Lloyd liner has a becoming or an unbecoming haircut. She answers that there is an underlying principle involved and one of such essential importance that to disregard it may lead to the devaluation of all that we have inherited from Greece, Rome, Byzantium, Persia, the Arabs, Pico della Mirandola, the Marquise de Rambouillet and Matthew Arnold. I must surely have noticed that the officer, although the front of his head is quite well designed— possessing forehead, eyes, nose, mouth and chin aligned with adequate symmetry—has, in regard to the back of his head, been less endowed. In fact the back of his head is flat and narrow and its junction with the neck is an inelegant junction, recalling that, not of a swan, but of a drake. In the days of civilisation, when taste and skill were applied to enhancing the merits of human personality and concealing its defects, the barber would have devoted his art to mitigating these mistakes that Nature had made. But now that we have entered the epoch of the common man the tendency is to cultivate uniformity rather than appropriateness, and thus the ship's officer had been given an American crop, which of all crops is, to the back of his particular head, the least suited. This, she says, is illustrative of what the Americans are doing to civilisations older than their own, shipping them, cropping them, distorting them, and in fact reducing them to their own mass standard of the Hemingway male. There is something in what she says, but I am saddened when I hear Americans criticised. They are so gentle really, so sensitive, and so subject to spasms of loneliness and self-distrust.

After dinner we go to the swimming pool, where there is to be a pillow fight under the arc lights. Those entering the contest succeed each other in heats. A stout white spar or pole is fixed across the bath; the competitors, each armed with a small pillow, straddle the end of the bar and then hitch themselves along it from opposite directions until they meet in the centre. When they are close enough they shake hands formally and then the whistle blows. Seldom do they have more than one pillow-slash at each other, since the very act of slashing upsets their balance and they topple off sideways into the pool. This is a perfect instance of Bergson's definition of the "imposition of the automatic" as an occasion for laughter; these men, so intent, so muscular, so careful, suddenly lose control of their balance and tumble like inanimate puppets into the bath below. We do not wait for the conclusion of the contest, but it looks as if the young American giant is bound to win, since he is so huge and godlike that when his antagonists see him hitching his mighty thighs along the pole towards them, they fall like ripe apples into the water, paralysed by fear.

As we walk back along the deck we pause as always to gaze at the stars. V. remarks that one of the mistakes of Nature is to have provided the earth with but a single satellite when she might just as well have given us the nine that she accorded to Jupiter. How wonderful it would be, when ploughing on a calm night through the Indian Ocean, if we could see nine moons above us, radiant in the luminous sky. They would whirl around us like globes, like crescents, or like gibbous lights. I remark that if this were so, it would be even more difficult than it is today to calculate the tides at London Bridge. Moreover, even as the Pacific Ocean was formed by the moon leaving us, so also might two whole continents swing away from us to form these satellites. "It might be America!" she remarks hopefully. "Or Eurasia," I add with equal hope. What I like about V. is that she is always having odd ideas. What have I done, O mighty Poseidon! to deserve so entrancing a companion?

She is disappointed that on this journey we have seen no phosphorus. When she travelled out to join me in Persia in 1926 she had gone by P. & O. to Bombay, and both wake and prow throughout her journey had been illuminated by phophorescent waves of beauty. It is all due, so Mrs. Carson informs me, to the absence of shrimps, or rather to the fact that in this area of the ocean shrimps lose their attraction for each other and that their passion is spent. The phosphorus, it seems, is occasioned by the unrequited ardour of the female meganyctiphanes; in these deep waters either her ardour has been requited already, or is less overtly ardent than in the Arabian Sea. Mrs. Carson, I have noticed, possesses both a lyrical and a scientific disposition:

Out over the plankton meadows [she writes] of the North Atlantic the dry twitter of the phalaropes is heard for the first time.

We ourselves have heard no twitters, whether wet or dry. But V. at dawn today did see a white bird with a long neck

flashing, probably a strayed cormorant from Réunion or Madagascar.

Wednesday, February 27

It is rough and the pool has become a *Wellenbad* again.
The log registers 525 miles since noon yesterday and it looks
as if we should this time pass Mauritius in the dark. We have
a drink with the captain before luncheon. He admits that there
has been some trouble with the Indonesian staff but he does
not regard it as serious. They used, he tells us with a sigh, to
be such a happy crew, looking forward to the day when they
would have saved enough to retire to Madura, build a little
house, plant a few banana trees, and live happily ever after
with their wives and children. But recently the Communists
have arrived to assure them that they are wage slaves, trodden
under the heel of the whites, whose arrogance and cruelty is
now a thing of the past. When simple folk such as they are are
assured that they are profoundly miserable and exploited, they
begin to develop all the symptoms of melancholia. It is not
that there is any danger of mass desertion, since the Indonesians on board are well aware that their present job, what with
salary, maintenance, tips, and other forms of gain, is highly
lucrative. But they are no longer as gay or friendly as they
used to be, and this saddens the captain's generous heart. He
tells us that on one voyage the Rotterdam Lloyd made the
experiment of engaging Italians to replace the Indonesians; on
reaching Sydney the Italians deserted, were arrested by the

police of New South Wales, and had to be repatriated by air at the company's expense.

We work all day. The sun sets in a blaze of glory and darkness almost immediately descends. After dinner we sit with the Stedalls and talk with them about cormorants, plankton, meganyctiphanes and other protozoa. Stedall knows more about such things than we do ourselves.

5

Thursday, February 28

The water in the pool this morning is almost unpleasantly muggy. The air-commodore, who rises early, ascends to the bridge and discusses with the navigating officers the state of the weather and the prospects for the day, assures me that the temperature of the sea this morning is over 80 degrees. We are out of the tropics, having crossed the Steenbokskeerkring, or Tropic of Capricorn. But it seems that a hot current runs from Malaya all the way down to the south of Madagascar and keeps the thermometer high. The sea around us actually flashes with vivacity. The log at noon tells us that we have been 521 miles since yesterday. It is in truth with giant paces that this ship, in sunlight and starlight, strides from Asia to Africa. We are perfectly cool in our cabins and we spend the whole happy day working, V. on her *Grande Mademoiselle* and I reading Kierkegaard.

V.'s only complaint against the authorities in this ship is that they do not provide the passengers with sufficient information. Why, for instance, did they not confess on the way out that the mail bags had at Cape Town been put in error upon the steamer and not flown back to Rotterdam by KLM? Why were we not told of the cyclone which, by prowess of navigation, we avoided when in these very waters on the way to Ceylon? Why is there no barometer on board, or at least a notice to tell us of the daily temperature of air and sea and the prospects for the next twenty-four hours? V. says that the captain and staff of the *Willem Ruys* do not treat their passengers as rational beings. While taking immense trouble to provide for our security, health, cleanliness, comfort, and amusement, they fail to give us the interesting information which we so much require and deserve. It is on this, their reticence, that ship rumours feed. She says that the officers of the mercantile marine are akin to hospital matrons, publishers, and government departments, in that they regard information, and even truthfulness, as "bad" for their patients, authors, and subjects. I think she is right, but mankind must be judged and managed, not according to the standards of reason possessed by the educated, but by the emotions of the uneducated, which dominate ninety-nine per cent of mankind.

Friday, March 1

We are now southeast of Madagascar, in those waters where that persistent and talented ichthyologist, Professor Smith, discovered the coelacanth after five years of surmise and research. We are also, I suppose, in the region of Lemuria, or Gondwana land, the lost continent which once united Africa, Asia, and

India and where now this lovely ocean seethes. I read Kierke-gaard happily, becoming more and more concentrated on the essential Self, and less prone to speculate about lost continents and prehistoric fish.

Leonard Forman, the herbalist, comes up to have a drink with us, and to return Wurtzburg's mighty tome on Raffles which I had lent him. He tells us that when he is installed in the herbarium at Kew he receives from time to time from remote missionaries in Malaya or Celebes dried specimens of plants which correspond to no known genus. His delight at receiving these desiccated particles is equal to that of Professor Smith when he met his coelacanth. He shows us some of the photographs he has taken in the jungle. We do not dare to ask him the names of the trees and shrubs depicted, since, unlike Confucius, he has a disregard for ordinary names. It would be like asking my son Ben, in his capacity of editor of *The Burlington Magazine*, what the drawings of Paul Klee "are intended to represent."

When I go down to dress for dinner I pass on the staircase an unknown Englishman who exclaims to me as I pass him "South Africa 521." I assume at first that he is informing me of our exact distance from Durban, or possibly of the rate of exchange now being offered by the Suid-Afrikaanse Reserve-bank for the Las Palmas peseta. He notices my momentary perplexity and adds, "Just got the latest Test Match report from the wireless operator." I am annoyed by this. While I have my delicious bath of steaming Indian Ocean water, and my even more delicious shower bath of sweet water, I examine the cause and nature of my annoyance.

Always, in such sessions of self-examination, I begin by

seeking for the motive of vanity, since it is invariably present on occasions of causeless irritation and must be identified and isolated before one investigates other motives. I had been irritated in the first place by the assumption on the part of a total stranger that I must necessarily share his interest. He was taking me for granted as an ordinary elderly compatriot of the public-school type, and I dislike being taken for granted or placed in a category. To that extent my irritation could be ascribed to personal vanity, or even conceit, and since I take much pride in my natural modesty, I felt appropriately ashamed. Yet this was not the only explanation.

If the man had remarked, "It seems cooler this evening," or, "It looks as if we were in for a rough night," he would also have been taking it for granted that we were sharers in a common experience. Yet I should not have felt the slightest annoyance. Why should this reference to a cricket score have set my nerves jangling? Had I, when descending the staircase, remarked to him *"O! L'île Bourbon—fatidiques rivages!"* (since we had passed the latitude of Réunion during the early hours of the morning and I had without success been trying to get this line right in my memory) he would have been justifiably outraged. Why therefore should I have been annoyed that he, returning from the wireless cabin on the top deck, should have repeated to me a sentence which, in his head, was also running?

I realised that his remark had touched an ancient wound. It had revived the pang of humiliation which, more than half a century ago, I used so often to feel when confronted with my inability deftly to play games with hand, or toe, or bat, or ball. But surely, I reflected, it is irrational at my age to be wounded by the memory of a humiliation experienced when I was at school. It was absurd for a grown man to feel, when descending the staircase of the *Willem Ruys* in the middle of the Indian Ocean, the same stab of pain that he had been caused, between 1896 and 1904, in the playroom of The Grange, Folkestone, or on the fields of the Wellington College, Berkshire. There must surely exist some more serious and deeper occasion for my annoyance.

I am a patriotic person. I believe that on the whole my fellow countrymen are more honest, more kindly, more efficient, and more inventive than the inhabitants of other countries. I care deeply for their repute. When they behave out of character (as in the Suez Canal escapade) or manifest too overtly their distaste for thought, I feel perturbed. Thus the interest that they take in Test Matches (which seem to me to occur with undue frequency and to be repeated month by month in every area of the Commonwealth and Empire) and their facile assumption that all other Englishmen, whatever may be their age or occupation, should share this interest, strike me as unintelligent. What can it possibly signify, I often ask, if eleven men from South Africa strike, cast, propel, or catch a ball with greater force or dexterity than eleven other men from Middlesex? It saddens me that my countrymen should be so indifferent to the important and so fascinated by the transitory; so unaware of the durable and so preoccupied with the immediate. As I fixed my little black evening tie, I found myself becoming angry all over again. Yet surely Plato, and even Socrates, to say nothing of the mighty Pindar, would have cared about who won the wrestling match at Olympia, and would have despised the man who had forgotten who won the quarter mile last year at the Isthmian? And surely Rufinus would have thought it eccentric and conceited if one of his colleagues in the foreign office at Byzantium had manifested indifference as to whether the Blues or the Greens had vanquished on Thursday in the Hippodrome?

I went down to dinner feeling much dissatisfied with myself. I explained my state of mind to V. She did not approve of my irritation, attributing it to the tricky arrogance of the intellectual. It was quite natural, she said, that this man should have assumed I was concerned with Test Matches, and it was friendly of him to pass on to me the information which he had so recently obtained. It would have been far more strange had I assumed that retired majors of the Indian Army should have been interested in Leconte de Lisle and that in any case football and cricket gave intense pleasure to countless decent people, who were not necessarily more stupid than I was, and who were the very stuff of which the British character was composed. "It would have saved the world much suffering," she remarked, "had Hitler been as interested in Test Matches as he was in Lebensraum."

On deck after dinner I encountered Sidney Culpeper. He took me by the arm, a gesture which I regarded as irrelevant and indeed out of character. "Isn't it splendid," he said. "I hear that the South Africans are all out for 521."

XI. MORGENSTER

1

Saturday, March 2

Were I a young man, I should spend several months learning Danish (a difficult language) in order to read Kierkegaard in the original. I should take a room in a pastor's house at Helsingor; I should feed on whey and cheese and soused herrings; I should go to church on Sundays; I should spend eight hours a day studying the works of the prophet; and on Saturday afternoons I should take the train into Copenhagen and ask the professor of philology to explain to me what Kierkegaard really meant when he used such conflicting words.

On Saturday nights, in order to clear myself of *Indesluttedhed*, I should visit the Tivoli garden in the company of some clear-minded friend of my own age. Garlanded with the white willow and the balsam poplar, redolent of sweetbriar and heartsease, we would ride on Jutland ponies together around the circuses, or swing in the gondolas of high balloons, or snap little rifles at the red, the magenta, and the golden balls which dance in the spray of fountains, or just sit under the laburnum trees drinking beer and brandy, discussing the nature of happiness, and listening to the brazen band. Then back I should return before midnight by the train to Helsingor; from my bare room I should gaze across the Sund at the lights of Halsingborg twinkling opposite and ponder, as I lay in my hard white bed, upon the solemn Swedes.

It might have happened, of course, that as I penetrated deeper and deeper into the life, the character, and the ideas of Sören Kierkegaard, I should have ceased to revere him as the prophet of existentialism, as the victim of the twin passions of despair and dread, as the champion and martyr of spiritual salvation. I might have developed a resistance against him, concluding that he was a repugnant egoist, a monomaniac who, had he not on October 2, 1855, dropped dead in the street at the age of forty-two, would, like Nietzsche, have taken leave of his mind.

There is much evidence to suggest that from his early childhood Kierkegaard was a stricken soul. His father, who was fifty-six years old at the time of his birth, was a fierce old gentleman obsessed by Hebraic theology and, in that he had seduced a servant girl, perpetually tortured by a sense of guilt. To the young Kierkegaard his father loomed as the personification of an all-powerful and vengeful Jehovah. An occasion appears to have occurred when the boy caught his father in a moment of abasement, ignominy, or degradation; he was shattered by this experience: it shook his confidence and caused "a sudden loss of support" which, as the behaviourists contend, is one of the few terrors with which all infants, whether they be born in Boston or at Enontekiö, are instinctively endowed.

As an adolescent Sören Kierkegaard indulged in perhaps imaginary dissipation, but on coming of age he recovered his religion and became engaged to Regine Olsen, the daughter of a respectable bourgeois family of Copenhagen. By then, however, the sense of mission, the conviction that he was destined for ever to exist as an outsider, or *"extraordinarius,"* the passionate desire to live alone with his God had come to cloud his affections. It may have been also that he then discovered that he was afflicted by some hidden illness or deformity, which he called his "thorn in the flesh" and which rendered him unworthy or incapable of conjugal relationship. In any case he broke off his engagement, much to the scandal of the Copenhagen bourgeoisie, and resolved, as a martyr-prophet, to devote the rest of his life to attacking his fellow citizens, to sundering himself from the crowd, to denouncing the hypocrisy of the Lutheran Church, to assailing all his former teachers and all his father's friends, to isolating himself within a high wall of unpopularity, to fighting passionately against his repressed atheism, to stripping himself of all convention and all rational habit and thus to stand naked and solitary in the presence of his own particular Jah. He persuaded himself that his betrayal of the unhappy Regine was justified by his belief that his duty to this God stood above all conventional honesty, that compassion was no more than "the most paltry of social dexterities," and that an exceptional genius, such as he was, had every right to practice what he called "the teleological suspension of the ethical." I quite see that, as a young man, I might have been disgusted rather than impressed by such arrogance of temperament. Yet it is also possible that my character might have been deepened and much improved by the study of this sombre, suffering soul.

"My whole life," wrote Kierkegaard, "is an epigram calculated to make people aware." Aware of what? Of the futility, in the first place, of what he called the "aesthetic" view of life, the belief in "immediacy," in the finite, in ordinary feeling and enjoyment. A man, if he is to fulfil his existence, must "commit" himself to an infinite idea, he "must hold fast to one thought." He must realise that the intellectual faculties are irrelevant to essential existence and that "faith" must always remain a difficult and dangerous choice which "reason" repudiates. "There is," he wrote, "struggle to the death between existence and abstract thought." Religion and philosophy were enemies, since the basis of religion was belief in original sin, which was a matter of revelation and not of logic. Truth is not to be found through learning or disputation but by an unquenchable thirst for God, a "whole-souled passion for infinity." He believed that, from that moment of revelation when he had experienced his Damascus on the heaths of Jutland, he had been "bewitched by God," as other men are said to have been bewitched by demons or fairies. To be satisfied with oneself, as oneself, is "demoniacal." The true individual, the man who penetrates to the secret of his existence, must cultivate inwardness, earnestness, and responsibility. An individual is not the universally human only, he is also an "exception"; he should strive to be the concrete embodiment of what all men have it in them to become. Life is but a secondhand affair, compounded of conventions, habits, and feelings; existence is something more than life; it is the Self stripped of all disguises and possessions. To reach that condition, to stand naked in the face of God, a man must cultivate the noble passions of despair and dread. Otherwise he will never achieve salvation.

Kierkegaard set great store by the proud passion of despair. "My grief," he wrote, "is my castle, which, like an eagle's nest, is built high up among the mountain peaks among the clouds; nothing can capture it." "I despair," he wrote again, "therefore I am capable of good." All forms of despair do not redeem; there is the demoniacal form which persuades a man to rest satisfied with his apparent self; there is the superficial form which seeks to find in external or finite circumstances the causes of distress. Redeeming despair is "a hot incitement, or a cold fire, a gnawing canker, the movement of which is constantly inward, deeper and deeper in impotent self-consumption." A man who experiences true despair is in despair, not because he has failed to achieve self-fulfilment, but because he is so constituted as to be unable to gain this self-fulfilment. True despair, therefore, is not despair about anything external but despair about oneself. It is by this that a man comes to realise "a self that is gained by infinite abstraction from the external; a naked, abstract self, in contrast to the clothed self of immediacy." Never to be aware of this transcendent self, says Kierkegaard, is to be guilty of "ethical stupidity."

Religious faith requires the conquest of reason, and therefore to believe in God obliges a man to take a terrible leap across the abyss which separates the rational from the transcendental. No man can make this choice, can undergo this frightful risk, unless impelled, not merely by the passion of despair, but also by the passion of dread. Kierkegaard was extremely subject to dread. "The whole of existence," he wrote, "frightens me, from the smallest fly to the mystery of the

Incarnation." Dread, he contends, is different from fear, since the latter relates to something definite, whereas dread is permanent, obscure, and dark. It is founded on a sense of original sin, and those men who do not possess this sense are akin to animals, who exist without a conscience or an aim. Dread is a sensation, almost a physical sensation. He compares it to the dizziness experienced by a human being when deprived of support or when he becomes aware of the vast chasm of the infinite that opens below and in front of him. Dread is both the desire for what one fears and the fear of what one desires; it occurs at the point of junction between reality and possibility; it serves to reveal the individual to himself and indicates to him the terrifying alternative between redemption and eternal punishment, between freedom and damnation. Dread is therefore a means of revelation. "He who has learnt rightly how to dread has learnt a most important thing." "The greater the dread, the greater the man." "Dread is the possibility of salvation, laying bare as it does all finite aims and disclosing all their deceptions." At the same time it is an egoistic or self-regarding emotion and if wrongly apprehended becomes "a womanish debility in which freedom swoons."

It is difficult to be sure with Kierkegaard, who often advocated contrasting solutions and who was apt to use the same word with different meanings, whether in fact he regarded dread as a useful or a disturbing element. His later disciple, Martin Heidegger, is more positive and more lucid. He asserts that dread, or *Angst,* is a mood rather than a feeling and represents the recoil of the self from the external world. It renders the individual conscious of his own insecurity and isolation in a possibly hostile world: it forces him to be responsible for himself, to choose between what is authentic in himself and what is unauthentic or assumed. It creates a feeling of loss of support, an impression of sliding as in some nightmare into the abyss, and tends to induce a man to doubt the truth of reality, even the truth of his own reality. To Heidegger, *Angst* is not, as it was with Kierkegaard, a special psychological accident, but an ethological fact, a component of all human character. It is clear that these thinkers believe that without this dread of failing to find fulfilment, a man is condemned to remain unfulfilled.

I find this a sobering reflection.

2

It is assuredly cooler. The air-commodore, who visits the bridge every morning before 6.00 A.M. and then plays deck quoits with his elder daughter, assures me that we are now beyond the Malayan current and shall soon come under the influence of the Arctic air stream. By noon we are on a line with Durban and have come 513 miles in the last twenty-four hours. Desiring something at once more robust and more compassionate than either Kierkegaard or Heidegger, I read William James's *Selected Papers*. I enjoy his New England briskness, certainty, and optimism. He shares my distaste for Rousseau, Obermann, and all escapists and defeatists. He does something to restore my troubled self-esteem.

After dinner we talk to the Stedalls about plovers' eggs. We have to put the clock back another hour; for me this always seems a denial, of at least a curtailment, of the living day; I do it with reluctance.

Sunday, March 3

During the night there was an electric storm of great intensity. V. had tried to wake me, but as usual I was plunged in so deep a slumber that she felt that to rouse me to consciousness would make such a noise that it might disturb Mr. and Mrs. Hyams, who inhabit the adjoining cabin. The storm broke about midnight and continued till about 2.00 or 3.00 in the morning. It was accompanied by torrential rain, but not by any hurricane, cyclone, or typhoon. The lightning flashed and shivered continuously and V. says it turned the ocean the colour of leaden blue. It was so intense that it put our wireless out of action and stopped all the electric clocks on board. I was sad at having missed this experience since we hate not sharing excitements.

At breakfast the air-commodore informs me that we can see the coast of Africa, and when we go on deck before luncheon there, on the starboard side, is a faint water-colour wash of lowlands backed by a faint blue line of hills. We must be opposite Port Elizabeth. We have done excellently through the storm, having covered 562 miles which, as far as I can recall, is the record for this voyage.

We are accompanied by a new species of gull—birds with yellow heads, elongated necks, and a rapid gliding motion. Stedall tells us that they are a species of gannet. He adds that there are two albatrosses sailing in our wake and tells us that these will follow the *Willem Ruys* until she reaches a certain degree of latitude, when they will swing round again and glide back towards the south and the Antarctic winds. To amuse Mrs. Gibson I bring on deck the pyjamas that Elvira made me from the handkerchief maps provided to airmen in case they were brought down in unknown territory. My own maps, which have faded much in the wash, depict in detail the islands of the empire of Japan. While Mrs. Gibson is engaged in studying my pyjamas and seeking to find the site of Hiroshima, I release upon the deck the mechanical serpent that I had bought from a street vendor in Singapore. It writhes atrociously and Mrs. Gibson recoils in panic. She hands me back my pyjamas and tells me that she herself possesses a blue nightgown upon which is embroidered in coloured silks a map of the Isle of Wight. "Does it include Bournemouth?" I ask her. "Certainly not!" she answers.

The weather, which has been rough all morning, changes suddenly and we enter calm seas. Again on our starboard side is a line of distant hills. V. is enraged at perceiving that other ships, mere cargo vessels or tankers, sail far closer to the coast than we do. She considers it inconsiderate of the captain to steer a course so far from land since he should realise that his passengers, having for days gazed out on the unvintaged sea, would be glad of a sight of the habitations and the works of man. As she utters this complaint I see a monster rise for a short two minutes from the deep. It must, I suppose, have been a whale or a sea elephant, but it turned slumberously in the trough of a wave and was gone before I could adjust my binoculars.

It is almost cold after sunset and the women appear for dinner with rich stoles of fur encasing their brown and naked shoulders. We are sitting in the saloon when we are accosted by an elegant young woman who introduces herself as Mrs. Firbank and asks for advice. She explains that her husband, who has remained behind in Malaya, was a cousin of Ronald Firbank and has now inherited his papers. When Ronald died some twenty years ago he left everything to his sister for life. This spinster, it seems, was an eccentric woman, who kept in tin boxes stored in a warehouse a vast accumulation of objects, including every scrap of paper that her brother had either written or possessed. She also had the habit (which is mentioned in Havelock Ellis) of ordering a dozen of everything that she bought. There would thus be twelve packets of hairpins, twelve tubes of tooth paste, and twelve knitted jumpers from Inverness. This elderly sister had died quite recently, and the husband of Mrs. Firbank had become residuary legatee. She was travelling home to deal with this inheritance and could we advise her what to do with Ronald Firbank's manuscripts and correspondence?

We tell her that she must be watchful, suspicious, and alert. There may be sharks who are on the look out for such material, who might hear what had occurred and who might pounce upon her in the hope of extracting unpublished material of which they would dispose to bibliophiles for many dollars. I was no expert in such matters and had only known Ronald Firbank very slightly. I advised her, on arrival in London, to write to Osbert Sitwell, who had been a friend and admirer of Ronald Firbank, and to ask him whether he knew of any active and honourable research-worker, who would help her to go through the papers and to decide on their disposal. "What name did you say?" she asks me innocently. I can well picture the astounded indignation of Edith, Sachie, Reresby, and indeed of Osbert himself, had they overheard this question. I retire to my cabin, write a letter to Osbert explaining the circumstances, and hand the envelope to Mrs. Firbank correctly directed to him at Renishaw. Having accomplished this good deed, I go down to dinner.

3

Monday, March 4

We come on deck at 7.30 and find that we are approaching Table Bay. The great precipices along the coast, which I gather are called "The Twelve Apostles," face the Antarctic with glittering calm. We turn towards the harbour but are delayed slightly, since another ship, having a man on board who needs urgent medical attention, demands and receives priority. So the *Willem Ruys* dawdles outside and we lean over the taffrail watching the penguins floating and ducking in our wake. I had always imagined the penguins to be tall bipeds, upright, sedate, and aligned in rows—seeming from a distance to be a company of Napoleon's old guard, arrayed in uniforms of white facings with blue jackets behind. But these animals are no more impressive than the ducks in St. James's Park. I accuse Stedall of having supplied us with false information. He says I am thinking of the pictures of the great auk or of the king penguins that breed in the Antarctic. These are the little Adélie penguins and almost another species. I am always impressed when experts are so considerate to the ignorant. Not that Stedall has ever pretended to be an expert; it is merely that he knows more about the creatures of the deep than either V. or I.

A cloth of cloud hangs over Table Mountain, sliding off the surface of the table and seeping downwards into the crags and precipices, "loitering," as Oenone observed of the mist on Mount Ida, "slowly drawn." It gives a West Highland touch to the scene, but across the bay the Hottentot Mountains, which were veiled on our previous visit, are this morning sharp and blue. Through my binoculars I scan the architecture of the town, which seems to me even more brainless than it did before. The redeemed foreshore is a wasteland between the harbour and the original edge of the town and constitutes at present *le plus vague des terrains vagues*. When they come to build upon it they will, I feel sure, erect rectangular blocks of houses, not realising that so high and dominant a background requires a flat foreground. There are three elephants strolling miserably up and down this deserted plain and from time to time sniffing with their trunks at the wild camomile that is sparsely scattered across the surface. But they are unlike the elephants of Ceylon; they belong to a recently disembarked circus and have been let out for their morning stroll. It angers me that this, one of the loveliest sites that I have ever seen, should be condemned to desecration by the ignorance of man.

We pass the narrow gap in the outer breakwater at 9.00 and are tied up to the quay at 9.30. We sit in the smoking room while the mail is being distributed and are there accosted by a woman and two men from the South African Broadcasting Company who desire to interview us. I go down to my cabin and sit on the chair while the interviewer perches himself on the bunk and the engineer (a slim and slightly bearded man) squats on the floor with his batteries, his flexes, and his other apparatus. I give smug and conciliatory replies to questions regarding the future of Indonesia and Ghana and whether I approve of the revolt of the external proletariat. My opinion on such subjects is as valueless as my views on thermodynamics, but I give it gracefully and reassuringly. I return to the smoking room where I find that our letters have been distributed. V., who has had many letters from home and is impatient to open them, is with her accustomed good manners being polite to the lady from the South African B.B.C. She then retires to her cabin and submits in her turn to a similar interview, which concentrates less upon the colour question than upon the merits of Kirstenbosch as compared to other botanical gardens.

I wait for her in the smoking room and have just started opening my letters when Peter Lycett Green appears. He has forgiven us for having, in momentary confusion, chucked him on our previous visit and has come to take us round and give us luncheon at Morgenster. He has been suffering from asthma and does not look well, but then asthmatic people vary in their appearance from hour to hour. I give him an orange juice, which is all the drink one can obtain when in harbour, and we sit there talking about life and letters until V. returns. Then at about 11.00 we at last disembark and enter Peter's car, which contains a poodle and Mr. Burnham.

He takes us straight to Kirstenbosch, not to the main gardens, which we had seen before, but to the adjoining nursery. We find it most interesting. He shows us the frames where, in little pans, they cultivate and propagate the fantastic vegetation of the Karroo desert. They are the strangest little plants that I have ever seen. At first sight they look like a group of fourteen or fifteen different sized pebbles mainly of a brown or dull grey colour. On closer inspection one sees that they are in fact growing plants, capable of expansion and division, and some of them bearing tiny little scabs on their surface which are no mere abrasions but organs of generation.

We then drive on to Groot Constantia. It stands in an amphitheatre of precipices and blue mountains, surrounded by vineyards and with a view across the Cape flats below it to the line of the Hottentot Mountains. It is approached through an avenue of gnarled oaks. Groot Constantia formed part of the estate acquired in the seventeenth century by Simon van der Stel. It included such other farmhouses as Klein Constantia, Hoop op Constantia, Witte Boomen, and Buitenverwachting, which is the Dutch for "Beyond all expectation." The present house was built by Hendrik Cloete in 1790, the architect being Louis Michel Thibault, pupil of Gabriel, and the plasterwork and decoration being executed by the German, Anton Anreith. The house was destroyed by fire in 1925 but reconstructed from the original designs and arranged and furnished as a national museum. One passes under the great white gable by a carved teak front door, above which is a niche and statue, into cool dark rooms, floored with Batavian tiles, roofed with neat beams, and containing specimens of Cape Dutch furniture and a few pictures. The stoep outside gives on to a terrace from which one descends by a few steps to a small garden. In the centre there is a placid pool enlivened by a single blue water lily standing pertly erect from its flat leaves. Beyond this is the wine store, a long white building with plaster carvings of urchins and grapes above the doorway and inside vast vats of highly polished wood and brass. All the buildings are white-washed, but as the surface of the walls are uneven the bright sun does not strike uniformly, but with all manner of shades and undertones. The roofs are thatched with the South African reed, which is unlike our straw thatching at home, since it is smooth and gives the impression of a moleskin cloth. As an example of simplicity, suitability, and elegance I should place Groot Constantia among the masterpieces of domestic architecture. Had the town planners of Cape Town developed the Dutch theme they could have created one of the most beautiful cities on this earth in place of the Victorian and Detroit jumble that now disfigures the site. V. and I again become angry at such lack of intelligence and taste.

We then drive to Morgenster, which is Peter's own house. It also is in the Cape Dutch style, with a fine gable enriched with baroque plasterwork, a stoep, and a library, drawing room, and dining room, in which his furniture, books, and pictures look fine indeed. He shows us his garden. It is a gardener's garden, displaying specimen plants and trees in little beds surrounded by stone copings. It is the wrong time of year, corresponding to our English August, and but few of these precious plants are still in flower. But V. enjoys it all immensely, since like most professional gardeners she derives ecstasy from reading the labels. We then have an excellent luncheon and are given Niederberg 1954, as good a white wine as I have tasted since I lived in Germany.

Peter drives us back to Cape Town and we stop at a shop which sells curios and other souvenirs designed for tourists. It contains Zulu shields, assegais, and knobkerries; views of Table Mountain painted upon slabs of local wood; lion's claws made into neat little brooches; and a variety of bags and belts constructed of zebra hides, and the skins of pythons and other reptiles. I am assailed by boat fuss, and V. with her usual unselfishness tears herself away from these delights, although unwillingly. We drive back to the dock, say good-bye to Peter, and clamber on board at 3.15.

We read our letters. As usual there are long, vivid, detailed and amusing letters from Ben and Nigel. Few men as busy as they are would take the trouble to write to their travelling parents at such length. We are grateful. Nigel says that the chairman and the local committee in Bournemouth East have refused to admit any new members to the Conservative Association, fearing that many of those who wish to retain Nigel as their sitting Member might outvote the caucus. I doubt whether they are legally entitled to establish a closed shop in this way. In any case their action is unfair and indicates that, not being sure of the justice of their attitude, they are determined to adopt totalitarian methods. I am disgusted and sad.

We cast off at 5.00. "There, you see," comments V., "I told you there was heaps of time, and we could easily have stayed another hour at that nice shop." It is not that she really cherishes a love for assegais or lion-claw brooches, but that she likes collecting her numerous Christmas presents well in advance and assumes that the simple recipients will welcome such outlandish objects. We watch the parapets of South Africa receding in the evening sun. It is cold and I wear my ordinary dinner jacket and not my white dinner jacket in the evening. Again we put the clock back an hour, which for me is always a small despair.

4

Tuesday, March 5

I spend the day reading, for the second time, *The Unquiet Grave* by Palinurus. I am aware that Cyril Connolly, when he wrote it, was in a melancholy mood. He was saddened by the war, obsessed by the invasion and occupation of France, and distraught by personal troubles. It was the memory of one of Virgil's loveliest hexameters that gave to the book both its title and its pseudonym. Yet it depresses me that this beautiful study should, like *The Waste Land,* have exercised so debilitating an effect upon the wills of the young.

I remember that two or three years ago I went down to King's School, Canterbury, to give a talk to their sixth form. When my lecture was over, I was shown the way to the station by one of the prefects, an intelligent youth, who had recently obtained a scholarship at Oxford. The great cathedral loomed behind us and in front, red and white and green, were the lights of British Railways. He told me as we passed through the town that the elder boys really enjoyed it when men of letters came down from London and gave them lectures. "It takes us," he said, "out of ourselves." I was pleased by this and asked him who, among living writers, he would most wish to hear. "Mr. Cyril Connolly," he answered. I did not suggest to him that of all the authors whom I knew Cyril Connolly was the one least calculated to "take" young people "out of themselves." I promised to approach the pundit and, in so far as I recollect, he was invited and went.

Unlike myself, Cyril Connolly is burdened with a sense of original sin. "Those of us," he writes, "who have been brought up as Christians and have lost our faith have retained our sense of sin without the saving belief in redemption." What is so depressing about him is that he believes the sense of sin to be a good thing and not a bad thing. He calls it "the taproot of the unconscious" and contends that Goethe and Voltaire are the only two first-class writers who never possessed it. I could think of others, but the point is well made.

I have noticed that those who believe in original sin tend, not only to deplore the evil of this earth, but also to love and cherish guilt feelings within themselves. It has always puzzled me why Cyril Connolly, who has afforded so much pleasure and given so much opportunity to younger writers, should nurture a load of guilt. True it is that on one occasion he filched three avocado pears from Willy Maugham's garden at Cap Ferrat, but this is not an episode that should weigh upon the conscience of a humanist. Yet he can write of "the accumulation of guilt and remorse which, like a garbage-can, I carry through life." Or of his "guilt-feeling about not being at work." I cannot believe that a man of his gifts and vivacity, educated at Eton and Balliol, can, except in moments of ill-health, feel any profound remorse for having dawdled in cafés in Paris or stayed in bed too long playing with lemurs. Such people, conscious of their own talents, are always on the verge of a masterpiece and suffer much from the intuition that their masterpieces, such as *The Unquiet Grave* or the *Journal Intime,* may prove to be confessions of their own lack of will power. It is not something that is due to external circumstance, since Connolly may be confident of writing an even greater work before he dies; it is a matter of internal humours and secretions.

Such accidie is in any case deplorable since it brings with it subsidiary distrusts and disappointments and weakens courage. Thus Connolly, like Baudelaire, is unable to contemplate himself without dismay. He sees himself as "a fat, slothful, querulous, greedy, impotent carcase," which is a most self-conscious thing to see. He is often visited by what he calls *Angst,* meaning thereby Kierkegaard's dread; namely a sullen combination of ennui, remorse, and anxiety. "Ennui," he writes, "is a condition of not fulfilling our potentialities; remorse of not having fulfilled them; and anxiety of not being able to fulfil them." What is so terrible about *Angst,* he tells us, is that it generates hatred, which is "crystallised fear." This is a suggestive comment. Does it explain why the nineteenth-century malcontents were merely melancholy, whereas the twentieth-century malcontents are indignant? This is a question which, as Mr. Colin Wilson would say, must be examined in a subsequent chapter.

Yet Connolly is no irredeemable pessimist. He regards escapist philosophies, even the teaching of the Buddha, as "a desperate stratagem of failure, the failure of men to be men." He believes that the pursuit of happiness must never be abandoned and regrets that we have lost the old Delphic formula which taught men that happiness could be found in the insistent practice of temperance and self-knowledge. "These are now," he writes, but not despairingly, "beyond the reach of ordinary people, who, owing to the pursuit of violent sensation, can no longer distinguish between pleasure and pain." He leaves us with the discouraging apophthegm that "nothing can be accomplished without fanaticism and without serenity nothing can be enjoyed."

"*Nudus,*" I fear, "*in ignota, Palinure, jacebis arena.*"

It is rough, with a following wind blowing up from the Antarctic. The two albatrosses, as Stedall predicted, have left us and turned round to their colder latitudes. The wind of our passage and the wind booming along behind us cancel each other out so exactly that I am able to light a match on deck. I do not bathe as it is too cold, but in the afternoon it clears up and the waves splash and sparkle in the sun.

Wednesday, March 6

Heavy clouds encircle the horizon and the sea is dark. I put on the python-skin belt that I bought in Cape Town, which encircles me exactly. I do not like it as much as the Indian belt I bought twenty years ago in New Mexico, since I have a feeling that the scales may peel off the surface. Moreover my Indian belt is broad and strong, whereas this python business is thin and scraggy and I do not feel myself (as Verlaine remarked when he was given a pair of braces to wear on his Belgian lecture tour) to be equally "*soutenu, maintenu, retenu.*"

The rumour spreads among the passengers that there has been a revolution in Java and that Djakarta is in danger of being invaded by rebel troops. The captain, who has had details by wireless, thinks the story is much exaggerated. All that has occurred is an expected difference of opinion regarding cabinet reconstruction between President Sukarno and the Vice-President, Dr. Hatta. But all those who know the condition of Indonesian party politics and the jealousy felt towards the government in Java by the other members of the Federation believe that sooner or later Sukarno will have to dispense with parliamentary government and establish either a personal dictatorship or government by an oligarchy. The captain knows quite a lot about Indonesian politics and, having a great affection for the people, adopts an attitude of sympathetic human distress towards their confusions and troubles.

I sit on deck reading, but see only one flying fish skimming from one wave to another like a small Woolworth mechanical toy.

We play Bingo after dinner but as always we win nothing. Mr. and Mrs. Gibson bet outrageously but take their losses with the calm to be expected of elderly gentlemen and ladies.

5

Thursday, March 7

It has rained hard during the night and the sky and sea are grey. I bathe hurriedly since, although we are well inside the tropics again, the water and the air are cool. I read again Colin Wilson's *Outsider*. I am not clear why my intellectual friends should so disparage him. I can quite see that passages in his book are both naive and pretentious but I understand that he is quite a young man and should therefore be pardoned if occasionally he loses his head. The sections that he devotes to Blake and Dostoievski seem to me industrious and subtle. I do not think that the learned or the middle-aged should snub ambitious young men.

In the evening, at 7.30, we catch up and pass a cargo steamer of the Rotterdam Lloyd. We salute her with ceremony. It is a lovely evening, with the sea a smooth maroon colour in the twilight and a young crescent moon beginning to glow above our heads. We fly the signal flag "G.F.S." which has nothing to do with the Girls' Friendly Society but is the Dutch equivalent of "Happy journey to you!" As we come abreast of the little steamer we send up slow red and orange rockets and hoot three times in our deep bass voice. A thin little hoot answers us across the now darkening waters. The flags fluttering, the red and orange rockets floating down gently with their parachutes, and the bright little moon above us compose a memorable effect. How proud must feel the mariners of the little boat, now dropping behind us, of this huge liner, made and manned by their countrymen, as it sweeps onwards, glowing on every deck with light and power!

After dinner there is an entertainment in the saloon. It is a repetition of the show we had on the voyage out. Selected male and female passengers are made to compete with each other in such tests as blowing up balloons, eating macaroni blindfolded, hanging out washing on lines, eating a dry rusk and then whistling into the microphone, and giving farmyard and other imitations. Then the games instructor and the swimming instructor take off their clothes, put on female bikinis, don comic hats, and do an imitation of American chorus girls singing whoopee songs. It is excellently done and they are almost of professional standard. In fact their mimicry is so apt that they seem indistinguishable from the visiting celebrities who on television start screaming and gesticulating before we have had time to turn the thing off.

V. has, owing to her Borgia blood, some affection for farce, but it fills me with impenetrable gloom. I move my chair out of the saloon on to the adjoining deck, where I can no longer see the two performers but can front the audience and watch their expressions of rapturous enjoyment. An elderly business man from the North of England, whom I have noticed sleeping in a deck chair after luncheon like a basking hippopotamus, is seated near me. He possesses a loud voice which he does not hesitate to demonstrate when speaking. His laugh is like the sound of thick linen being torn quickly by the machines of some satanic mill. He is entranced by the performance. "Excellent!" he shouts, and at one moment, "Positive genius!" I glance at him in disagreement, even in reproof. He does not observe or understand my look.

I sit on there, just outside the open saloon (since in hot weather the glass walls of the saloon can be rolled aside, turning it into an open air verandah), listening with one ear to the sighing of the Atlantic and with the other to the caterwauls issuing from the illumined interior into the tropical night. Always have I regarded myself as an Insider, born and nurtured in the optimism of the Victorian age, confident that the social structure around me is getting better and better each decade, and sharing contentedly in the simple pleasures of my fellow men. Suddenly I feel myself, like Mr. Colin Wilson, to be an Outsider expelled from delight into the fringes of the Atlantic Ocean, unable without falsity to echo the laughter of my fellow passengers or to reflect their happy grins.

V. notices my depression and assumes that I must have been

sitting in a draught and contracted a stiff neck. But when we go down to our cabins and I explain to her that I am an Outcast, she is sympathetic and amused. She argues that if, that afternoon, I had derived, as I did, so much pleasure from watching the children being given their swimming lessons, I ought to be able to derive equal pleasure from the after-dinner performances of the same swimming instructor, even if he was arrayed in a bikini with feathers on his head. To sit there in aloof suffering, unable to laugh or even to clap hands in applause, was a disgraceful posture, suggesting intellectual conceit. "But surely," I protest, "Raymond would have been equally miserable?" "No, he wouldn't," she answers. "He would have gone off to the smoking room and played bridge with Mrs. Hyams. You just seemed rude."

I retire to my bunk ashamed.

XII. EVENAAR

1

Friday, March 8

Walking back from the bathing pool this morning I meet Sidney Culpeper in his neat and perfectly ironed tussore suit. He is leaning on the balustrade with his elbows on the teak bar and his hands locked in front of him. The lapis lazuli in his signet ring is the same colour as the sea. "Good morning!" I exclaim in my dawn manner. "Oh, it's you," he answers. He begins to show symptoms of evasion, flapping the book he has picked up from the chair against his neat trouser leg. "Let's sit down for a bit," I say to him. "It's agreeable here in the cool breeze." Reluctantly he lowers himself into the chair beside me and directs his gaze to the horizon. The following dialogue then occurs.

H.N. "Do you ever suffer from *Angst?*"

S.C. "What's that?"

H.N. (taking a deep breath) "Well, *Angst* is the modern term for what used to be called "solicitude" and what Kierkegaard called "dread." It isn't fear exactly, since fear is a positive reaction against some realised menace or danger. It is a mood of constant although generally undefined anxiety and has many diverse components. It may be due to some actual or imagined weakness of the nerves or to hypochondria. It may be due to love. It may be due to a sense of original sin and an anxiety lest one be too earth-bound to enter into a state of grace. It may, as with dear good Samuel Johnson, come from a terror of death and the expectation of eternal punishment. It sometimes arises from religious doubt, or more often from the inability of a man to abandon rationalism and to surrender his mind to complete spiritual or idealogical conviction. It also comes from a feeling of guilt, which is an emotion different from that of remorse, being unconnected with any precise memory of previous sin. It is caused rather by acute dissatisfaction with one's own character. I have noticed that with intelligent people this dissatisfaction is frequently connected with the consciousness of their failure, either to achieve a harmonious personality, or to give full expression to what they know to be their own maximum capacity. Such people reproach themselves with sloth, which, as you will agree, is one of the major sources of causeless melancholy."

s.c. drops his accustomed tricks of evasion and stares away from me across the sea. His eyelids have ceased to flutter and he looks firm. "Sloth?" he asks. "Do you regard that as a sin?"

H.N. "As a misfortune, rather. We know so little still about physiology or psychology that it is arrant to define anything as a sin, unless it be cruelty or falsehood. These latter are deliberate acts and indicate an evil will. But sloth arises probably from some physical debility, difficult to diagnose but akin to, and often accompanied by, the defect of indecision. It is a great misfortune and often generates despair. Do you, Culpeper, suffer much from despair?"

s.c. "What do you mean by despair?"

h.n. "I mean *Weltschmerz*—the feeling that life on this earth is devoid of meaning or purpose. That all philosophies and religions are nothing more than words woven in differing patterns as amulets against panic, as phylacteries assumed by us slaves of destiny in the hope of fortifying the illusion that we possess free will. Despair is the child of dread and like its parent produces an almost physical sensation, a wave of dizziness or vertigo, as if we were sliding into an abyss. Kierkegaard assures us that the man who is unacquainted with dread or despair is sullied by ethical stupidity. What I want to determine to my own satisfaction is whether these two afflictions are inseparable from the gift of serious reflection; whether they should in fact be regarded as the sign and attribute of the superior man; or whether they are but seasonal maladies affecting those generations of mankind who happen to be born in periods of violent transition; or whether, like arthritis, they can be ascribed to purely physical causes such as the underdevelopment of the pituitary or the sick condition of other glands. Are you yourself much subject to causeless melancholy?"

s.c. (whose features have assumed almost a stern expression) "No—I often feel shattered by life, but I am not temperamentally a melancholy man. My despair is concentrated entirely upon myself. And my dread, my *Angst*, as you call it, centres around a definite, almost a concrete, apprehension."

h.n. "Definite? Concrete?"

Culpeper, who until then had been taut and tense, relaxed suddenly. He had decided to take the plunge.

"Yes," he went on, still staring away from me at the horizon. "I am constantly and definitely afraid of again going to prison. Twenty years ago, when I was just eighteen, I was given two years for what they called 'soliciting.' I had not been soliciting, I had been accosting; but I suppose that they thought I was too young to accost. You see my name is not Culpeper really, but Worsley. I come of a Manchester family, not from Kent. Luckily both my father and mother were dead when the thing happened and I have never seen my uncle again. My father was a very rich man and I am wholly independent. So when I came out of Wakefield after nineteen months in jail I bought a property in Somerset where I live. I took the name of Culpeper, since it was my grandmother's name. So you see, I live in constant dread of being found out or of the thing happening all over again. You see that, don't you?"

"Yes," I answered, "I see that."

This, I reflected, explains his spasms of evasiveness, as also his bouts of impertinence. He seeks by being rude to compensate himself for his humiliation. I was deeply touched by his predicament and its effects; but I knew that any expression of sympathy would be like the scrape of a bramble against a burn. So I went on talking in the same level tone of voice, appearing to take for granted what was in fact a surprising confession.

"I do not think," I went on, "that dread, despair, or melancholy which are produced by definite misfortunes or misadventures can ever be quite so destructive of will power as those which result from self-distrust. After all, one can get the best of external miseries by the application of reason. It is the inner canker, the secret virus, the undiagnosed debility, that make a man feel that nothing is worth while. It must be truly terrifying to feel that nothing is worth while."

s.c. "I never feel that."

h.n. "But of course you ought to do something to get outside yourself and away from it all. You'll never dismiss dread if you do nothing but collect jade. Surely you could find some job which would enable you to do good to other people?"

Suddenly he fell back upon the old evasive, prim, slightly contemptuous, Culpeper manner. "Moral earnestness. Woohoo!" he said. I suppose I looked a little hurt, since he became serious again. "But as a matter of fact," he said, "I do busy myself with outside work. I lecture regularly to the W.E.A. on oriental art and every term I give a course to students at Reading. This spring I am giving ten lectures on the Romantic movement. Then I have tutorials as well. Quite the busy bee. Hee-hee."

"So you know about these people?" I asked him. "You know about these discontented and angry young men and women? I should like to ask you about them."

He rose and started again to flick his book against his neat trouser leg. "Another time, I think," he answered sharply as he left me.

I was moved by this encounter, and when I got back to my cabin I told V. about it. "Poor boy!" she said. "Poor wretched boy! How unfair things are! Let's ask him to our cocktail party tomorrow!"

"Yes," I answered, "let's. But I think it would be better if you asked him yourself."

"Of course."

2

We are now on a level with Ascension again. The captain tells me that we nearly had a fire last night, since a woman had shaded her reading lamp by draping it in a silk handkerchief and when she left the cabin the handkerchief caught fire. Luckily the Javanese steward smelt burning and extinguished the flames before it became necessary to turn on the sprinklers.

I congratulate the captain upon the beauty of the scene that he had staged for us last night when he sent up the rockets to meet the crescent moon. He says that they were not rockets exactly, since they do not burst or explode in the air. They are flares attached to parachutes and are used as distress signals. I point out how awkward it would have been if other vessels crossing the South Atlantic had caught sight of these signals and hurried to our rescue. The Rotterdam Lloyd would have to pay hundreds of thousands of pounds in damages for salvage, demurrage, jettison; or barratry and all the other delinquencies and penalties known to marine law. He is amused by this and explains that before releasing the distress signals he had sent out a wireless message informing all circumambient shipping that if they saw the signals they were not to take them seriously, since they were gestures of greeting, not of supplication. I remark that surely this was a dangerous thing to have done. Supposing that the woman's handkerchief had in fact set fire to the *Willem Ruys*, then nobody would have taken any notice of our appeals for help: the mighty vessel would, as a charred carcase, have sunk with all on board. What

I like so much about Captain de Jonge is that he is always so amused when his passengers make silly remarks. His blue eyes dance with merriment.

There are shoals of flying fish this afternoon, and V. and I have never become bored by watching them. At the approach of the liner they scatter like a flock of starlings. When the sea is sharply rippled as it is today they do not fly as straight as they did when there was a satin surface. They deviate and twitch. But again we notice that they do not dive back into the water, but fall into it simultaneously with exactly similar patterns, as if one had thrown a pail of gravel into the sea. "Not a pail of gravel," says V., "a saucepan full of small peas."

I find that the Dutch word for Equator is *Evenaar* which as a word is far more evocative than our old mathematical term. Sydney Smith told Lady Holland that he disliked a man because "I heard him speak disrespectfully once about the Equator". He would not have spoken thus disrespectfully had it been called *Evenaar*. V. has a passion for the Equator and is annoyed with the captain for crossing it in the dark tomorrow when there will be no light to see it by.

Saturday, March 9

It is V.'s birthday today and I sing "Happy birthday to you" through the bathroom door. Later I give her a piece of soap which I bought at Wynberg when on our way to Groot Constantia and the topaz which I acquired so surreptitiously while waiting for our luncheon at Kandy. She delights in its sparkling colour and says she will have it set as a brooch when she gets home. She also gets three greetings telegrams by wireless, a feat which strikes us both as miraculous.

I bathe. The temperature of the water in the bath is 79 degrees and my weight is 11 stone 9. I think the machine must be out of order, since in spite of my daily walk round the deck I must surely register more than that. But if the machine be lying, then it is a polite lie and rejuvenating.

We work and read all day. V. has written some forty thousand words of *La Grande Mademoiselle,* but does not think that she will be able to finish the book by the time we get back to England. And then will come all those interruptions and *Mademoiselle* will be put away into a drawer until the long dark autumn evenings come. She does not, I fear, possess my gift of concentration, being so polite to those who intrude upon her that she becomes distracted. She says that my habit of disregarding all interruptions or obligations is not due to superior powers of concentration but to the fact that I do not mind being rude. I fear there is something in this criticism. I do not, I hope, enjoy being unkind; but certainly I am uncivil to people who are so insensitive that they do not realise that their dawdling and adhesiveness is a waste of other people's time. Yet her sublime patience with dawdlers ends by wearing her down.

Before dinner we give a little party in the smoking room for the Gibsons and the Stedalls in honour of V.'s birthday. We have a constant stream of champagne cocktails from seven until eight. Sidney Culpeper, in a neat suit of some thin blue material, joins us. He is very shy and our hearts go out to him. Before going down to dinner we walk along the deck to get some air. V. observes, close under the side of the ship, the shape of a vast fish swimming in panic. I say it is a coelacanth and that one can detect its feet. She says this is nonsense, that there are no coelacanths this side of Africa, and that it must be a shark or a whale.

After dinner we talk to the Greens for a bit and then go to the stern to gaze once again, and possibly for the last time, at the southern stars. It is a wonderful sight with a calm sea and the young moon glittering in our wake. There are no stars at all to be seen, not even Magellan's Clouds, and V. complains bitterly at the fatuity of the constellations decorating the Southern Hemisphere. There is a dance being held on the second-class deck, which is as wide as the terrace of a hotel at Miami and glitters with coloured lights. By the swimming pool, isolated from this revelry, we find Leonard Forman, seated alone on a teak bench. He says that he has come there to be out of the noise. He says that he is longing to reach Southampton since sea voyages bore him stiff.

As we walk back to our own section of the ship V. expresses indignation that any young man of health and talent should ever be bored. "Why doesn't he dance," she asks indignantly, "or at least play deck quoits?" "But he may loathe dancing," I answer loyally, "and may be as bad at games as I am." "Then he ought to read," says V. "I have no patience with young people who suffer from boredom." I like Leonard Forman much, although I admit that, having spent his young life drying plants, his capacity for more vivacious pleasures may have become a trifle desiccated. I suggest to V. that he may have absented himself from the throng in order to indulge in a session of sweet silent thought. Or that he may be suffering from *Weltschmerz*. Or that he may have left his tender heart behind him at Bogor. Or merely that, being a man of evident sensibility, he is afflicted by the intolerable beauty of the night. *"Le soir,"* I quote from Madame de Moailles:

> *"Le soir, était plus beau qu'on imagine;*
> *J'avais pitié de moi."*

But V., who is deeply tolerant of those who have fallen by the wayside, like Sidney Culpeper, cannot stand people becoming bored. She regards it as a denial of life. And, oh blessed Aglaë, how I agree with her!

3

I foresaw when I was choosing books for this journey that, if I passed my whole time among the malcontents, I might lose all humanistic self-assurance and be left with a taste of ash in the mouth. I have therefore brought with me, in the Everyman edition, a few books by sturdier philosophers, or gentle optimists, or clever men who had retained their faith in God. I have brought Kant and Hume and William James and John Stuart Mill and Bishop Gore. This sounds a formidable library, but in fact the thoughts of these great men were contained in tabloid form, to be taken, on retiring to rest, as quinine pills.

I am afraid that Mill, who meant so much to me when I was at Oxford, now seems too plausible, assured, and passionless to prove of much solace to those who suffer from dread and despair. Most of the ideals that he preached have today been realised and would appear but smug illusions to the angry young. Yet from those thin academic lips there do issue sentences which express, although with a greater assumption of infallibility than I should ever dare to emulate, several theories that I believe to be correct. He admitted that happiness, and even contentment, should never, by the superior man, be regarded as ends in themselves. "It is better," he writes, "to be a human being dissatisfied than a pig satisfied; better to be Socrates dissatisfied than a fool satisfied." Nor did he believe that happiness, except in transient moments of ecstasy, could ever be achieved. The most that man could hope for was "not a life of rapture; but moments of such, in an existence made up of few and transitory pains, many and various pleasures, with a decided predominance of the active over the passive, and having as a foundation of the whole not to expect more from life than it is capable of bestowing." He felt that those who were unable to adjust themselves to their environment were doomed to melancholy, since they were flouting "the desire to be in unity with our fellow-creatures which is a powerful principle in human nature." This is not a principle that operates with any continuous force upon the thoughts and feelings of modern malcontents. John Stuart Mill would not have regarded their sorrows with sympathy. "When," he writes, "people who are tolerably fortunate in their outward lot do not find in life sufficient enjoyment to make it valuable to them, the cause generally is: caring for nobody but themselves."

When I read Mill today I am haunted by the spectre of Jeremy Bentham sitting bolt upright in his box at University College, dead, fully dressed, and smiling unctuously.

It is David Hume whom I now find invigorating, being fortified by his massive Scottish sense and his firm Scottish style. Edinburgh must indeed have been Athenian in his century.

Moreover, one of the memories which on the rare occasions when I feel glum always restores my gaiety, is that of the scene which occurred when Rousseau became suddenly suspicious of the Scottish philosopher when they were travelling together from Paris to London. They were sitting silently beside the fire in an inn and Rousseau, as was his wont, began to wonder whether Hume had made fun of him behind his back and whether he really admired or liked him as much as he had hoped. The sequel is described by Rousseau as follows:

Having thus reflected, I was presently seized with remorse. I despised myself for my suspicions. Finally, in a transport of emotion, which I shall always recall with pleasure, I flung myself on his neck, embraced him eagerly, while bathed in tears and almost choked by sobs. In a strangled voice I ejaculated the words "No! No! David Hume cannot be a traitor. He is either the best or the meanest of human beings!" Hume returned my embraces with civility, and, gently tapping me on the back, repeated several times in a good-natured and equable tone: "Why, what my dear Sir! Nay, my dear Sir! Oh! my dear Sir!" He said nothing more. I felt my heart yearn within me. We went to bed.

Hume may have been self-satisfied, but he certainly hated gush; he even went so far in his dislike of overtly expressed emotion as to condemn poets as "liars by profession." He was the calm brand of rationalist who defined faith "as more properly an art of the sensitive than of the cogitative part of our nature" and who asserted that "all knowledge degenerates into probability." "Any hypothesis," he wrote, "that pretends to discover the ultimate original qualities of human nature ought at first to be rejected as presumptuous and chimerical." The words "at first" strike me as an engaging human touch.

I am sure that Hume was right in stressing the importance of habit and of the association of ideas. He had some conception, also, of the troubles of the modern mind. He realised that "pride" produced a happy feeling and that "humility," or what we should call a feeling of inferiority, created an unhappy feeling. He refers specifically to "the uneasiness of being contemned."

Hume was not an overt atheist, and in fact dismissed the agnosticism of Spinoza as "a hideous hypothesis." Nor was he tolerant of beliefs other than his own. He is perfectly beastly, for instance, about the Catholics, whose faith he derided as "a strange superstition" and whose devotions he dismissed as "mummeries" practised "for the deliberate purpose of enlivening impressions, and therefore ideas, and therefore belief." Yet Hume, for all his inconsistencies and gaps in logic, was a muscular thinker; he never whined.

William James also, unlike his slow sad brother Henry, exercised a tonic effect. I admit that there was about him a touch of New England heartiness which was liable, in the hands of other, brisker people, to degenerate into the doctrine of virility for virility's sake. But, after reading so many spineless confessions, I am enhanced by his faith in the value of effort.

He was convinced that happiness could be found in self-fulfilment and that this could be achieved only by the expenditure of energy, "by the amount of effort which we can put forth." "Wherever," he wrote, "a process of life communicates an eagerness to him who lives it, there the life becomes genuinely significant. Wherever it is found, there is the zest, the tingle, the excitement of reality and there *is* 'importance' in the only real and positive sense in which importance ever anywhere can be."

He distrusted all forms of escapism, which he called "moral anaesthesia," and he regarded "the habit of inferiority to our full self" as a disgusting habit. He despised those who denied life, and who in their aversion from activity "collapse into yielding masses of plaintiveness and fear." "The heroic mind," he wrote, "does differently." He even went so far as to discourage introspection, on the ground that it might lead to self-absorption. "Strong feeling," he wrote, "about oneself tends to arrest the free association of one's objective ideas and motor processes. We get the extreme example of this in the mental disease called melancholia."

I suppose young people in America and elsewhere still sometimes read William James. I regret that I never had the good fortune to know him. He certainly impressed Gertrude Stein most valuably, and she was not a woman who was impressed by the old-fashioned. To me he seems a salutary moralist.

Bishop Gore, for his part, possessed a sensitive and less boisterous soul. He regards the Buddhist doctrine that men should by the elimination of desire strive to reach the end of sorrow as a self-regarding doctrine and as therefore "abhorrent." He is convinced, with Kant, that the only absolute evil in this world is "the evil will," and that, since the majority of mankind possess good wills and not evil wills, there remains great hope of human perfectibility. Our modern world, which is so sick with uncertainty, could be healed by confidence in this absolute, and young people should begin by persuading themselves that life is good and that man should make the most of it.

The essential injunction formulated by Bishop Gore—who was an intellectual and therefore disinclined to be pragmatic—was that at least we should cultivate a feeling of moral responsibility. Socrates tried to inculcate this doctrine, but he was perhaps too ironical and argumentative. Plato rendered it implicit in his idealism, but Plato is too vague for our amoral generation. The Stoics believed in it as a "duty," but their outlook was too dispassionate to affect or console the inner conscience. It was the Jews—whose harsh intolerance might seem ill-attuned to Bishop Gore's Christian gentleness—who convinced men of their moral responsibilities by convincing them of original sin.

Bishop Gore contends that all the great religions in the world have had this in common, namely, that, finding man obsessed by his dread of invisible hostility, they provided him with a sense of dignity and courage by implanting the belief in perfectibility. All good doctrine inculcates personal responsibility, if only in the form that every man is born with certain natural virtues and defects and that it is his "duty" in life to develop the former and to repress the latter. For him the conception of moral responsibility is closely connected with the conception of free will. In short, he believes that the universe is part of one whole, and expressive, in some sort, of one purpose, in which every individual is called upon to co-operate with intelligence and effort. I see what the bishop means, but I am very bad at visualising the universe in theological terms.

4

Sunday, March 10

A hot day with a following wind. We crossed the Equator during the night and this morning there occurred a repetition of the Neptune ceremony. I fail to understand the significance of this renewed baptism, since all the passengers, apart from those who were born in Batavia and have never left it before, must already more than once have crossed the line. Anyhow V. and I ignore the ceremony and spend a busy morning writing and reading in our cabins.

There is an epidemic of colds on board. V. contends, and perhaps rightly, that it is due to the fact that passengers become heated playing quoits or rushing round the deck and thereafter sit with open pores directly under some electric fan. I suggest that, since most of them have lived for years in the tropics and must therefore know that it is dangerous when perspiring thus to sit, their stiff necks and bronchial troubles must arise from some other cause. She says that what one learns from experience is that nobody ever learns from it. She is herself very careful to avoid draughts and electric fans, moving her gimlet to those few tables where no fans revolve.

They are in this boat so scrupulous, or perhaps so doubtful, regarding the cleanliness of their passengers that, when I pass the bathing pool on my circuit this afternoon, I see that it has been emptied and is being carefully washed and scoured by Indonesians with their trouser legs turned up to the knees. When I pass it on my ninth round the cleaning process has been completed and the Atlantic is boiling fresh and bubbling over the blue tiles. Mrs. Gibson, who is a much travelled woman, tells me that after we leave the Canaries the bath will be closed and that its rounded O will be filled to the lip with tomatoes being exported from Las Palmas to Rotterdam.

Already they are playing off the final heats of the deck tennis, quoits, and ping-pong competitions. The Stedalls, who engage with prowess in these pastimes, but who have failed to win in the semifinals, are evidently under the impression that there has been some dirty business somewhere. Being interested in sports that are played unsportingly, I press them to tell me exactly who cheated whom. They shake their heads sadly, being too gentlemanlike to say more. I suggest to them that it is the game that matters and not who wins it. Again they shake their heads with deliberate discretion implanted on their features. "We should not wish," they seem to imply, "to divulge what we have seen or know." This confirms me in my opinion that competitive games, especially when they occur between teams of different nationality, do not create concord or happiness, but leave behind them the suspicions of distrust and the poisons of hatred. "Anyhow," remarks Stedall, in his easy White's Club voice, "let's say no more about it." So off he goes with his binoculars to gaze at gulls. Mrs. Stedall remains in the saloon stitching away at the appliqué work which I first noticed, before I ever got to know these agreeable people as we were steaming almost two months ago past Finisterre.

Mrs. Gibson in the evening tells me that her friend the purser had informed her that I was to be asked at the farewell dinner on Sunday to make a speech on behalf of the British passengers. She had suggested that I might not care for making after-dinner speeches and that it might be better to invite the air-commodore. The purser replied that, whereas I had made the journey out and back, the air-commodore had not. "And in any case," he added, "Sir Harold wears the right tie." Mrs. Gibson, who is quick at the uptake, realised that the purser was referring in this ambiguous phrase to the undoubted fact that I was educated at one of our leading public schools. For the moment I am quite pleased at being thus classed as an Insider. But then I reflect that the purser can never have read *Some People* and that, being of a critical, if not of a rebellious, nature, I do not enjoy being thus taken for granted by a Dutchman as a member of the Establishment. Mrs. Gibson chuckles at my discomfiture, but I feel old, desiccated, and classified like a dried leaf in Leonard Forman's herbal.

This incident creates within me a T. S. Eliot mood. I see myself as "an old man driven by the Trades to a sleepy corner," and in fact, if the air-commodore be correct, and he is always correct, we are entering the trade-winds area. I pace the deck reflecting upon all that I have failed to experience or to accomplish:

> *Footfalls echo in the memory*
> *Down the passage which we did not take*
> *Towards the door we never opened*
> *Into the rose garden.*

Yes, I have become "an old man, a dull head among windy spaces," and what is so bad about it is that I realise that by no artifice or courage can I recapture what has gone:

Because I do not hope to turn again
Because I do not hope
Because I do not hope to turn.

Round and round the deck I pace, turning always along the promenade, into the second class, round the sports deck, back by the swimming pool, reflecting that what renders old age intolerable is that it deprives one of the ecstasy of expectation. I know that if the unexpected were now to occur it could only be of some unpleasant nature. My contentment is no more than a passive refusal to envisage the horrible event. As such it is a despicable mildness, a retreat from all devouring thought. I ought, I know, to be angered by this realisation. "Do not," wrote Dylan Thomas:

Do not go gentle into that good night,
Old age should burn and rave at close of day;
Rage, rage, against the dying of the light.

I ought, I know, to observe from my sleepy corner the "hyaena of despair"; but I observe nothing of the sort. All I observe is Mrs. Boynton, who by now has reached the concluding chapters of *The Expansion of Christianity*.

Monday, March 11

The wind changes and we have definitely entered the area of the trade winds, Tom Eliot's reference to which had so deeply depressed me yesterday. The deck steward has run out of my brand of cigarettes and the book matches which hitherto V. has obtained so readily from the barman are falling short. It is much cooler and the passengers have ceased to flaunt their naked limbs.

"I have been thinking," Culpeper remarked to me this afternoon, having reverted to his virginal manner, "of what you said about sloth as a cause of melancholy." "It was not an original reflection," I answered. "It has often been noted before. Even the scholastics, who were so unobservant of human nature, agreed that the lack of any useful, or even practical, occupation was a major cause of accidie." "And what is accidie?" he asked. "It is the medieval word for what has later been termed causeless melancholy, or ennui, or *Weltschmerz*." "Well," he continued, "I was reading my Bible this morning as I always do and I found in Proverbs a quotation which confirms your theory that sloth creates dread or fear. I have written it down for you." At this he extracted from his pocket a wallet of crocodile skin on which were the initials S.C. lettered in gold. "Here it is," he said. "The slothful man," I read, "says there is a lion in the way; a lion in the streets." I was impressed by this quotation, since it seemed to suggest both the *Angst* which indolence inspires and the tendency of lazy people to attribute their sloth to external causes. I put the quotation into my own grubby wallet and thanked him.

It is quite cool at night and we sit, after dinner, not on deck, but in the saloon. Our Indian summer's gone.

5

Tuesday, March 12

I wake up suddenly in the early hours of this morning and

feel the ship straining in an odd way and the engines groaning slightly. It only lasts for a few seconds and I put it down to imagination. But at breakfast the air-commodore tells us that there was a submarine earthquake during the night, the news of which has been wirelessed to us from London. Naturally we hope that strange white fish, perhaps even a coelacanth, will be ejected by this explosion from the bosom of the deep and even that wet islands will rise around us, inhabited only by two stranded flopping whales. V. is enchanted by this idea, feeling that if only we could be marooned on one of these dripping rocks she would be able to finish *La Grande Mademoiselle* before we disembark.

The air-commodore assures her that there are no baby Krakatoas to be seen and that the sea is clear. Other rumours dash and flame around the ship. A Portuguese vessel, in distress off the Rio de Oro, has wirelessed for help and we are dashing to her assistance. One of the children on board is missing and he must now be floating in the Atlantic being munched by sharks. As always, there was some slight foundation for each of these rumours. A ship, which may well have been a Portuguese ship, since they are a nation of navigators, had in fact wirelessed an appeal but other and more unoccupied vessels had already turned to help her. A little boy had in fact been missing for a few hours, but it was found that as a joke he had locked himself in the bathroom belonging to a friend. He was soundly slapped and his yells, so Forman told me, resounded throughout the stern of the boat.

We work all morning and then go on deck. It is cold and rough, those who are still determined to sit out on deck have put on jerseys of Shetland wool, and the sliding doors of the saloon have been closed against the wind outside. Even the great wooden punkahs which all these weeks have revolved in the smoking room and the saloon have been switched off and stand immobile.

In the afternoon it becomes warmer and calmer. V. comes on deck. One of the Dutch sailors, a boy of seventeen, climbs over the side in the setting sun. He is doing nothing more important than cleaning or painting the inside of a lifeboat. But his hair is of spun gold, his face that of a Bronzino, and his naked torso is irradiated by the sinking sun. V. rightly says that he is perhaps the most beautiful of all the beautiful sights that we have seen.

At night takes place the farewell dinner in the dining saloon. I was accosted before we went downstairs by a major, who had heard that I was to reply for the English-speaking passengers and who asked me to say a special word of thanks to the captain and the ship's officers for the wonderful way in which they had treated British service officers going on leave. I was surprised by this request, since I did not quite see why members of the armed forces travelling in the *Willem Ruys* should have expected to be treated either better or worse than ordinary civilians. He was somewhat inarticulate on the subject and merely said, "Oh, you should see how they treat us on our own troopships." I consulted the air-commodore, who is a sensible man, and who confirmed to me that the service passengers were specially grateful and would be obliged if I would utter a word of thanks on their behalf.

The Rotterdam Lloyd are, as I have frequently observed, a most hospitable line. We are given an excellently devised dinner with champagne, burgundy, and liqueurs at the expense of the company. The system followed is the same as that for the farewell dinner that we had two nights before we reached Singapore. The speeches take place, not at the end of dinner, but in the interval between the hors d'oeuvres and the main meal. This is an excellent practice, both for the speakers and for those who have to listen. Among other great advantages it renders the speeches short.

The captain as usual makes a charming speech, enlivened by apposite jokes. He says that the wireless says that there has been no winter at all in Europe and that in London yesterday the thermometer registered as much as 70 degrees on the roof of the Air Ministry. Our friends when we land will mock at us for having sailed all the way to the tropics, when we could have enjoyed perfect summer weather had we remained at home. To these comments we should reply that we had been told that the Suez Canal was frozen and were therefore obliged to go round by the Cape. That would puzzle them.

I then leave my table, walk to the microphone set up at the foot of the staircase, and make my little speech. I bring in about the gratitude felt by the service passengers, although it still does not seem to me a relevant or necessary thing to say.

There is dancing afterwards, but V. and I go to our cabins at 10.00. The *Willem Ruys* ploughs onward to the north.

XIII. GRAND CANARY

1

Wednesday, March 13

I spend the morning going through my notes on the books I have been reading during the last eight weeks.

There is no doubt that a sea voyage, when there are no committees to attend, no telephone to tinkle, and no kind casual friends to drop in, does provide one with opportunities of continuous reading such as no other form of holiday can provide. Moreover, the three categories I have chosen—namely, study and annotation, instructive reading, and bunk books—help me to vary concentration and to prevent the veteran brain cells from becoming clogged.

I used to think that the perfect holiday was to motor with V. in France or Italy or Spain, since it was the sole form of leisure which prevented us from reading all the time. Having no confidence in my gifts as a motorist, V. would drive the car herself, while I sat in the seat beside her, scanning maps and giving instructions. It is true that she also distrusted my talent for map reading and would pay slight attention to the guidance that I gave. Yet these journeys provided blissful intervals of comparatively void repose. I now feel that motoring holidays, delightful though they be, are in comparison distracting and exacting; what the congested brain really needs is a necklace of uneventful days, in which the static and the dynamic are exactly balanced. Moreover neither of us has ever found the habit of continuous reading to be any strain upon the nerves. Thus when I contemplate the bulk of the notes that I have taken since we left Southampton I feel curiously refreshed. But have they, as I intended, added anything substantial to my knowledge of melancholy? At least I feel clearer on the subject than I did before.

I had from the outset decided to separate what I have called "causeless melancholy" from the several moods of depression occasioned by recognisable external or internal events.

Obviously a person can be afflicted with external disadvantages which render him or her pessimistic. The most common of these are an unhappy childhood, a series of unsuccessful love affairs, a nagging wife, an ill-tempered husband, uncongenial employment, persistent failure, acute poverty, the denial of opportunity, or misadventures attributable to the injustice or malice of mankind. In addition to this there can exist certain other misfortunes, which might be described as "internal" misfortunes and which persuade people that life upon this earth is profitless, purposeless, and unfair. Such misfortunes are ambition in excess of will power or capacity, extreme personal ugliness, an envious or jealous disposition, self-pity, religious doubts, or a more than average lack of physical or moral courage. Such causes of melancholy are recognisable: they can sometimes be surmounted and often, in maturer age, as with Werther and René and Childe Harold, they lose their virulence.

Yet the most general, although often unrecognisable, causes of melancholy are physical causes. Most of the malcontents whose cases I have considered have been cursed, either with some deformity which hampers biological fulfilment, or with some functional weakness which prevents the easy elimination of waste products. Thus Sainte-Beuve, and I suspect Rousseau also, suffered from hypospadias; Lucretius seems to have been impotent, and Kierkegaard had his "thorn in the flesh"; Baudelaire, Nietzsche, Verlaine, and Byron were all afflicted with underdevelopment or sickness of the pituitary; and almost all sensitive men and women are apt, during the stages of puberty and adolescence, to be assailed by a conflict between yearning and inadequacy which renders them sad. Even those malcontents, such as Sénancour and Amiel, who enjoyed average good health and the external circumstances of whose lives seem to present no apparent grounds for melancholy, may, for all we know, have inherited some glandular deficiency and have been poisoned through their lives by excessive secretions of bile and gall.

It is no adequate explanation to assert that such men were rendered miserable by a deeper insight into the emptiness of existence, or into the presence on this earth of greed, stupidity, cowardice and malevolence. There must have existed in themselves some defect, or quality, to account for this hyper-sensitiveness, for their tortured awareness of a universal emptiness culminating in the flames of hell. I have come to the conclusion, therefore, that there is no such thing as "causeless melancholy." Some malcontents are rendered pessimistic by recognisable external or internal events; others are miserable for no apparent reason but owing to their "disposition," which in its turn is the result of unapparent physiological flaws.

Although I have abandoned all intention of discovering the causes of melancholia, I have been interested in identifying some of its more curious symptoms, or characteristics. Of these I should select three effects that seem to be shared by all malcontents, whatever be their diverse temperaments and circumstances. These are: (1) a peculiar sense of insecurity, (2) guilt feelings generated by a failure in self-fulfilment, and (3) a special inability to adjust themselves to reality.

The nervous condition created in them by their feeling of insecurity may, for all we know, be due, as the behaviourists would suggest, to sudden loss of support when young—to having been dropped at the age of a few weeks by nurse or mother, to having been suddenly deprived of a mother's love, or to having been exposed in childhood to repeated bickering between mother and father. I have often been assured by schoolmasters or those who specialise in child psychology that in almost all "difficult" cases one can trace a divided or an unhappy home. It is recommendable that parents should recognise how important it is to restrain their fury in the presence of their children and not to throw knives, spoons, plates, or puddings at each other when innocent little eyes are looking on. A morbid cell of insecurity may thereby be created and inflammation set up.

This feeling of insecurity is not, I think, confined to those who have been born and bred in epochs of violent transition. It may be that those who when young have been infected by the wild hopes aroused by victories or revolutions experience in the after vacancy a special form of disillusion which may lead to cynicism, a distrust of human effort or intention, and a sense that all the uses of this world are unprofitable, flat, and stale. It may be that those who in their youth live in constant apprehension of some atomic hecatomb are more inclined to pessimism than were those to whom wars were sparkling adventures undertaken only by the naturally gallant and conducted with discriminating weapons. Yet on the one hand, cases of apparently causeless melancholy can be observed in the most static periods, such as those of the reigns of Queen Victoria or Louis Philippe, when the climate of the time was one of rigorous optimism. And on the other hand, it is the middle-aged people, rather than the adolescents, who feel that the prospect of universal obliteration renders energy purposeless.

The sense of insecurity which is peculiar to the malcontent is a subjective emotion, and not one that is caused by any definable apprehension. It produces spiritual dizziness, akin to the physical dizziness experienced by those who, owing to some illness or accident, have lost the faculties of balance and are constantly afraid of tumbling off heights, rolling into gulfs, or finding the pavement in Piccadilly gaping at their feet.

The second common symptom of seemingly causeless melancholy is the uneasiness engendered by failure to justify promise. Infant prodigies, and those horrible children who win television competitions, are especially subject to this disappointment. Those parents who are cursed with these early flowering plants should excerise great restraint in not flattering their prodigies in private or public; they should teach them that the fact that in March one may bloom as a prize daffodil makes it most unlikely that one will ramp as a Eucryphia in August. Expectation of success, if wholly unfulfilled, is certainly a melancholy situation, and, since it is unbearable to face the fact that one is less gifted at the age of thirty-five than one was at the age of six, people seek to attribute this decline in mental power to some external event. I admit of course that indolence, indecision, and procrastination, with the persistent guilt feelings they generate, are a constant source of melancholy, but I should not call it causeless melancholy. The latter, if in fact it existed, would be far more horrible, opaque, and frightening, and might be caused by a sudden collapse of will power, or by realising the awkward fact that some geniuses are really not so bright at forty as they were at six.

It is not the infant prodigies only, the scholarship boys, the double firsts, or the winners of the Prix de Rome, who are visited by disappointment at not having realised the rewards promised by their early eminence; older men and women are also afflicted by these moods of self-reproach. Many of them attribute their failure to external circumstances, to the envy of others, to the fact that they were born "unlucky," or to the ill chance that they have never been accorded scope or opportunity for the full expression or expansion of their natural gift. There are some, however, who possess the discernment to realise that their character is weaker than their intelligence and that they lack the will power to give full effect to their talents. Such people suffer acutely from "guilt" and attribute their failure in self-fulfilment to the parasite of "sloth," which has nibbled and discoloured the pink buds of their childhood and adolescence. It is indeed remarkable to find how frequently in the confessions of malcontents the word "guilt" and the word "sloth" accompany each other on the same page. Yet in fact laziness is largely a matter of habit and requires but a slight movement of the will to be rendered unhabitual.

A third characteristic which can be observed as common to all malcontents is an aversion from reality, or the inability to accept the external world. This is no ordinary problem of adjustment and is not identical with the accustomed conflict between the internal and the external, the individual and the community, the conformer and the rebel, the insider and the outsider. It is something more unusual and mysterious than this. It is a fundamental ineptitude to take reality for granted or even to believe in its existence. Again and again have I found malcontents who not only doubt the reality of existence but suffer panic moments when they doubt their own reality. "Am I really I?" they ask themselves, and this question invariably arouses within them the twin passions of dread and despair.

I am prepared to admit that those who suffer from these terrifying disabilities and apprehensions may be of finer temper than those who manage to dismiss such conflicts from their consciousness. But I have not been considering respective merit: I have been concerned with trying to discover what it is that makes men and women unhappy without a recognisable reason. I am now convinced that there is always a reason, however obscure. It may happen that future physicians will discover some hormone the injection of which will mitigate these miseries. Meanwhile my compassion for malcontents has been much enhanced by reading so much about them.

2

After luncheon we are in sight of the Grand Canary, and when I go down to V.'s cabin I find a note propped up on her dressing table by a spoon. It tells me that she has gone up to the observation saloon and will I follow her there? I do so and we gaze at the island as it slides past us on the bow.

The flanks of the Grand Canary are treeless and of a peculiar dark brown colour, different from the fawn of Persia or the crystalline grey of Greece. We see the small peninsula, the Isleta, on which the harbour and docks have been constructed, a mile or two outside Las Palmas itself. There is a gigantic steamer straight ahead of us which we take to be a Cunarder or a P. & O.: but when in half an hour we catch up with it we find that it is but a coastal steamer of a few hundred tons. Such are the deceptions of nautical visibility. We enter the harbour at 4.45 and are tied up to the quay by 5.30. There is a blockage of passengers aligned for the gangway and some comradely chaff. We get on shore at 6.00.

The mole is long, narrow, and congested with crates of oranges and tomatoes. The first fifty taxis have been engaged by some tourist agency for an excursion of sorts, and we have to walk for at least half a mile. Eventually we find an empty taxi, but it is pointing in the wrong direction and is obliged to turn round in the narrow space left between the sea and the orange crates. It seems to me to manoeuvre recklessly near the edge. Remembering how Venizelos once toppled into the harbour at Brindisi and had to be fished out with a boat hook (*Seianus ducitur unco*), I insist upon V. disembarking from the taxi and I do so myself. Eventually the manoeuvre is accomplished and we drive off into the town.

We leave the harbour installations of the Isleta, drive across the isthmus, on the other side of which flashes the beach of Las Canteras with its striped tents and parasols, and are taken by our taxi to the smart hotel. V. has a repugnance for smart hotels and bangs on the window of the cab, exclaiming *"Correos! Correos!"* thereby indicating to the driver that we do not wish to see the beastly hotel but to post our letters. So he swerves under an arch and draws up in a courtyard where there are damsels in native dress selling red carnations to tourists. We wave them aside petulantly and enter the adjoining post office, where there is a charming official who sells us stamps. Then off we go into the old town, past the Chapel of San Antonio Abad, where Columbus attended Mass, and into the Plaza Santa Ana where we get out of our taxi and look around. There are palm trees in two trim rows; a mud-faced cathedral; and the statues at the entrance to the garden of the wild dogs that gave the islands their name. There is a statue of a lop-eared Labrador, one of a bull terrier, and one of an animal distantly resembling a red setter. They do not strike us as in the least reminiscent of the wild dogs which once swarmed in the island and which must have been like the pariahs of old Stamboul, the Molossians of Arcadia, or the angry, furry sheep dogs that attack one in the arid uplands of Iran. But they are nice statues and we buy post cards of them to send to Philippa, with whom even the fiercest Molossian becomes a lap dog.

Then we drive to the main shopping street, named the Triana, like the quarter of Seville from which V.'s Andalusian ancestors derived. We leave the taxi outside a cinema and walk up one side of the street and down the other side, gazing at the shops. I buy a nice leather bag for Elvira, which has obviously come from Tetuán, and V. buys another bag of Las Palmas origin which is draped in red and green fringes hanging down like seaweed. We also try to buy some of those Spanish cigarettes which we had so much enjoyed when at Cadaqués, but we have forgotten their name. So we buy book matches instead, and a melon, and a tambourine, and some more picture post cards. Then we drive back to the boat.

After dinner we lean over the side staring at the lights of the town. There are the usual lights that fringe the coast road and the gardens, the higher neon lights in the new town, the dimmer lights of the old town, and some lights that climb steeply up the hill, indicating residential streets. There is a bright moon and we can see the line of hills fringing the bay of Las Palmas and a huge distant peak, still illumined by the afterglow of the sunset, which I tell V. is the Peak of Teneriffe, although I well know that it must be the Cruz de Tejeda, the highest of the Grand Canary mountains.

We notice that the chairs are set out in rows in the main saloon and the deck steward tells us that they are expecting a troupe of dancers from the town who will entertain us with local songs and dances. Knowing Spanish unpunctuality, I doubted whether the troupe would arrive before our ship sailed, but the steward assured me that they had already come on board and were now doing their stuff in the second-class saloon. We hesitate to visit them, expecting that it will be an artificial performance and one that we shall dislike. In the end we go down there and are amply rewarded.

The troupe consists of some twelve people, six men and six women, with a small guitar band and a man with flaxen hair who yells Canarian songs. The women dancers wear the local dress, a coloured skirt and bodice, a tiny hat shaped like a *sombrero cordobés* and worn over one eye, and below it an embroidered kerchief which falls as a mantilla over the hair and neck. The men to my astonishment are dressed in white kilts or fustanellas like evzones; they have bare knees and feet. The band begins to thrum, and with a gliding motion they link hands in the sesquipedalian rhythm of a *sardana*. We had watched this lovely dance in the square at Cadaqués, when the waiters, the waitresses, and the cashier from the hotel would dash out in sudden ecstasy, turn a measure or two, and then hurry back to serve coffee on the terrace. Surely this must be the most ancient, as well as the loveliest, of all Mediterranean dances, deriving from the Turbasia, the round dance of the dithyramb, which I have witnessed during Holy Week in the tavernas of Attica and Thebes. It possesses a more sustained continuity of tune and movement than any other dance I know, giving to the heads and bodies of the dancers an undulating movement of strange grace. The Indonesians have crowded into the packed saloon and watch these intricate movements of the feet and arms with awed delight. I have never seen them more animated, not even when they first caught sight of the volcanoes of Sumatra. V. and I stand there entranced.

We then return to our own saloon, where we find the passengers still ranged in rows waiting for the dancers to come up from the second class. We sit with the Gibsons for a while. They have been dining on shore at a tavern that they recalled from earlier days. We do not wait to see the dancers again, since we do not wish, by repetition, to blur our first impression of surprised delight.

The ship does not leave Las Palmas until midnight, and the cranes scream and clatter above our heads, to the accompaniment of boisterous applause and laughter from the saloon.

3

Thursday, March 14

We are at sea. The stewards and staff have changed from their white duck into black suits and trousers; their dark uniforms do not seem to fit them as well as did their white uniforms; they look short and drab, which makes us feel sad. The swimming pool has been closed for the remainder of the journey. We are facing north.

Before luncheon we have drinks in the smoking room with the Gibsons. They tell us that after we had gone to bed last night the troupe danced and sang quite beautifully. Then two awful things happened. One of our elderly fellow passengers, who had been dining on shore, rose from his chair and clasped one of the Las Palmas girls round the waist. It was not quite so horrible as it sounds, since they did not attempt the *sardana*, but merely danced together for a short while to some Argentine melody that went quite well. But then a woman, who must also have been dining on shore, descended from the observation saloon, from the balcony of which she had been applauding the dancers, seized hold of one of the young men in fustanellas, and started to do a comic turn, in which she caricatured a Spanish dancer, exclaiming *"Olé"* from time to time in a breathless voice. It must have been this performance that had evoked the riotous and ribald applause which had reached us in our cabins amid the bumps of the tomato crates and the whining of the cranes. The Gibsons had been shocked by this exhibition. V. and I were more than shocked, we were angered and saddened. Since here we recognised The Enemy —that creeping infection of vulgarity that will subdue the world. Like the sand of Arizona it seeps stealthily, obliterating our ancient monuments and temples, filling even our gardens with its gritty dust.

While pacing the deck after luncheon I asked myself why this story had filled us with such anger and gloom. It cannot have been a Frenchwoman who perpetrated this infamy, since she would have had too much taste; it cannot have been an Italian, since she would have known that men are but seldom attracted by the jocose; I fear she must have been British, or perhaps American, or even Dutch. Nor was it the woman's performance that irritated me only, since she may have been tipsy in her vaunting, and unaware. It was the loud applause with which the passengers greeted her exhibition that was so depressing. Probably none of them, as individuals, approved of her action; but as a mass audience they were moved to assent. Yet they must have realised that the *sardana* as danced by the troupe from Las Palmas was a perfectly authentic performance and one which was executed with tradition, beauty, and skill. To applaud a caricature of such tradition and training was to manifest insensitiveness to values and that inability to distinguish between the authentic and the unauthentic which seems to me one of the major symptoms of vulgarity. V. and I felt that the intense pleasure we had derived from watching the dancers had in some way been sullied by these guffaws.

Anyhow we are now 217 miles from Las Palmas and on a level with Marakesh. There is a northeast wind blowing and few people sit out on deck. Even the Chinese lady has appeared in a padded coat and skirt, decorated in the Chiang-sui tartan. It is all very sad. Our Indian summer has gone.

4

Friday, March 15

The thermometer in my cabin, which for so many flying-fish days registered 75, is now below 60; at night I take my London greatcoat from its hanger and put it over my bunk; it looks most urban. We pass Lisbon during the morning, but as usual the rain clouds hang heavy over Cintra; we see nothing at all. I send across the waters my blessing to Dick Ward, up in his little room above the Tagus, and my curse to the old beldame who, in the guise of a Portuguese night nurse, shoved a syringe into my sciatic nerve.

It seems that our rage yesterday against the woman who aped the *sardana* was founded on insufficient evidence. The Stedalls tell us that, so far from being an American who caricatured Spanish dances, she was a Hungarian of excellent family who had spent ten years in Málaga being trained as a dancer and that she danced better than the whole troupe combined. But when we repeat this to the Gibsons they snort with indignation. Of course the woman was American, or anyhow Dutch, and her vulgarisation of the performance was inebriate and crude. "There!" exclaims Mrs. Gibson, pointing an accusing finger, "there is the woman herself!" I follow the finger and observe one of our fellow passengers who had often struck me as possessing a manly face and conceited hair. I have long since reconciled myself to the fact that ship's information is seldom either unanimous or precise.

After luncheon we pass between the Berlenga Islands and the coast of Portugal. All I see is a white lighthouse, a building that looks like a prison, and two very green fields. The Portuguese coast remains a blur through the mist. V. starts her packing which, considering the number of earthenware pots, walking sticks, feathers, orchids, lion's claws, zebra bags, python belts, and batik that she has acquired, may constitute a problem. Fortunately in the course of her foraging expeditions among the alleys of Colombo, Singapore, and Djakarta she has also acquired baskets of many strange shapes and sizes: the one, I suppose, will fit into the other.

I observe that now that we are approaching the end of our voyage relations between passengers are becoming more intimate. Not only do the women now address each other as "dear" or "Gwendolen," but they pass a hand across each other's stoles or shoulders with a stroking movement, signifying affection. Even I made bold to cross the floor of the smoking room and to ask Mrs. Stanley, a jolly American widow who reminds me of Elsa Maxwell, whether I might be so bold as to enquire what was the splendid fur that she was wearing. "Blond mink!"

she answered, as flattered by my question as I was awed by her reply.

After dinner we sit in the saloon and are shown coloured slides of Dutch cities, tulip fields, and fishing boats. I enjoy that sort of thing. From tomorrow onwards we have to pay cash for any drinks we order; our confident Asian days of chits have passed; we are entering the chill suspicious latitudes of the North.

I had an interesting talk with Sidney Culpeper this afternoon. Much as I relish his impertinent pose, amused and touched though I am by his defensive giggles, I have long since realised that essentially he is a serious and sensitive person, who has endured and enjoyed experiences different from my own. The years he has devoted to instructing the proletariat and lecturing at provincial universities enable him to supply information which I might otherwise have missed.

"Supposing," he said, when I passed him for the third time during my walk round the deck, "supposing that I joined you for a bit?" I was pleased by this suggestion, since it showed that his self-assurance in regard to myself had been increased and not diminished by his confession. Like so many epicene men of my acquaintance, Culpeper walks firmly, taking long measured strides as if setting out along the valley of Khatmandu on a two months' expedition to the Himalaya. In my little canvas shoes I trip beside him.

"Well," he began, "have you discovered the cause of causeless melanchloy?"

"No," I answered, "I have merely convinced myself that there is no such thing. Melancholy is caused, either by external circumstances, or by defective glands. Having read the confessions of typical malcontents from the fifth century B.C. down to the very brink of existentialism, I have come to the conclusion that pessimism is almost always caused by the bodily humours. These poisons produce insecurity, dread, guilt, despair, maladjustment, and doubts regarding reality."

"Then have you decided why it is that, whereas the nineteenth-century romantics were just unhappy, the modern romantic is angry as well?" He glanced at me sideways with two faint lines of scornful amusement forming under his nostrils and at the edges of his mouth. I could see that the rude, nagging, outrageously impertinent Culpeper was not far away.

"Well," I began, drawing a long breath and adopting what I fear might be described as my didactic tone, "well, my conclusions are something like this. The feeling of flatness left over after the excitements of the French Revolution and the Napoleonic Wars, the disappointment and disillusion created by the betrayal of so many ideals, produced among sensitive people a revulsion against immediacy and a desire to escape from their fellow men and to nurse their wounds amid the eternal solitudes of nature. They had observed how the greatest upsurge of idealism that the world had ever witnessed could be diverted, used, and degraded by the ambition, turpitude, or weakness of individuals: they had seen glory in its most dramatic form and it had all ended in the picture of an obese and jaundiced little man gazing at the receding cliffs of Ushant from the deck of the *Bellerophon*. Many of them had lost their religious faith and all of them had been deprived of any confidence in the value of human effort or the integrity of human motives. Worst of all, in this atmosphere of universal disillusion, they could not find within themselves the will power or the energy for action; they became afflicted by the most destructive form of accidie, the feeling that nothing really mattered and that there was nothing that anyone could do. The more virile among them, such as Alfred de Vigny, preached stoic resignation; the less virile, such as Lamartine and Leopardi, crept into corners where they cried. They experienced deep and pregnant unhappiness; but they had lost the energy to experience rage."

"And did you," asked Culpeper, "reach similarly confident conclusions regarding the modern generation?"

"Yes," I went on, undeterred by his disdain, "I think I have. The main difference between the young men and women of today and those of 1820 is that our revolution is still continuing, whereas theirs ended, or seemed to have ended, at Waterloo. The younger generation of today is not perturbed, as the early romantics were perturbed, by the loss of religious faith. Young people, in England at least, have retained their belief in social justice as an attainable ideal and have not therefore lost their energy or collapsed into apathy. Thus unlike their forebears they are not resigned but impatient. It is their impatience that accounts for their anger. I find it an encouraging symptom.

"For the moment, of course, their anger is concentrated against those who, directly or indirectly, they consider responsible for the fact that what they wanted to happen has not as yet occurred. They may admit that we have achieved a high degree of social security, and that the ideal of equality of opportunity has almost been realised, but they are enraged to observe that we are no nearer than we ever were to the classless state. Moreover even the greater educational and occupational

opportunities that they have now been accorded contain elements of irritation. Equality of opportunity implies a tenser
degree of competition, and they feel surrounded by people
similar to themselves who are striving fiercely to snatch their
jobs. And even though, at their technical schools and universities, they acquire a great amount of knowledge, they do not
acquire the humanities, which are the foundation of style. Naturally, when they encounter people who have enjoyed the priv-
ilege of a luxury education, they are angered by what must
seem to them effortless and unmerited intellectual and social
ease. I assure you that I feel embarrassed when I meet these
angry young men."

"Woo-hoo!" said Culpeper. "That was a good one! I see that
you have been mugging up John Osborne and Kingsley Amis
and John Wain. But have you ever actually *met* an angry
young man? I assure you he is a myth, even as your causeless
melancholy proved a myth. In the last ten years I have got to
know some four hundred young men and women of the middle,
lower-middle, and working classes, and believe me only some
of them have the time or the imagination to feel discontented.
Most of them are just louts or puddings, who allow life to
slide by them unperceived, and are intent only on passing exams
and getting jobs. In their rare moments of reflection they concentrate their musings upon food, sex, motor bicycles, beer,
pull-overs, and the local dance on Saturday evening. The tiny
minority of those who stray beyond the barriers of habit scarcely
worry at all about the contrast between knowledge and education, between content and style. When they feel angry, they do
not, as you imagine, become enraged with social *injustice,* but
with social *justice.* What they hate is this beastly Welfare State,

which mothers them, and disciplines them, and fusses over them, as if she were a matron looking after little boys in a school sanatorium. They are not in the least grateful at being spared the hazards which caused their grandfathers such aching anxiety: they are the modern romantics who yearn for adventure and resent being regarded as entries under age groups in an institutional card index. They long to escape from their sanatorium, to differentiate themselves from the morons who share with them these abominable equalities of opportunity, to escape into newer countries where they imagine they will encounter delicious dangers and reap shining rewards. I should call them restless rather than angry. And when I get a chance I encourage their rebellion good and proper. Hee-hee!"

"Oh dear!" I murmured as I continued for a while to flap in my rubber shoes beside him along the deck of *Willem Ruys,* "Oh dear!"

4

Saturday, March 16

Time ceases to be a necklace when only two beads remain on the string. We are already afflicted by *Abschiedsstimmung*. I pay my bills; I sort out the tips which I shall distribute tomorrow into envelopes marked with the recipient's name; we go up to the bridge and present Captain de Jonge with a book from each of us *avec dédicace;* in return he gives us some Dutch translations of Yeats. An Indonesian steward goes round extracting from the slots in the deck chairs the name cards which they have carried, through cloud and sunshine, during the last eight weeks; he puts them in a large cardboard box which had once contained many hundreds of cigarette cartons; he then empties the box into the Bay of Biscay and I watch the cards fluttering like the trail of a paper chase towards our wake.

At 6.30 I see the light of Ushant stabbing the gathering darkness with monotonous insistence. I am alone in the prow. I bow low three times with hands joined like those of a Buddhist priest, paying my tribute to the ancient parapets of France. I then see that a Dutch businessman arrayed in a thick ulster has been watching me with curiosity and compassion. It is irritating thus to be caught in a moment of dramatic sentiment. I go down to my cabin, have my last bath of fierce sea water, my last shower, and don my tuxedo. After dinner we dance, or rather they dance, in the saloon. The band plays *"Que serà serà,"* but without much conviction. We step out into the night and see that the fog is swirling along the deck and dimming the rows of lights. Above us the foghorn booms.

Sunday, March 17

V. is wakened during the night by drunken voices in the corridor; strayed revellers, after a farewell party, are making their way to an adjoining cabin for a final drink. At 2.00 A.M. the foghorn starts again, as we creep slowly up the misty Channel. I drop to sleep, feeling uneasily that we shall be very late at Southampton.

I wake at 7.00 to find we are in the Solent and opposite Cowes Castle. By the time we have finished breakfast we are entering the docks. The rain pours down on the slate roofs of the warehouses, which glitter grey under low grey clouds. At 9.40 we leave the *Willem Ruys* by the covered and illuminated gangway and enter the terminal building. We sit on the green benches, buy the Sunday papers, and wait patiently to be informed that the customs are ready to examine our luggage. We had been told that the special train for London would leave at 11.30 and get us to Waterloo by 1.00, and we had told the car to meet us there at that hour. But we are now informed that the train will not leave Southampton till 12.40 and will only reach London after 2.00. We telephone to Sissinghurst and manage to catch the car before it leaves and to warn Copper that we shall be an hour late. Along the green benches of the terminal all manner of rumours begin to circulate among our former fellow passengers. There has been a strike of dock workers; the customs officials refuse to leave their beds on Sunday mornings; the mails had been piled in the hold above our luggage with the result that all the mailbags have to be sorted, checked, and unloaded before a single suitcase can be put on shore. By that time V. and I have read our Sunday papers down to the poultry news and are becoming restless. Delay is always tiresome, but unexplained delay is excruciating.

We are thus seated when V. gives a sudden exclamation of delighted surprise, and there are Nigel and Philippa advancing towards us. They had had the greatest difficulty in being admitted to the terminal and Nigel had been obliged, much to his embarrassment, to divulge his quality as local M.P. Other people who had come to meet their relations were kept resolutely crowded behind a barrier for four hours. Nigel was indignant about this and undertook to complain to the Ministry of Transport. He was told by the supervisor that the reason for this inconsiderate and exacting segregation between the landing passengers and their nearest and dearest behind the barrier was that those returning from the Far East were all too apt to slip little packets of opium, hashish, or heroin to their shore confederates. V. was indignant at this flagrant example of red tape; even my civil-service mind suggested that there had been some lack of co-ordination between the several departments responsible for the prevention of drug traffic. We sit on there talking to Nigel and Philippa, while the children of the passengers play with their toy trains and motor lorries along the wide floor space of the terminal. Nigel describes to me the present situation in his constituency; his Association have instructed their branches to boycott him ruthlessly; I am infuriated by such Nazi methods, but Nigel takes them with his usual tolerance. At last the loud-speaker blares, the gates into the customs shed are flung open, and our luggage, which is heaped in a pile beside the counter, is passed through with a quick gesture of magenta chalk. We enter the special train; Nigel and Philippa sit beside us for a bit and Philippa has a cup of British Railways soup. Then they leave us. As the train slides out we catch a glimpse, between the interstices of the customs shed, of the great flanks of the *Willem Ruys* shining in the rain. We wave a fond farewell.

The train chunks across the network of rails that serve the various docks and wharves. At the gate of one of the many level crossings a grey Rolls-Royce is poised with Culpeper at the wheel and a chauffeur beside him. I wave at him frantically as we chug past; but he does not see me.

We reach Waterloo exactly at 2.00 P.M. and are met by Copper, the car, a bewildered Rollo on his lead, and Colin, whose auburn head towers above the other passengers. We stop for a moment at the Albany, where we have some coffee and sandwiches, and then through familiar wet roads drive down to Sissinghurst. We get home at 5.10 while it is still light enough to see that the orchard is ablaze with daffodils.

Thus ends our Journey to Java, the happiest journey that even we have known.